JEAN LINDEN

Explorer
Master of the Orchid

JEAN LINDEN

Explorer
Master of the Orchid

Nicole Ceulemans

With the collaboration of
Guido Braem
and
Ronnie Viane

Edited by
Guido Braem

From the late fifteenth century onwards, the many voyages of discovery from Western Europe were all undertaken by sea. The development of shipping, advances in cartography and improved technical equipment encouraged exploration in ever more distant regions. During the seventeenth and eighteenth centuries, these voyages steadily became less the preserve of fortune hunters and adventurers and more the work of medical men and botanists. Commissioned by heads of state or botanical gardens, they sailed to record the natural history of far-flung lands.

From the beginning of the nineteenth century, yet another kind of explorer began to emerge. In addition to their scientific agenda, many expeditions now also had commercial aspirations.

In Western Europe, which was reaping the fruits of industrialization, there were wealthy customers for exotic plants, animals and all kinds of collectable objects. In particular, the cultivation of rare plants from remote areas was becoming the rage. Many expeditions were undertaken, partly out of scientific interest but also to import seeds and plants into Europe where they found a ready market.

The Société royale d'Agriculture et de Botanique de Gand, founded in 1808 to support the developing horticulture industry, did not equip any expeditions itself but provided a forum where collectors and growers could bring their latest specimens to public notice by means of competitions and exhibitions. By around 1830 there were two exhibitions a year, a winter and a summer one. In 1839, on the occasion of the thirtieth anniversary of the first winter exhibition of 1809, an international exhibition was held that aroused a great deal of interest. It was such a magnificent success that it was decided to organize such an event every five years. These five-yearly exhibitions later became internationally known as the Floralies of Ghent.

In 1845, on the occasion of the second quinquennial exhibition, the Société royale launched it own journal. The *Annales de la Société royale d'Agriculture et de Botanique de Gand* not only reported on newly imported plants and their nomenclature, growers and suppliers but also, under the editorship of Charles Morren, the latest discoveries in the world of horticulture, with reference to foreign publications and tips for the amateur horticulturalist. During the five-year life of this journal, 291 lithographic plates were published.

The botanical discoveries of the young Jean Linden were likewise greeted with enthusiasm. In 1846 the Société royale published an account of the expeditions made by Linden in Central and South America, the journal editor writing the prophetic words: "The history of Belgian ornamental plant cultivation will in the future have to take account of Mr Linden's work. Many of the plants he has imported are already circulating in the trade today". Fifty years later, on the death in 1898 of this famous explorer and expert on orchids and ornamental plants, many of the plants imported by Linden were commercially available. They generated a significant income for many nurserymen.

Unlike many plant hunters who went to work purely for commercial reasons, Jean Linden had a botanical interest in many species, not just the orchid. It is thanks to him that we have so many varieties of fern, palm, begonia, bromeliad, and so on.

A remarkable fact about this praiseworthy explorer was that, decades later, he could still describe exactly the place where he had found a specific species. He gladly put his knowledge at the disposal of horticulture. Both in Brussels and Ghent he succeeded in educating the growers of ornamental plants away from their traditional practice of cultivating orchids from mountainous regions in glasshouses that were much too hot and humid. He did this, not only by participating in the exhibitions of the Société royale, but also through his highly regarded and remarkable publications. It can be said of Jean Linden that, in addition to his scientific merits, he also had outstanding commercial talents. In him, moreover, scientific discipline, a feeling for new discoveries, a love for botanical science and an aesthetic sense were harmoniously combined. It is these qualities that have made Linden an important historical figure. It is these same qualities that are so highly valued in scientific research at our universities today. The many readers of this excellent publication about the life of Jean Linden will undoubtedly agree.

Count de Kerchove de Denterghem

ACKNOWLEDGEMENTS

Nicole Ceulemans

Jean Linden ranks among those members of society who contributed to the economic prosperity of 19th-century Belgium and Luxembourg and the cordial diplomatic relations enjoyed between these two countries. Unlike his contemporaries in business or politics, however, his name has virtually vanished from the collective memory. Realising one day that I was related to him, I began to dabble in some vague research. This amateurish 'occupation' soon developed into a more systematic activity, which gradually took over a great part of my life.

After a decade of investigation, the material I had collected far outstripped my original, naïve curiosity and any family interests. Jean Schuermans, my husband, convinced me I should assemble my findings into a book. My first thanks thus go naturally to him: he was constantly at my side and unhesitatingly accompanied me to Venezuela and Mexico. Neither must I fail to mention my aunt, Andrée van Overstraeten-Bavelaar, who provided me with my first documents and thus the foundations of this work.

My next step was to seek the opinion of Jan Martens, Director of Fonds Mercator, whom I first met at Kinshasa University. Although he had never heard of Jean Linden, he found the subject matter intriguing. Jan advised me to embark on a Linden biography with the aid of one of his regular collaborators.

A number of encounters were providential in forwarding my task. Here I would like to express my gratitude to those who gave me invaluable assistance throughout, in the hope that I have not overlooked anyone.

By comparing the obsession with orchids, which is perhaps not so well known now as it once was, with the more widely known tulipomania, Hubert Darthenay helped me appreciate the historical importance of Jean Linden and indicated the main lines my work should follow.

Meeting Professor Guido Braem and hearing him talk of Jean and Lucien Linden as if they were his own relatives was a revelation, given that I, their descendant, knew virtually nothing of them. Long before me, he had

« Jean Linden at the Horticultural Society of London, circa 1860.

Frontispiece:
Haemanthius lindenii, species discovered in the Congo by Auguste Linden during the 1886 expedition. First flowered on the continent in 1890. Plate from *L'Illustration horticole*, 1890.

turned his attention to what he called the "Linden dynasty" and was clearly delighted to learn that a more in-depth study was under way. Guido was my inspiration at every stage of the book, with his encouragement and fund of botanical knowledge where my own was lacking.

Denis Diagre, the historian, traced out for me the general development of horticulture and botany in Belgium and provided much-needed tips on navigating the labyrinth of libraries and archives. Ronnie Viane, professor of botany, shed light on residual problems in my research. Lucien Debersaques, librarian at the Société royale d'Agriculture et de Botanique in Ghent, Professors Bamps and Robbrecht of the Jardin botanique in Meise and Jan Balis were my guides in the study of archives and herbaria respectively. Finally, Antoinette Reuter arranged for me to consult the Luxembourg archives. I must also acknowledge the appreciable help given by the Belgian embassies in Bogotá and Caracas. In the Columbian capital, Professor Santiago Díaz Piedrahita of the Academia Colombiana de Historia was another vital source of assistance. Frans M Feij and Marianne Born-van der Linden made access to the writings of Nicolas Funck so much easier with their carefully nuanced translations.

My recognition and warmest thanks are also extended to Fabrice Biasino, whom I met through Natacha Langerman. His patience and his command of the *mot juste* contributed to the synthesis of countless ideas and assemblage of the many pieces of this puzzle — the fruit of my research — into a coherent whole. Last but not least, the results would have come to nothing without the labours of the Fonds Mercator team, the Bureau La Page and photographer Hugo Maertens. To all those mentioned, my sincerest gratitude. Through the grace of each, Jean Linden has at last emerged from his unjustified oblivion.

Nicole Ceulemans, October 2005

Note to the Reader

To facilitate the presentation of large amounts of scientific and historical data, the authors have observed the following conventions…

In the body of the text, plants are allotted by their current scientific names. The exceptions are plant-hunters' travel accounts, other quotations, and captions to original illustrations, where we have reproduced the old fashioned classifications – including any period errors or inconsistencies of spelling, the term [*sic*] denoting their deliberate introduction.

The enormous sums once lavished on plants or botanical expeditions are given in the currency of the period, together with their equivalent in euros and pounds sterling today.

Finally, to reduce the length of the footnotes, two horticultural journals, *L'Illustration horticole* and *Le Journal des orchidées,* have been abbreviated to *IH* and *JO* respectively.

CONTENTS

IN SEARCH OF JEAN LINDEN

1994-2005

Lucienne Linden.

y grandmother, Lucienne Linden, loved talking about her "Belle Epoque" in Brussels. She was highly dramatic, giving colourful descriptions of the luxury and ease of the bourgeoisie before the Great War in Belgium; before everything collapsed. She owed these golden years to her grandfather, Jean Linden, who dedicated his whole life to his "darling daughters": his orchids. When he died in 1898, Lucienne was 12. She well remembers this great, imposing man, especially his kindness and good humour.

"Lulu", as we affectionately named her, talked of Douke, the governess who never left her side, of the cupboard where the jewellery was kept, of the journeys to Switzerland with the whole household. She would describe the luggage compartment of the train where the trunks were stored, the hat-boxes and their suite. She also recalled her grandfather's open-air receptions and winter gardens, where King Leopold II was a familiar sight. High society guests would come and admire the newly introduced exotic plants.

I was a little girl then, and I would listen, wonder, and dream ... these were tales of another world, with an exotic aura. These are the memories of happy days, when the whole family would talk of "Grandfather Linden" and of "our Toucouyou Island". Yes, it was a fact: somewhere in the southern seas – we did not know exactly where, but it was somewhere near Cuba – there must have been an island that Jean Linden was given in reward for services rendered! We only have a few souvenirs of these family tales that have now passed into legend. There was Marie, the doll that came from the workshops of the notorious Jumeau brothers in Paris. Lulu was three when her grandfather gave her this doll. He bought it in Paris when he visited the 1889 World Exhibition. Marie is as tall as a two-year-old child, and wears tiny felt shoes, which are now half-eaten by moths. Yet her white lace dress

Marie, the doll given by Jean Linden to his granddaughter Lulu.

‹ Lucienne Linden (on the left) with her parents Lucien Linden and Marguerite Van den Hove, with her sister. The figure at the window is probably Jean Linden. 1890s.

and hat, which is plumed and covered with flowers and graces her long hair, still lend her the allure of a great lady. She is the incarnation of my grandmother's stories. Marie was given to me when I was nine, and she is still here by my side, keeping me company.

It may seem strange today, but nothing from the "Linden Dynasty" and too few testaments to the activities of Jean have been handed down through the generations of his family. Of course, there were some photographs scattered through their various display cabinets, yet none of my relatives knew about the history of orchids, of their discovery, their culture, or of Jean Linden's passion for the extraordinary plants that he introduced to Europe. The only sign was the family tradition at funerals of placing a *Cattleya* bloom in the coffin.

In Venezuela, 1998.

I did not quite know whether I could believe Lulu's beautiful tales or in the significance she accorded her grandfather. Yet, one day, my aunt Andrée brought me a copy of the special issue of *La Semaine horticole* that was published on the death of Jean Linden. The journal includes the report of the Venezuela expedition, with a mention of Tocuyo. The sound of that name immediately triggered the memory of my childhood's exotic dreams. I quickly pinpointed Tocuyo de la Costa on a map of Venezuela dating back to 1840. It was no island, but that did not matter: town or river, Tocuyo did exist, and it now became imperative that I go in search of my legendary forebear.

The only archive I had was an obituary, the above-mentioned issue of *La Semaine horticole* and one of Lucien Linden's books, *Les Orchidées exotiques et leur culture en Europe*, which had miraculously escaped the dispersal of family heirlooms. I found the first autographed text of Jean Linden in Paris. It was a scrap of paper so thin as to be transparent: in 1845, he wrote a few words to Adolphe Brongniart, a botanist who ranks amongst the most eminent 19th-century taxonomists of the Muséum national d'Histoire naturelle, recalling his return from Colombia. Colombia! My heart was pounding. From then on, my ever-increasing curiosity fired my research.

MY "TOUCOUYOU"

Following in the footsteps of my great-great-grandfather was like a treasure hunt! Each clue brought me closer to this man who had captured my imagi-

La Semaine horticole, special edition of
12 February 1898, p. 61.

Lucien Linden, *Les Orchidées exotiques,* 1894.

nation. My search was more of an archaeological excavation. I visited Kew
Gardens and the Lindley Library in London, the Botanical Gardens of
Brussels and Geneva, the Muséum national d'Histoire naturelle in Paris, the
Bibliothèque royale de Belgique and the Archives générales du Royaume in
Brussels, the Mundaneum in Mons, the archives and library of the Floralies
in Ghent and several archives in Luxembourg, Mexico, Venezuela and
Colombia. Little by little, I created a small library of most of the articles
and books relating to Jean Linden. Whenever possible, I acquired copies of
his publications.

Sorting through papers and microfiche was no longer enough, however.
I had to find my grandfather's "Toucouyou" and get a taste of the South
American atmosphere he had imbibed for over a decade. Accompanied by
my husband, Jean Schuermans, I started on the trail of Jean Linden in
Mexico and Venezuela. Although I sometimes felt sensitive to this invasion
of his privacy, I gradually formed an image of Linden that was rooted in
reality and could be compared to his legendary, glorified persona. The
archives – unveiling the explorer's substantial correspondence with ministers, scientists, bankers and diplomats – enabled me to establish travel itineraries unknown at that time, as well as to identify the plants collected and
their places of discovery. In these archives, I also found references to some
of my ancestor's close family members, such as his half brother and sister,
Louis-Joseph and Catherine Schlim, and particularly Nicolas Funck, a fundamental figure in the Linden context.

CATTLEYA MENDELI

The result of these ten years of piecemeal research is the discovery of a man of his times. In 1835, taking advantage of the drive for expansion by the young Belgian state – a precursor to the colonies – young Linden used his contacts to live out his passion, creating the desire to possess a priceless, luxury article: the exotic plant, with a focus on orchids and palms. His early successes fuelled his creation and development of the horticultural industry in Belgium.

Beyond a simple factual chronology, however, I wanted to structure this monograph by exploring different aspects of the life of Jean Linden. His clear passion for orchids serves as a core theme for the whole study. One soon realizes that the three expeditions he led in Latin America constituted a critical stage in his evolution as a naturalist. Upon his return to Belgium (after a brief stay in his native Luxembourg), he did not confine his activities to running his horticultural companies but continued the trend of sending specialist collectors to import exotic plants as yet unknown to Europe. At the same time, he evolved as a society figure, equally at home in the company of scientific personalities, leading industrialists, political figures and diplomats. Financial prosperity, directing the activities of his collectors and personal networking thus represent the three main aspects of the life of Jean Linden, apart from his expeditions. A chapter by Guido Braem gives us an overview of the specialist publications to which Linden devoted himself and, finally, the last years of his life and the succession of the Linden dynasty lead us to an evaluation of his place in the history of botany and industrial horticulture.

In Venezuela, people transfer the cattleyas from the wild to their immediate environment (hedgerows etc.).

‹ *Cattleya mendeli* [sic].
Illustration from the *Lindenia*.

THE YOUNG LINDEN

1817-1835

It would be futile to try to capture Jean Linden, his expeditions and his entrepreneurial success without locating him in his historical context. The turning point in this man's life, in 1835, was a direct consequence of the political situation of a state that was in its initial stages of development. [1]

We frequently forget that, in those days, Belgium and the Grand Duchy of Luxembourg were one unity. Belgium had acquired its independence in 1830 and, on 21 July 1831, the fledgling country witnessed its first king take his oath, in the church of Saint-Jacques-sur-Coudenberg. Less than two weeks after his accession, however, the head of state had to prove his mettle as commander-in-chief of the armies: William of Orange, first king of the Netherlands, rejected the treaty of XVIII Articles that had been ratified by the various European powers. He planned to re-conquer the southern part of his kingdom by force. The defending forces of the infant Belgium were neither well equipped nor adequately trained. Furthermore, it was trapped in its status of neutral state, rendering it something of a buffer zone between the Netherlands, France, England, Prussia and the Austro-Hungarian Empire. Without the providential assistance of its French neighbour, it would almost certainly have disappeared from the European map. Faced with a military defeat that questioned its capacity to defend itself, Belgium had to accept a new treaty at the end of 1831. In the treaty of XXIV Articles, the northern part of Limburg and half of Luxembourg were given back to the Dutch king. As King William did not ratify this revised treaty, however, Belgium continued to enjoy the provinces for another eight years. It came as a shock, therefore, when the Netherlands finally ratified this second agreement in March 1838 and England and France put pressure on Belgium to fulfil its conditions.

‹ Jean Linden. 1870s.

1. For an overview of the geopolitical situation in Belgium's early years, see: Els Witte and Jan Craeybeckx, *La Belgique politique de 1830 à nos jours. Les tensions d'une démocratie bourgeoise*, Brussels, Labor, 1987; Comte Louis de Lichtervelde, *Léopold Ier et la formation de la Belgique contemporaine*, Brussels, Librairie Albert Dewit, 1929; Carlo Bronne, *Léopold Ier et son temps*, Brussels, Paul Legrain, 1971.

View of Luxembourg from Clausen, 1814.

This political episode explains why a significant number of figures in Belgian history, be it political, cultural or scientific, were in fact natives of Luxembourg. Many citizens of this former province attained the highest civilian and military positions, as evidenced by Jean-Baptiste Nothomb and, later, by minister Emmanuel Servais. Jean Linden was another of these great men.

During the nineteenth century, the European landscape progressively metamorphosed as the industrial revolution gained pace. The nascent Kingdom of Belgium was also changing in this regard. Brussels was evolving from week to week, embracing the technical progress that was revolutionizing commerce and transport. In fact, never-ending building sites as we now experience in Brussels, are nothing new. Without listing these architectural developments, it is interesting to note that the Brussels of Linden's youth – as well as his native Luxembourg, both far from being European capitals – did not look anything like the places we know today. Devoid of congestion or pollution, Brussels was still limited to the central pentagon and crossed by the River Senne with unbroken views. In May 1835, the railway reared its head in the shape of the first steam locomotive on the allée Verte. It is possible to imagine Jean Linden witnessing this spectacular opening a few months after his arrival in Brussels. This particular traveller did not get a chance to experience the new means of transportation until ten years later, however, when he returned from his lengthy sojourns in Latin America.

If these environmental factors essentially developed at the end of the nineteenth century, some can be linked to the activities of Jean Linden. At the instigation of the authorities, whose aim was to make Brussels a botanical city,[2] the horticulturist developed an important complex of greenhouses that directly impacted on the regional development of the capital and its suburbs. Some of these sites eventually disappeared in the relentless programme of urban renewal in the capital. On the rue Vautier, the house of the director of the Parc Léopold – where Linden would live until 1896 – is the only remaining witness of his presence in the city. In 1835, however, the young Linden could hardly have foreseen the impact he would later have on the urban fabric and citizens of Brussels.

The landscape was not solely disrupted by technical and scientific progress. There was also a fundamental shift in thinking across Europe. In a positivist drive to expand horizons and foster economic growth, national authorities launched multiple initiatives and explorations. Science, knowledge and curiosities were now the concerns of a whole society eager to change its environment and way of life. The natural sciences, in particular biology and botany, were universally acclaimed. The appeal of science and economic ambition merged together in the great expeditions launched by various European countries. Belgium aligned itself with this approach and was quick to dispatch scientific missions to different continents. These expeditions covered different disciplines, from mineralogy through zoology to geography and botany. The latter enjoyed a fashion revival in the first half of the nineteenth century, as witnessed by the development of institutions for botanical studies.

In France, the Muséum national d'Histoire naturelle opened its doors in 1793. In England, too, the scientific domain was already well established by the beginning of the nineteenth century. Sir William Hooker created a scientific department at Kew Gardens in 1841, which would soon be renowned for its herbarium, library and museum of economic botany. Kew would also become prominent in the dispatch of collectors abroad, whose role was to introduce unknown plant specimens into England.

The coverage of these expeditions in the press sparked major interest amongst the general public as well as within scientific circles. A pioneer of the nineteenth century, the German naturalist Alexander von Humboldt (1769-1859) undertook a long journey to South America with Aimé Bonpland, from 1799 to 1804, an initiative that was emulated by countless followers. In 1803, the President of the United States, Thomas Jefferson,

Opening of the first rail terminus in the allée Verte, Brussels, 5 May 1835.

The director's house still stands today at the back of Parc Léopold, in the shadow of the European Parliament buildings.

2. This ambition was already evident in the 1820s, when King William I of Orange named Leyde as the country's zoological capital; he also planned to turn Brussels into "the botanical capital of the kingdom of the Low Countries". Denis Diagre, *Le Jardin botanique de Bruxelles*, lecture at Brussels University, 27 March 2004.

commissioned two explorers, Captains Meriwether Lewis and William Clark – complete with military escort – to establish a commercial route from Missouri through the Rocky Mountains to the Pacific. This mission would take three years.

Von Humboldt's influence spread to Belgium, where Latin America began to generate fashionable interest. In its infant state, however, Belgium was feeling its lack of geographers. The Vandermaelen brothers[3] created the first geographic company in Brussels in 1830. Philippe (1795-1869) was a self-taught geologist and Jean-François (1797-1872) a horticulturist. The two brothers, both passionately interested in cartography and the natural sciences, were particularly sensitive to the echoes of the voyages of von Humboldt. In 1832, they risked their fortune and reputation in discovering the world, sending their assistant Gédéon Crabbe and their gardener Deyrolle to Brazil for a 16-month period. Later, from 1835 to 1840, the Vandermaelen brothers would finance the expedition of botanist and geologist Henri Galeotti (1814-1858), whom Jean Linden would encounter in Mexico.

Following the example of the cartographic brothers – as well as the personal interest of King Leopold I in Latin America – the Belgian government commissioned a scientific and economic expedition to Brazil. This is where Jean Linden enters the picture.

JEAN LINDEN

On 12 February 1817, his father, Antoine Linden, a Luxembourg clockmaker, was physically incapable of going to the town hall to register the birth of his son. He had pneumonia, from which he would die a couple of months later, leaving two children: Marie and Jean. A year later, his young widow Marie Becker (1791-1834) married François-Henri Schlim (born 1791). He was also a clockmaker and the son of a printer. He enrolled in the Belgian army from May to August 1831, wherein he was commissioned as a lieutenant in the seventh infantry. Upon his return, he opened an inn in Luxembourg, which he called "À mon idée". The father of five children, he died on 3 February 1833, 18 months before his wife. Two of his direct descendants also became naturalists: Louis-Joseph Schlim (1819-1863), who accompanied Jean Linden to New Granada, and Catherine, born on 2 April 1824.

Jean Linden.
Watercolour portrait from around 1845.

3. For a concise introduction to the brothers Philippe and Jean-François Vandermaelen, see the recent work *Cent trésors de la Bibliothèque royale de Belgique*, Brussels, Fonds Mercator, 2005, pp. 190-193 [section by Marguerite Silvestre], which accompanies the exhibition of the same name.

Raised by his mother and stepfather amongst professional, creative, educated and independent artisans, Jean Linden was early exposed to the rigor and scientific precision that informed his profession as an explorer and collector. He studied at the Athénée royal de Luxembourg, an old Jesuit college founded in 1603. The school had abandoned its old-fashioned educational methods, based on the translation of classical texts, to embrace new subjects such as mathematics, languages and science. Linden exhibited a particular interest in the natural sciences. His passion for nature inspired his travels through the countryside of Luxembourg and Belgium, collecting plants under the supervision of eminent botanists (see also the chapter on Jean Linden and his networks page 163).

On 2 February 1834, on the eve of his departure for Brussels, Jean found himself an orphan with the death of his mother. We do not know how the family coped following their tragic, double bereavement. All we know of this time is that the eldest daughter, Marie, married a Luxembourg civil servant, Arthur Herschen. As for Jean himself, he entered the newly founded Brussels University where he pursued his scientific studies. He was amongst the first 96 students of the institution, which was then situated in an annex of the Palais des Beaux-Arts, on the rue de la Régence. He pursued courses in geology, geography, zoology and botany, in particular with Professor Jean Kickx (1803-1864), a botanist and professor of malacology. Linden maintained links with the professor in Ghent until 1864.

L'Ancienne Crèche seen from the Chemin de la Corniche. Drawing of the Reuter family home in Luxembourg by Adolphe Eberhard.

L'Athénée royal de Luxembourg. Painting by A.M. Jobard, 1825.

It is interesting to consider why Linden chose neither the Leuven University nor Ghent University, both of which were well established with departments fully equipped for his training. It seems that the choice of university did not rest on its attributes and competences as a centre of learning, but was linked to the burgeoning network of contacts the young native of Luxembourg was enjoying among the political leaders of the newly independent nation of Belgium. Through François Tinant, Linden would become the protégé of Jean-Baptiste Nothomb, then Minister for Public Works, who also had regular meetings with Philippe Vandermaelen and was a passionate supporter of the latter's project to map Belgium and Luxembourg.[4]

In 1835, the Belgian government undertook to sponsor a scientific and commercial mission to Latin America: more specifically, Brazil. They first visited members of the Académie royale then Brussels University with the aim of finding the "scientist in a million" who could take charge of the expedition. A young, 18-year-old student met with general approval. From then on, every biography of Jean Linden speaks of a "brilliant student", "botanist chosen by the Belgian government", etc. In the spring of 1835, Jean could not have pretended to be an experienced scientist competent in botany, astronomy, mineralogy and ethnology. Yet rumours of his imminent departure were circulating by August, though he had only started his courses in November the previous year. As a result, the academic contribution of the student could not have amounted to much beyond a few scientific principles and sessions of plant collecting with Tinant. It is possible that yesterday's reality was a lot simpler than that of today ... The prospect of a voyage of exploration destined for great discoveries is bound to have tempted a vigorous young man with nothing to lose. He may well have heard of von Humboldt through his narrative accounts, which were published in 30 volumes from 1807 to 1834. Linden was capable of marching or horse riding all day long, of using a rifle and swimming. He was clearly cast in the same mould as naturalist explorers. Linden's burning interest in botany and the support of his relations probably took care of the rest.

When he arrived in Brussels, Jean Linden was alone and unknown, yet his sojourn in the Belgian capital would be brief. It was merely a springboard to adventure on the far side of the Atlantic. Immersed in a society that promised great opportunity, the young student grabbed his chance to make a swift impression in scientific circles. Linden progressively estab-

4. *Ibid.*, p. 190.

lished a highly respectable place for himself amongst members of these sets whose credentials were already established, such as Vandermaelen, Tinant, Dumortier and even Nothomb. In September 1835, he left Brussels with two of his student colleagues: Nicolas Funck and Auguste Ghiesbreght. The latter would support Linden throughout his expeditions, whereas the former would become a lifelong friend and collaborator.

Nicolas Funck

I only discovered "Uncle Nicolas" – as Lucien Linden (Jean's son) often referred to him – when I found the commission for the second voyage of my great-great-grandfather. He is, however, inextricably linked with the life of Jean Linden. Nicolas Funck (1816–1896) was also born in Luxembourg, the son of a contractor and bricklayer, Michel Funck, and his wife Marguerite Urban. He studied architecture in Brussels, probably at the Académie, and was chosen to accompany Linden as illustrator and diarist on his first two expeditions. The friendship between the two men was further strengthened when Funck and Linden married two Luxembourg sisters, Catherine and Anna Reuter, on 9 April 1849 and 13 October 1845 respectively.

Nicolas Funck would forsake his initial profession of architect for zoology. When his friend encountered some difficulties in his position as director of the Zoological Gardens in Brussels he left Luxembourg, where he was teaching natural history at the highschool Athénée royal, and moved to the Belgian capital, helping his old friend before succeeding him in 1861. Two years before, in 1859, he had become the editor-in-chief of the *Journal d'horticulture pratique de Belgique*, following in the footsteps of Henri Galeotti.

Without doubt, his eloquent pen has enabled me to fill the blank pages of Jean Linden's life. His journal (*Reise-Errinnerungen*, drafted in German and so far unpublished), in which humour and poetry set the tone, injects new life into these expeditions. The writer gives free rein to his political opinions, along with vivid descriptions of social conditions in the countries they traversed.

In *Le Journal des orchidées*, Lucien Linden speaks in turn of Nicolas Funck's interventions: "My uncle Funck related anecdotes of his voyages [...]. He was a humorous and lively guest. Later on, he would leave his mark as a modest and conscientious scientist."*

Funck can never be separated from Jean Linden. In addition to his appointment as director of the Cologne Zoological Gardens in 1870 – a position he held until 1886 and in which he welcomed on a visit in 1875 the Brazilian emperor, Dom Pedro II, whom he had met 40 years earlier in Rio de Janeiro – he managed the society Flora, an association linked to the Cologne Botanic Gardens.

His name is also to be found amongst the administrators of the Linden family companies and in the birth registers of the Linden children. He constantly figures at the heart of Jean Linden's closest circles. He remained faithful to the natural sciences, as one of the founding members of the Société des Sciences naturelles in Luxembourg, for which he organized exhibitions and ornithological displays. He was also an honorary member of the Ghent flower show committee (Floralies) in 1878 and 1893. Nicolas Funck died in Luxembourg on 10 August 1896, two years before his "old friend". The botanist Schlechter would name an orchid genus *Funckiella* [more generally, and erroneously, spelt *Funkiella*].

* *JO*, 1896, p. 185-186.

THE ADVENTURE

Brazil   1835-1837

Mexico   1837-1841

Venezuela and New Granada   1841-1844

THE FIRST EXPEDITION

Brazil 1835–1837

In the course of just ten years, Jean Linden undertook three major expeditions. Although officially commissioned by the Belgian government, his explorations were also backed by other interested parties. This was not an unusual situation: at the time in question, numerous vessels carrying Western scientists were plying the southern seas in quest of new discoveries. On board the *Beagle,* for instance, Darwin was exploring South America, Australia and the Galapagos Islands between 1831 and 1836. These voyages were ostensibly scientific in nature, but were often motivated by the possibility of future economic advantages.

The first destination of Linden and his companions was Brazil, which in 1835 had started commercial negotiations with Belgium. A trade and shipping treaty between the Netherlands and Brazil was, in fact, already in existence, having been signed under William I.[1] In an attempt to revive it, in 1834 the diplomat (and occasional watercolourist) Benjamin Mary was put in charge of negotiations for a new agreement. The resulting document was ratified on 22 September 1834; on 27 June 1835, Belgium also founded the Société universelle de Commerce et de Navigation.

The way was now open for other ventures. A certain Guinard, a trade agent, was commissioned to draw up a report on Brazil. On 26 June 1835 on board the *Caroline,* he drew up a detailed analysis of the country's markets, local crafts and traditions. He added: "I believe I have also fulfilled the government's intentions by bringing back from Brazil seeds and shrubs whose description or nomenclature will be found along with samples and details filed as follows ... Having managed to establish a friendly correspondence between the curator of the Imperial Gardens in Rio and the administrators of the Horticultural Garden in Brussels, I have, as far as I can see,

View over Rio Bay, detail. Drawing by Benjamin Mary, around 1834. Rio de Janeiro, collection Paulo F. Geyer.
‹‹ *Vera Cruz,* 1844. Engraving by Moritz Rugendas.
‹ Map of Rio de Janeiro, around 1840.

1. Trade and shipping treaty with Brazil, 20 December 1828. Passim.

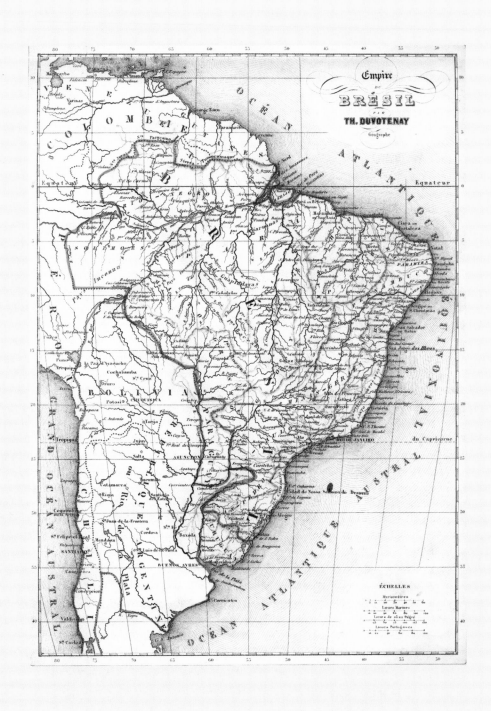

rendered an important service to everyone connected with botany and horti-culture. During the establishment of this correspondence, Senhor Brandão, the curator of the Imperial Gardens – who has honoured me with his esteem and, dare I say, his friendship – has authorised me to offer the administrators of our Botanic Garden all that Brazil possesses in the way of plants, shrubs, seeds, etc., in exchange for plants from Belgium ..."[2] This is followed by a catalogue entitled: *List of plants and seeds brought back from Rio by Mr Guinard on behalf of the government and forwarded to the offices of the Minister of the Interior.*

This was the background of the expeditions led by Linden and commis-sioned by the Belgian government. No written record, however, can be found of the orders for the first voyage to Brazil. The only – uncorroborated – men-tion asserts: "The voyage is authorised by the Belgian government on behalf of the Emperor of Brazil."[3] In fact, Linden and his companions did meet the emperor, Dom Pedro II, who was then just 14 years old.

Explorers were usually recruited from amongst botanists and geologists. Closely connected with Nothomb, a member of the government, the brothers Vandermaelen, Barthélemy Dumortier or perhaps Jean-Baptiste Meeûs may have been influential in the appointment of

Linden. Dumortier left the following note in his correspondence: "Mr Dumortier announces that Linden and three other naturalists propose to leave very shortly for northern Brazil, where they intend to spend several years studying the flora and fauna."[4] In addition, the Société royale d'Horticulture, of which Jean-Baptiste Meeûs was president, entrusted Linden with the shipping to Brazil of crocus, tulip and daffodil bulbs, together with asparagus and melon seeds, in exchange for plants from South America, a list being available on request. The aims of the Société royale d'Horticulture had scope beyond the botanical, however: many of its mem-bers were from families of merchants and leading bankers.

Linden was 18 when he accepted the offer of the Belgian government: "I was a student in the Science Faculty of Brussels University when, in

‹ Map of Brazil in 1840.

Santa Cruz. 6 November 1837. Emperor Dom Pedro. Drawing by Benjamin Mary, 1837. Rio de Janeiro, Paulo F. Geyer collection.

2. Report addressed to the Minister of the Interior, 26 June 1835. Brussels, Archives of the Ministry of Foreign Affairs.

3. Marks Klein, *Le Tour du monde des Luxembourgeois*, Foetz (Luxembourg), Éditions Kremer-Muller & Cⁱᵉ, 1995, p. 59. The author does not identify his source; he may have found this information in the newspaper articles that appeared after Linden's death.

4. The fourth man mentioned was a certain Jacquet, of whom no trace can be found in the records. Brussels, Archives of the Ministry of Foreign Affairs.

September 1835, the Belgian government entrusted me with a scientific mission to South America, at that time still almost unknown, assigning me two colleagues, Funck and Ghiesbreght."[5] We have already described, in the preceding chapter, the famous "Uncle Nicolas". Linden's other companion, Auguste Ghiesbreght (1810-93)[6], was older than he by seven years. Ghiesbreght would participate in the first two expeditions. After studying medicine in Paris, he volunteered in 1830 to fight in Belgium's war of independence. He, too, was a student at Brussels University, meeting Linden and Funck in Brussels in 1834. After the second expedition he settled in Mexico, continuing to collect a wide range of plants that he sent back to Europe from 1852 onwards. He practised as a doctor among the natives of Chiapas, dying in 1893 at San Cristóbal de las Casas.

"Our preparations were quickly made and at the end of December we disembarked in Brazil after a difficult three-month crossing."[7] This was Linden's sole account of the first expedition; the other facts only became known through Funck's somewhat fragmentary report. This did, however, reveal much of interest concerning daily life on these exotic missions. In his writings, Lucien Linden describes the departure from Antwerp in 1835: "How many times did Uncle Nicolas describe to me how they left Antwerp! Besides their letters of credit, the three young travellers were burdened with a heavy bag of coins to cover initial expenses. They were taking turns carrying the bag. Suddenly one of the group, exhausted, refused his turn and put down his burden, right in the middle of the Meir in Antwerp, declaring he would carry it no further ... I never found out who it was, or who eventually picked it up."[8]

The *Journal d'Anvers* of Saturday, 25 September 1835 announced "the departure of the Belgian schooner *Clémence* under Captain Knudsen, bound for Rio de Janeiro with a mixed cargo" – gin and cheeses, for the most part. "The *Clémence* was a modest vessel to say the least, an old-fashioned Dutch schooner known as a *galiasse*, rounded identically at stem and stern, coated all over with a layer of pitch, hardly elegant, with a capacity of around 300 tonnes deadweight. She was one of the old types you still see on the Mordyck and the Dutch canals; on either side were what looked like wooden wings that could be lowered in turn so that the vessel did not drift too far when tacking into the wind. Bunks were installed in cupboard-sized spaces (66 x 181 cm). Billeted in pairs in these compartments reserved for us in the upper cabin, we scarcely had space to dress and undress, and each man had to wait until the other had finished."[9] The ship's complement consisted,

Le bateau à vapeur anglais *Attwood*, cap. Morfée, ven. de Londres, avec passagers et diverses marchandises.

Au bas de la Rivière.

Un brick mecklenbourgeois, venant de Riga, chargé de bois et un pleyt belge, venant de Londres, chargé de diverses marchandises.

DEPARTS, DU 25 SEPTEMBRE.

La galiotte belge *Clémence*, cap. Knudsen, all. a la Rio-Janeiro, chargé de diverses marchandises.

La goelette russe *Imatra*, cap. Nordling, allant a Méditerranée, chargé de mecaniques et diverses marchandises.

AMSTERDAM, 24 SEPTEMBRE.

Dette active	*int* 2 ¹/₂	54 ¹/₂	Ardouin	*int* 5	41 00
» »	5	101 ⁵/₄	Cer Nap Fal.	5	00 00
» différée		1 ⁵/₈	Rus H. 1798	5	104 00
Bil de change		24 00	Dito 1828	5	104 ¹/₂
syndic. d'am.	4 ¹/₂	94 ⁹/₈	Dito 1831	5	98 00
» »	3 ¹/₂	79 00	Inscrip. rus.	6	69 ¹/₁₆
Soc. de Com.	4 ¹/₂	111 ⁴/₄	Lots de Pol.		149 ¹/₄

Extract from *Le Journal d'Anvers*, 26 September 1835.

5. J Linden, in *JO*, 1894, p. 21.

6. For information on Auguste Ghiesbreght, see José Rovirosa, "Vida y trabajos del naturalista belga Augusto B. (Bonifacio) Ghiesbreght, explorador de México", *Naturaleza*, 1889, 2/1, pp. 211-217.

7. Jean Linden, *op. cit.*, p. 176.

8. Lucien Linden, *JO*, 1896, p. 185.

9. Nicolas Funck, *Reise-Errinnerungen*, Luxembourg, 1909, 1915-1920, 1922.

View of the "trapiche" of Itaguahy, September 1836.
Drawing by Benjamin Mary, 1836. Rio de Janeiro, Mario
Pimenta Camargo collection. Inside the sheds on the
banks of the Itaguai river, slaves were secretly
disembarked for the Brazilian coffee plantations.

beside the master and the first mate, of eight sailors and four passengers, including our explorers. A volley of gunshots signalled their departure. As the *Clémence* left the estuary, the young travellers suffered their first unpleasant experience of the voyage: a violent storm that raged for three whole days off the Isle of Walcheren.

The Atlantic crossing followed the obligatory route via Madeira and the Canary Islands. The heat was overwhelming; there were few distractions, and the smallest event onboard became the focus of everyone's attention. One day, the capture of a blue shark led to a surprising discovery: when opened, its belly was found to contain "a boot probably belonging to a sailor who fell overboard and sadly never saw the light of day again".[10] The shark was stuffed and sent back to Europe as a trophy. Later, not far off the Brazilian coast, a sail appeared on the horizon. Delighted at the prospect of possible company after twelve weeks of solitude, the crew altered course to meet the stranger. As they drew closer, things took a turn for the worse: the other vessel's port side was lined with cannons. With her four rifles and two pistols, the *Clémence* was hardly equipped to resist a pirate attack. There was nothing reassuring about the mystery vessel: her crew were a motley, unprepossessing bunch. Their captain, a mulatto, hailed the explorers' ship in French through his megaphone, demanding her name, port of origin and cargo. He also enquired about any warships in the vicinity. The black pirates

10. *Ibid.*

then lost interest and made off at high speed. A few days afterwards, in Rio Bay, Linden and his friends witnessed the same pirate ship being towed in by an English frigate – she had been captured the day after this disturbing encounter on the high seas.

Three months after their departure from Antwerp, on 27 December 1835 the three adventurers landed in Rio de Janeiro. Their uneventful arrival is confirmed in a letter to Dumortier. "At Rio", wrote Funck, "the high society of the time was composed of representatives of friendly nations, naval officers from England, France and the USA, various naturalists, scholars and princes on study trips to Brazil".[11] Linden, Funck and Ghiesbreght were welcomed by the Belgian Consul, Adolphe Tiberghien, for whom they had letters of recommendation signed by the Minister of Foreign Affairs at home. They were received very warmly and invited to stay with the consul.

The following day they called on Benjamin Mary, appointed the first representative of Belgium in 1832. He had resided from February 1834 in Catete, the aristocratic quarter of Rio, near the Praça Flamengo. He was highly regarded in the city, for both his diplomatic skill and affability, and his talent as a landscape painter. He became a friend to the young explorers, who had cause to be grateful for his advice and protection. Benjamin Mary was also the nephew of Joseph Parmentier, a native of Enghien and a famous botanist and horticulturist, who specialised in tropical flora. It is thanks to

11. *Ibid.*

Mary's watercolours, which reproduce in fine detail the luxuriance of the

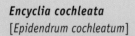

Encyclia cochleata
[*Epidendrum cochleatum*]

Of medium height, this epiphytic orchid occurs throughout the Caribbean Islands, southern Florida, Mexico, Central America and even the northern countries of South America (Colombia, Venezuela, Guyana) where it flourishes at altitudes of 100-2,000 m. 38*Encyclia cochleata* is structured as a small, tightly knit group of pseudobulbs. The inflorescence produced at the top of this slightly flattened organ, which is ellipsoid or pear-shaped, can sometimes reach a height of around 50 cm and comprises numerous flowers opening successively in an extended season.

Although known since the work by Plumier on Jamaican plants (1703), it was first properly described by Linnaeus in his famous *Species Plantarum* of 1753. In his *Flore de la Guyane* (1955), Lemée eventually transferred the species to the genus *Encyclia*. Today it remains extremely popular among orchid growers. [Guido Braem]

*Rio de Janeiro. Panoramic view of the plain to
the north of the city.* Drawing by Benjamin Mary, 1837.
Rio de Janeiro, H. von Martius collection.

virgin forests, that we can appreciate the flora of 19th-century Brazil. The
first excursion of Linden and his companions was made to the Botanical
Gardens at the foot of Mount Corcovado. As they made their way along
Botafago Bay towards Tynco, they encountered hundreds of trees, shrubs
and flowering plants – including palms, sapodillas, avocados, pepper and
vanilla – which they recognised from their studies of the few meagre specimens in European greenhouses. They spotted their first "parasitic" orchid,
as it was referred to then – *Epidendrum cochleatum,* already familiar in
Europe – clinging to the trunk of a *Carica papaya* and stood in wonder
before the Royal Palm *Oredoxa regia* – the largest of the New World palms,
which forms majestic avenues.

One excursion succeeded another for the three Belgians. On Mount
Corcovado they discovered tillandsias, numerous ferns and some impressive

1-2. Cattleya crispa, pendula. 3-6. Cheiranthera linearis, All.Cunn.

Laelia crispa
[Cattleya crispa]

Initially classified by John Lindley in 1828 as *Cattleya crispa,* this splendid orchid was renamed *Laelia crispa* in 1853 by Heinrich Gustav Reichenbach. The new nomenclature is based on the number of pollinia, *Cattleya* possessing four and *Laelia* eight. Endemic to Brazil, *Laelia crispa* grows at altitudes of 600-1,200 m in the states of Espírito Santo, Rio de Janeiro and Minas Gerais, as well as certain southern regions of Brazil. It is a large plant: its pseudobulbs can attain nearly 30 cm in length; they are compressed, with furrows on the flat surfaces. Above these the leaves grow up to 30 cm long and 5 cm wide. The inflorescence is generated from the apex of the pseudobulb and bears up to ten flowers, each of them some 13 cm in diameter and truly dazzling. The sepals and petals are white with purple basal tint.
The labellum has a yellow base, striped with purple at the centre; the apex is also purple, but reticulated with darker purple veins. The column is white, again with purple base. [GUIDO BRAEM]

Zygopetalum mackayi
[Zygopetalum mackaii]

This remarkable orchid was named in honour of James Townsend Mackay (1775-1862). He was a gardener and botanist of Scottish origin who worked principally at the University of Dublin. In the first place, William Hooker classified the plant as *Z. mackaii* in the *Botanical Magazine* for 1827. Today, his spelling error is usually corrected (*mackaii* becoming *mackayi*). *Z. mackayi* is an impressive species. The pseudobulbs are 5-10 cm in height and surmounted by two or three smooth leaves with a leathery texture, bright green but turning yellow with age. An inflorescence up to one metre tall rises from the base of the pseudobulb. It bears five to twelve flowers of 7-9 cm in height. These are highly perfumed, long-lasting and waxy.
The greenish-yellow sepals and petals are marked with large, irregular spots varying from reddish-brown to chestnut. Broad and flattened, the labellum is white with a network of dark red to bluish-violet veins.
Z. mackayi is endemic to Brazil where it is encountered in the states of Minas Gerais, Espírito Santo and Rio Grande do Sul. Its habitat is usually grassy plains or prairies. [GUIDO BRAEM]

bamboo. Another day, Mary took them by sailboat to Fort Santa Cruz and to the island of Boa Viagem. There they observed plants never seen before, such as *Vellozia* and *Barbacenia*. On a steep slope they found orchids in bloom: *Stanhopea tigrina* and *Laelia crispa* (already introduced to Europe) as well as the rarer *Zygopetalum mackayi*. On another occasion they experienced the delights of the Tejuco Valley, famed for its shoreline and waterfall.

For their explorations on foot, Linden and his friends proudly donned their "explorer's gear". They had turned impromptu designers, cobbling together a form of dress considered most appropriate for travelling naturalists. "It consisted of trousers and a loose jacket made of grey cloth, a wide-brimmed, Mexican-style straw hat and leather waders that came up to the knee [sic]. This costume was completed by a lacquered belt with a hunting-knife suspended over the left hip, and a small axe – not forgetting a rifle, specimen box and butterfly-net."[12]

The outfit caused a sensation. If their arrival in Rio had passed more or less without notice, this was certainly not the case when they went out for the first time attired in this fashion. "We were the objects of universal curiosity, not only on the part of the Brazilian-born black and white community but also of the many French people in the rua da Ouvidor, down the whole length of which we walked."[13]

A fortnight later, they completed preparations for a trip into the interior. To save money, Linden, Funck and Ghiesbreght used horses destined for the Swiss settlement of Morroquemado ("Burnt Mountain" or Nova Friburgo), one of their halting-places along the way. In this town, founded in 1825, the three men rented a house from a certain Proust, formerly a pharmacist from Saint-Malo. They also used a warehouse and garden to store the plants and animals they had collected until they could be dispatched to Europe.

Their route took them through Praya Grande, Alcantara and Cassaraban. As they headed for San Antonio, they lost their way in the virgin forest at night and made for a point of light in the darkness. Juan de Aguilar, "a well-read, highly educated man", received them with much courtesy. The following day, on the excuse that their horses and mules could not be found in the coffee and sugar plantations, their host invited the explorers

Édouard André: Le Voyage dans les Andes, around 1875. The frontispiece of this work published by the Société nationale d'Horticulture de France shows a "tourist outfit" identical to that described by Nicolas Funck.

12. *Ibid.*
13. *Ibid.*

to spend a further four days on his estate, such being the tradition of hospitality on a Brazilian Fazenda. Linden and his companions were to profit regularly from this custom, experiencing a decided pleasure in being able to converse with European settlers, partake of excellent wines imported from France and have a sing-song round the piano when encouraged to do so by the master or mistress of the house. On occasions, Funck was surprised to find them singing with Linden the popular French song: "J'irai revoir ma Normandie!" (I'm off back home to Normandy!). Such was their lifestyle at the inn on Mount Clara, or the home of a Frenchman near Aldeas das Piedras.

In the equatorial forest at the foot of the Organ Mountains, giant trees with massive trunks buried in the undergrowth, bushes and creepers alternated with elegant palms and ferns as tall as fully-grown trees. Funck was awestruck by a group of broad-leaved caladiums, dwarf palms (*Chamaedorea*), bromeliads and tillandsias. In his report he describes the cries of the monkeys and parrots and "the romantic song for which Actaeon would interrupt his hunt, Mary her prayers, and Orpheus lay aside his lyre".[14] The collecting went at a very good pace, with orchids already making up the majority of their specimens. From a single trunk they took no less than thirty specimens of the genera *Maxillaria*, *Cattleya*, *Epidendrum* and *Stanhopea*. On another occasion they cut down a tree and "procured a hundred orchids of twenty different species, without counting the bromeliads, caladiums, etc".[15]

The route taken by Linden in Brazil is unclear. The report of Funck, the diarist to the expedition, comes to a sudden end with the dispatch of crates to Antwerp, via Rio, on leaving Morroquemado. The same report – announced in Brussels as being the first part of a longer text at a reception hosted by the Académie royale in 1836 – appeared in instalments in Luxembourg between 1909 and 1920. No trace, however, has yet been found of a second part.

In the meantime, the three companions had declared their ambition to scour the provinces of Minas Gerais, Goiás and Mato Grosso, "which offered more of interest in the way of the natural sciences".[16] We know through Linden that he "successively explored the provinces of Rio de Janeiro, Espírito Santo and Minas Gerais with his companions, and then

‹ *Rio de Janeiro. View of Sugar Loaf Moutain and Fort St-John. 19 octobre 1837.* Drawing by Benjamin Mary, 1837. Rio de Janeiro, H. von Martius.

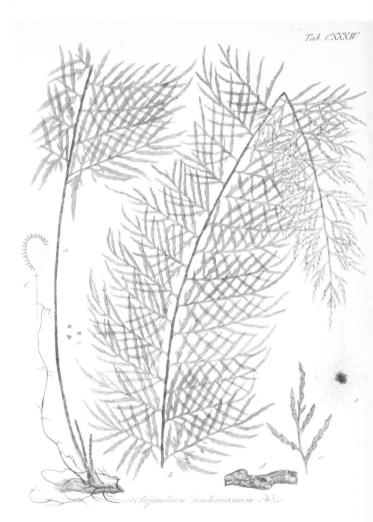

Polypodium lindenianum.
Plate from *Farnkräutern*, 1851.

14. *Ibid.*
15. *Ibid.*
16. *Bulletins de l'Academie royale des Sciences de Belgique*, 1836, p. 199.

Oncidium limminghei (now known as *Psychopsiella limminghei*). Plate from the *Lindenia*.

continued alone, on horseback, through the southern provinces of São Paulo and Santa Caterina".[17]

During 1836 and 1837, Belgium keenly followed the adventures of the young explorers. Barthélemy Dumortier kept his colleagues at the Académie in the picture through the contents of letters from Brazil, in between the arrival of crates full of natural history specimens. At the end of March 1837, the expedition returned home accompanied by further considerable collections. The young explorers were welcomed with great enthusiasm, surrounded as they were by the aura of exotic travel. Their arrival was mentioned in *Le Courrier belge* of 3 March: "Linden, Funck and Ghiesbreght have returned from Brazil. They left towards the end of 1835 to attempt a scientific expedition into the interior with the financial backing of the government and private funding bestowed by His Majesty the King. They have brought back with them a splendid collection of plants, including several species not yet cultivated in Belgium, as well as many rare animal species,

17. *JO*, 1894, p. 21.

amongst them thousands of insects and three or four thousand birds."[18] A few days later, the same newspaper revealed: "Among the items brought back were five thousand living plants, which the Minister of the Interior has shared out between the universities of Ghent and Liège, and the explorers have been received in Brussels by Their Majesties the King and Queen."[19] A further article states that King Leopold, in the presence of Prince Albert from England, presented each member of the expedition with a gold medal in token of his appreciation and satisfaction.

Few traces of any scientific feedback from the expedition have been recorded, however. Apart from the tally of specimens given in the press, there is no known document that analyses the quality of the collections shipped back to Belgium. (We shall have occasion to note, in examining the later expeditions, that some of the batches suffered from the long sea journey.) Nor do we hear of any scientific advances that resulted over the following few years. Was any attempt made to capitalise on the many discoveries through exhibitions, publications or scientific papers?

Notwithstanding the above, the new Kingdom of Belgium remained eager for this type of scientific undertaking. "Our young state," asserted the Académie royale des Sciences in Brussels, "must support these expeditions, and the government must provide new funding".[20] This plea was to be answered a few months later. The scientific agenda was to be complicated, however, by the introduction of a number of commercial and industrial aims. These saw a subtle change in relation to the first momentum of positivism and philanthropy supplied by the 19th-century Belgian middle classes.

18. *Le Courrier belge,* 3 March 1837.
19. *Ibid.,* 8 April 1837.
20. *Loc. cit.*

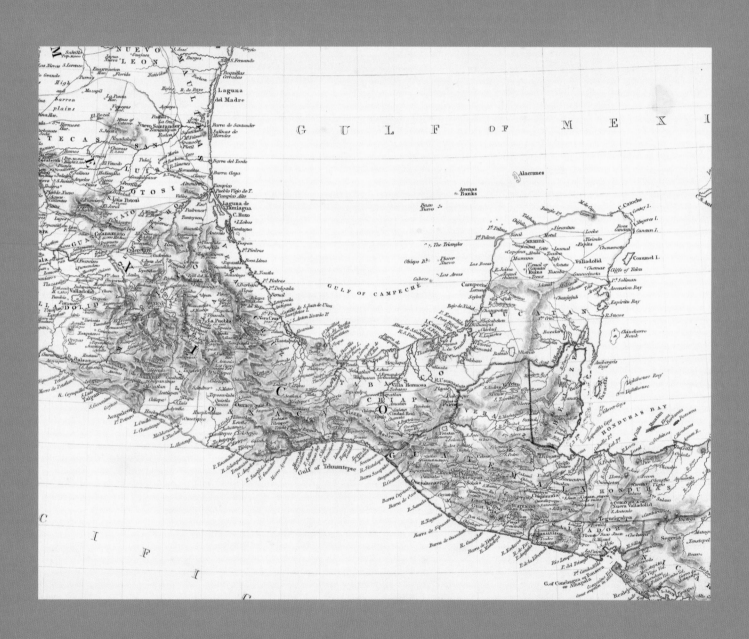

THE SECOND EXPEDITION

Mexico 1837-1841

Palenque, February 2003.

Soon after the return of Linden and his companions in March 1837, a second expedition was mounted in the hope of further discoveries. This new undertaking was much better documented than the first. It appears that the preparations and aims were given more careful thought, that the Minister of the Interior issued more specific instructions and that Linden himself conducted his researches more systematically. The wonder of a young man on his first journey had given way to more rational leadership.

For my own part I discovered quite a few traces of Jean Linden during my two stays in the states of Tabasco, Chiapas and Yucatán in February and December 2003: roads, villages and haciendas where the Mexicans have preserved a memory of the passage of the three young explorers. Their journeys were all the more real to me after my own adventures. What follows are the recent impressions of a great-great-granddaughter retracing the footsteps of her ancestor, interwoven with historical facts and material from the diaries of Nicolas Funck, Ghiesbreght and Galeotti.

In September 1837, the Belgian government entrusted Linden, Funck and Ghiesbreght with a new mission to Latin America. The orders for the expedition signed by King Leopold on 7 September reveal a more detailed programme. The territories listed in the document are vast, stretching from Cuba to Colombia via the various countries of Central America: Honduras, Guatemala and Panama. In actual fact, Linden followed a quite different itinerary: after a stopover in Cuba, the team made leisurely progress through parts of Mexico, visiting Veracruz, Jalapa, Mexico City, the Anáhuac plateau, the volcanoes of Popocatépetl and Iztaccihuatl, the Cofre de Perote and Mount Orizaba, as well as the entire eastern slope of the Cordillera, Oaxaca and the states of Tabasco, Chiapas and Yucatán.

‹ Map of Mexico in 1840.

Mount Orizaba, 2003.

What is more, the interests of science were not the only concern of the expedition, as its brief made clear. Belgium had recently appointed its first Minister for Trade and Industry and the explorers were required to obtain and communicate to the government information of interest to industry and commerce: for example, on consumer products and exports. Shortly before their departure, the three young men received further, final instructions concerning this additional aspect of their mission. In particular, they were required to furnish the minister "in the shortest time possible"[21] with a detailed report containing any piece of information that might assist the implantation of Belgian commercial enterprises in the countries visited. Actually, the travellers followed these orders only vaguely, leading to an animated correspondence between the ministers concerned and something of a political conflict.

We also have details of the budget for this expedition.[22] Each member received, as his total monthly allowance, 470 francs (2,250 euros). Some 5,000 francs (24,000 euros) was supposed to cover the costs of the sea crossing and the preparations. Finally, 1,000 francs (4,800 euros) were allotted to offset expenses arising from illness or the purchase of animals for the state collections. Guaranteed for three years, this enormous budget nevertheless proved insufficient: the expedition was

21. Brussels, Archives of the Ministry of Foreign Affairs, dossier 2014.

22. Royal decree dated 7 September 1837.

23. Jan Possemiers, *Les Belges et le Mexique*, Louvain-la-Neuve, Presses universitaires de Louvain, 1993, p 11.

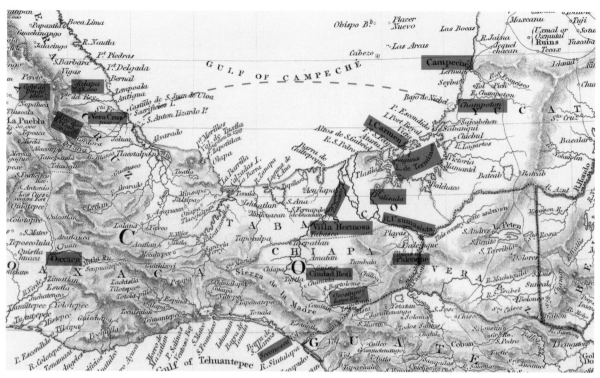

Map of Mexico in 1840. Detail showing sites visited by the three explorers.

obliged to spend an extra year in Latin America, in difficult conditions and penniless.

The second departure of Linden and his fellow travellers was made from Le Havre in September 1837. The Belgian merchant marine had been severely reduced in size since 1830 and only the ports of Le Havre and Hamburg operated regular links with Cuba. In the meantime, Belgium had recognised the republic of Mexico in 1836, so it was of paramount importance to conclude shipping and trade agreements there. Brussels hoped to install a plenipotentiary in Mexico City, plus a few unsubsidised consuls in the main ports. At this very moment, Baron Félix de Norman (1804-60) was preparing to visit Latin America on personal business. On 10 October 1837, the Belgian government entrusted him with a "special mission" – in fact, commercial espionage.[23] A major landowner in Kempen – as well as burgomaster of Westmalle – and a keen agronomist, he was anxious to study the farming methods of Latin America and prospect the market for a possible gin distillery. With his secretary, Arnould Oboussier, de Norman accompanied Linden, Funck and Ghiesbreght during the sea crossing. The five men reached Havana in the early days of December 1837. No written record of this voyage has come down to us: all we have is a sketchy mention by Nicolas Funck of being shipwrecked on an island.

Mountain view of Mexico, 2003.

MALPIGHIA ILICIFOLIA MILL.

Linden, for his part, remained very evasive about his itinerary and for good reason: he had already realised the huge personal financial advantages that could accrue from such expeditions. The burgeoning horticulturist and businessman in him counselled against divulging the source of his specimens. Botanical espionage was already a real danger, with some of his fellow collectors happy to confuse rivals by laying false trails.

In my attempts to re-create their itinerary I had only the account of their climb of Mount Orizaba and the shipwreck. I therefore followed the trail of the crates of plant and animal specimens dispatched to Belgium: their labelling revealed the route the expedition had taken and sometimes the actual source of the specimens.[24]

In Cuba, the group harvested a large number of plants. It was there, on the rocks of the Mesa de Mariel, and not in Brazil,[25] that Linden discovered *Malpighia ilicifolia*. He did not, however, collect specimens at the time, but was to return in 1841, bringing the species back to Europe for cultivation. When he died half a century later, it was a spray of these flowers that was laid on his heart.

During his stay in Havana, de Norman was present at various negotiations between Mexico and France. He had a foreboding of what was to become known as the "Pastry War" and the blockade of all Mexican ports by France.[26] With remarkable prescience, he judged circumstances favourable for extending Belgian commercial interests in Mexico to the detriment of France, visiting Mexico City at the end of January 1838 when most of the delegates had left the capital.

The causes of this war remain vague. The conflict lasted for several years and seriously complicated the lives of our naturalists and the dispatch of their specimens. Concerned by the rising tension, on 8 January 1838 the Belgian government ordered the expedition to "attach itself to the diplomatic mission that Belgium is sending to Mexico".[27] The three members hastily abandoned their quest on the island and made for the Mexican coast, though not before sending off a first batch of plants collected during their two-month stay. The consignment – documented in a catalogue – reached Antwerp on 23 April; King Leopold I was informed of their arrival the following day by the Minister of the Interior. The consignment was forwarded to the Botanical Gardens in Ghent, but after examining and drawing up an inventory of the specimens, the staff announced they had arrived in a poor state, apart from a parcel of seeds from Havana intended for the Société d'Horticulture de Bruxelles and

‹ *Malpighia ilicifolia.*
Plate from *L'Illustration horticole.*

24. See, for example, the illustration on p. 72.
25. Jan Possemiers, *op. cit.*, p. 33.
26. The "pastry war" (*Guerra de Pasteles*). *Loc. cit.*
27. Brussels, Archives of the Ministry of Foreign Affairs.

Mr Vandermaelen, Director of the Établissement géographique de Bruxelles. At the same time, the Société royale d'Horticulture expressed a desire for some of the specimens "for the Botanical Gardens in Brussels, where the school has just been entirely renovated, despite the Society's unhappy finances".[28]

After their arrival in Veracruz, Linden, Funck and Ghiesbreght stayed a week in Jalapa to explore the surrounding country. They met up with de Norman again a few days later in Mexico City, but did not stay – the young explorers were eager for further discoveries.

My trip to Mexico began at El Mirador in February 2003. I had been intrigued by a couple of sentences in the brief biographies of Linden: "They set up base at the Hacienda del Mirador, a German settlement in the state of Veracruz ... There they encountered Henri Galeotti, a traveller and explorer who had established botanical stations both there and in Zacualpan."[29] Galeotti was a geologist and mineralogist of great standing in the academic community of Brussels and had been sent on a scientific mission by the Vandermaelen brothers. My awareness of this expedition and the botanical station whetted my curiosity. I decided to make El Mirador my base for retracing the route followed by Linden during his four years in Mexico.

Mount Orizaba. Present-day view and engraving by Moritz Rugendas, around 1858.

El Mirador and Mount Orizaba.
Engraving by Moritz Rugendas, around 1858.

In February 2003, I had only Ghiesbreght's terse account of climbing Mount Orizaba to guide me to the hacienda in question: the trio were staying in "a village near Orizaba". The letter adds: "Our first day's walk brought us to San Juan de Coscomatepec."[30] At Fortín de las Flores – a propitious name for our search – a kind local confirmed the existence of a German or Swiss botanical station. Following his estimate of a day's journey from Coscomatepec, the only place in the vicinity marked on the map, we arrived in the Tatutla region, near Huatusco.

Besides discovering the Hacienda del Mirador, I had the pleasure of meeting the descendants of the founders of the station and, through the testimony of Mrs Hildegard Growmann and her son, Jorge Müller, El Mirador became a reality. Her enthusiasm kindled by our arrival, the old lady recounted the history of the family, who still own the hacienda. Its story began in 1824, when Carl Christian Sartorius left Germany to try his luck in Mexico. With the purchase of some 4,000 hectares at Acasonica and the hacienda at El Mirador, he formed a large estate that soon began to prosper. He welcomed many European visitors, researchers, explorers and naturalists; El Mirador became internationally famous, with even the Emperor Maximilian of Mexico being received there some time before his

28. Meise, Archives of the National Botanic Garden of Belgium.

29. A. Lasègue, *Le Musée botanique de Benjamin Delessert*, Librairie de Fortin, Masson & Cᵢₑ, 1845, p. 240.

30. Auguste Ghiesbreght and Jean Linden, letter addressed to a friend (identity unknown), 15 October 1838.

Barranca de Santa María with the heights of Mirador and the volcano Orizaba. Engraving by Moritz Rugendas, around 1858.

The Mirador botanic station is still mentioned in history textbooks today.

Hacienda del Mirador, February 2003.

execution. The royal visit is commemorated in the diary of Sartorius, which an emotional Mrs Hildegard then showed us. The typewritten pages contain numerous descriptions of the hacienda, its buildings and activities. These were followed by an endless list of visitors. Among the names were those of Jean Linden and Ghiesbreght; the German Carl Hartweg, travelling for The Horticultural Society of London; Moritz Rugendas, the painter; and the botanist Carl Bartholomaeus Heller. Curiously, there is no mention of Galeotti or Funck. Throughout its history, El Mirador was to serve as a temporary base for travellers, bringing a touch of civilization to a spot that is miles from the nearest town.

There is no doubt, however, that Galeotti stopped at El Mirador. The accounts of the climbing of Mount Orizaba, particularly the one by Ghiesbreght which appeared five months after the ascent in *Le Courrier belge* of 7 March 1839 – "Belgians Scale Orizaba: Four-Man Team on Volcano" – are positive proof of his presence and collaboration in the botanists' expeditions. After all, one of the aims of this perilous operation was to collect specimens of solidified lava at an altitude where vegetation gave way to glaciers.

The rest of the journey involved exploring the region around Oaxaca. The three had left the state of Veracruz just before the French attack on the Mexican port of the same name on 11 February 1839. On their return to the city they dispatched part of their collection, proposing to take ship to Campeche. The war dragged on, making things difficult for the expedition, and money began to run out. A violent dispute appears to have broken out in Veracruz at the residence of Édouard Strybos, the Belgian consul, involving de Norman and Ghiesbreght.[31] It was around this time that Ghiesbreght made a round trip to Belgium to settle some pressing matter. Linden and Funck put in at Campeche with the aim of exploring Yucatán and then descending to Tabasco and Chiapas.

I found some difficulty in tracing the route of the three Belgians from Campeche. To try to learn more and visualise the possibilities open to them at that period, I journeyed to Yucatán. In addition to the information above,

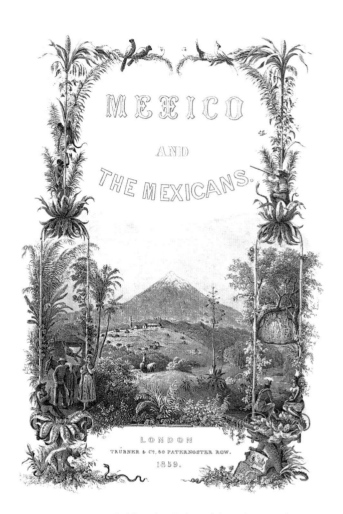

Carl Sartorius, *Mexico and the Mexicans*, London, 1858. Title page with engraving by Moritz Rugendas.

31. Jan Possemiers, *op. cit.*, p. 33; Brussels, Archives of the Ministry of Foreign Affairs, dossier 2014.

32. Ing José N. Rovirosa, *Pteridografía del sur de México*, Mexico, 1909.

33. The *cronistas* in Mexico are public historians: they represent, to some extent, the popular and local memory in areas where libraries and archives have not been opened or have barely been developed. The most informative one I met was attached to the Archives of the City of Macuspana, Tabasco.

34. *The State of Campeche*, Mexico, Ed Nueva Guía, 2002.

I also had with me the notes made by José N. Rovirosa (1849-1901)[32], a Mexican botanist from Macuspana in Tabasco. Once in Yucatán, I was lucky enough to meet one of his descendants. José Rovirosa was a typical 19th-century scholar: erudite, and fascinated by everything to do with nature. Much younger than Linden, he never met him, but seems to have known Ghiesbreght. Through long conversations with the *cronistas*[33] of each town I succeeded in establishing a plausible itinerary for the explorers: Campeche, Laguna de Términos, back to Campeche, on to Frontera, Palizada, San Juan de Tabasco (now Villahermosa), Teapa, Palenque and Ocosingo, down to the Pacific coast, Soconusco (Huixtla) on the Guatemalan border, and a final return along the Gulf of Mexico via San Cristóbal de las Casas. So I began in Campeche, a town now classified as a World Heritage Site by UNESCO. What was once a thriving port[34] extremely attractive to pirates has given place to a small, chic city, its restored houses recalling the days of its glory.

The creation of Brussels Botanical Gardens

The Botanical Gardens, Brussels.
Engraving after Gineste, around 1830.

The first botanical gardens in Brussels were established in 1796 to preserve the collection at the court of Nassau. Situated at that time off the rue Montagne de la Cour, they were very soon extended by the addition of tropical greenhouses.

In 1826, during the Dutch occupation, the site was taken over for other purposes, but a limited liability company, Koninklijke Maatschappij van Kruid-, Bloem- en Boomkwekerije der Nederlanden, was set up to safeguard the collection.

In 1829 the company moved into new premises designed by the architect Tilman-François Suys. At first, the activities of the Botanical Gardens were of a commercial nature, with great emphasis on the development of links with the Dutch colonies. The Belgian revolution of 1830, however, had serious repercussions on the financial position of the gardens. In the flurry of patriotic changes following independence, the Dutch company was renamed the Société royale d'Horticulture de Belgique (1837). Throughout the nineteenth century, the institution was always short of funds, despite the progressive sale of land at the west of its property to accommodate a new railway station, the Gare du Nord. In the end it was the tireless efforts of Barthélemy Dumortier that staved off complete disaster; in 1870 the state acquired the Botanical Gardens, and from then on its primary task was the organisation of expeditions conducting scientific research into botany and horticulture.

Henri Galeotti

A Parisian by birth, Henri Galeotti (1814-58) took Belgian citizenship in 1843. As a geologist and mineralogist, he was sent by the Vandermaelen brothers on a scientific expedition to Mexico from 1835 to 1840. It was during this extended stay that he established a botanical station at the Hacienda del Mirador, near Veracruz. He also wrote a report on his climb of Mount Orizaba.*

On his return to Belgium, he went into the horticultural business in Schaerbeek, but his efforts failed in the wake of the economic crisis of 1848; he appears to have possessed little commercial acumen. Abandoning business, he obtained the post of director of the Botanical Gardens in Brussels in 1853 – a post he would hold until 1857. In that year he began to edit the *Journal d'horticulture pratique,* but died a few months afterwards.

* "Galeotti, Enrique, Ascención al Pico de Orizaba", *Boletín del Instituto nacional de geografía y estadística,* 1861, 1, pp. 271-273. The account dates from 10 September 1838.

Odontoglossum pendulum formerly known as *Oncidium galeottianum* in honour of the explorer Henri Galeotti, founder of a botanical station in Mexico.

Carl Theodor Hartweg

Born in Karlsruhe in 1812, Carl Theodor Hartweg was working in the same field in the early 1840s as Jean Linden, and in the same area of the world. After studying botany in Karlsruhe and Paris, he offered his services to the Horticultural Society of London, which sent him to explore Mexico and Colombia. Hartweg scoured Mexico from 1836 to 1840, the large number of plants he collected forming the subject of a paper – *Plantas Hartwegianas* – that was published in 1839. He also seems to have been attached to the family of Carl Sartorius by a strong bond of friendship.

Linden met Hartweg for the first time in Chiapas around 1839-40, a few months after the former visited El Mirador. In a way reminiscent of Stanley's later encounter with Livingstone in the Congo, the two explorers met at a bend on the trail leading to Comitán on the Mexico-Guatemala border, respectively exclaiming "Hartweg!" and "Linden!" though they had never seen each other before. Their paths had nearly crossed several times during the previous few years and each knew the other by reputation – but chance never brought them together. They were to meet again in Colombia in 1842 between Villa Purificación and Popayán, and a third time in Bogotá. On his return to Europe, Hartweg was appointed Superintendent of the Schwetzingen Gardens in Baden. He died in Baden in 1871.

‹ Campeche, a city now designated a World Heritage
Site by UNESCO. Neoclassical houses and the
Instituto Campechano.

In 1839-40, a disaster threw the smooth running of the expedition
into turmoil. Jean Linden fell seriously ill, stricken by "a violent attack of
the *vomito negro*, which Europeans call yellow fever".[35] Evacuated immediately to Laguna de Términos (modern Ciudad del Carmen, between the
Gulf of Mexico and the rivers issuing from Chiapas), he survived what was
thought to be certain death: in 1862, no fewer than 27 French soldiers
would die from this disease.[36] "A natural haemorrhage saved his [Linden's]
life, but it took a painful three-month convalescence before he could
return to his collecting."[37] After his recovery he rejoined Funck and
Ghiesbreght and the three embarked for Tabasco. As I strolled around the
town, I could not help picturing my unfortunate ancestor on his sickbed in
such uncomfortable conditions.

After stops in Frontera and Palizada – traditionally a smugglers' hide-
out – the team members made their way to Chiapas. "In these unexplored
states, they made numerous botanical discoveries and also came across the
colossal ruins of the ancient Mayan cities of Palenque and Ocosingo. The
former was buried amid dense forests watered by the Río Usumasinta, the
latter situated in a cold, fir-clothed region extending from Ocosingo to the
territories of the Lacandon Indians."[38] According to José N. Rovirosa,
Linden and his party were the first botanists to explore these areas. At about

35. *Plantae Columbianae*, 1863, p. XLIX;
The Garden, 1879.

36. Archives stored in Laguna de Términos.

37. *Plantae Columbianae, op. cit.*

38. Jean Linden, *Rapport sur le voyage scientifique
exécuté sous les auspices du Gouvernement belge.*

the same time, the Mayan ruins were brought to the world's attention by John Lloyd Stephens, an American lawyer, diplomat, businessman and "antiquarian" (1805-52), whose fascinating narrative – *Incidents of Travel in Central America, Chiapas and Yucatán* – appeared in 1841 with watercolour illustrations by the English artist Frederick Catherwood.[39]

His account has much in common with that of Linden. The information he provides on flora and fauna, the local inhabitants and the difficulties of travel due to the revolution provides a valuable complement to the report of the Belgian botanist. Though the two teams crossed the territory in opposite directions and never met, Stephens having left from northern Guatemala to make his way back up to Yucatán via Palenque and Ocosingo, his famous publication does mention three Belgian travellers. The Mexican government had forbidden foreigners access to the ruins of Palenque but the author asserts: "Dr McKinney had heard that three Belgians had travelled to

Near Laguna de Términos.
December 2003.

Ciudad Real with the express intention of seeking permission to view the ruins, and had been refused."[40] The probability of bumping into citizens of a nation only ten years old in these desolate and virtually unknown regions must have been negligible. The comment by Stephens does, however, enable me to date the journey of Linden to Palenque prior to 14 May 1840.

Very little documentation has survived concerning the final days of Linden's second expedition. His own narrative mentions a foray into northern Guatemala – then in the midst of a revolution – before returning along the Gulf of Mexico "making for Soconusco (now Huixtla) and the coast of the southern sea".[41] (The reference is to the Pacific.) According to the scant biographical data available, the three explorers had to return by the same route, travelling first to San Cristóbal de las Casas on the way to Teapa, where they stayed several months before leaving the country at Campeche.

39. John Lloyd Stephens and Frederick Catherwood, *Incidents of travel in Central America, Chiapas and Yucatán*, New York, 1841.

40. *Ibid.*

41. Jean Linden, *Rapport... op. cit.*

Panoramic view of Palenque. Colour lithograph by
Frederick Catherwood, 1844.

 In September 1840, Funck and Ghiesbreght re-embarked for Brussels
at Guadalupe de Frontera. They left Linden on the American continent
"detained by a fever". Eventually he returned home via Havana and the
USA. The three naturalists met up again in Brussels on 20 December to
supervise the unpacking of their crates. On that day, the Chevalier du Bus
de Gisignies officially confirmed to the Minister of Public Works, Jean-
Baptiste Nothomb, that the inventory was under way. While the scientific
community and public opinion were full of praise for the expedition, the
minister was describing it as a failure. He had hoped to derive from it some
advantage for trade and industry and perhaps a means of establishing
Belgian commercial interests in Latin America; the explorers, however, had
sent neither the promised materials nor the information requested. This
was a major disappointment. Even while the mission was underway, discord
had grown between the ministries, with the usefulness of the expedition
being fiercely debated.

Carmencita: A Romantic Interlude

I was intrigued and somewhat amused by a passage I noticed in a later account. It persuaded me to interrupt the thread of my narrative to relate a slightly more whimsical incident in the Mexican adventures of my distant ancestor. Jean Linden fails to mention – and I do not blame him – a prolonged stay at the hacienda belonging to the governor of Tabasco: he was to reveal something of the secret only at the end of his life. When asked: "Did you ever have any amorous encounters during your trips?" he replied: "Me? Amorous encounters? Never ... Well, yes, once, you know. After a series of hikes through the virgin forest, we arrived one day in a state of utter exhaustion at a vast hacienda where we were offered hospitality. ... Our host had a daughter, Carmencita, 15 or 16 years old, a real Creole beauty. We became close friends; morning and evening we rode together about the huge estate. One evening, after supper, sitting on the veranda in the tropical night, I mentioned my impending departure. She rose and took my hand, looked into my eyes and whispered: "Jean, please don't go!" Never in my life have I felt such emotion, and I promised to stay. During the night, however, I packed my bags and fled, after telling my peons where I was headed and where to meet up with me. The fact was, I had a fiancée at home."*

The woman he describes as his "fiancée" was not Anna Reuter, "the only love of his life", whom he was to marry on 13 October 1845, but someone unknown to us who failed to wait for Linden and married someone else in the meantime. Following the account of José N. Rovirosa and the testimony of a *cronista* with whom I spoke during my visit to Villahermosa in 2003, I was able to place this incident near Teapa, an agricultural region where the valleys formed rich farmland and the forests on the high ground abounded in orchids. The story of Carmencita would end there but for a few lines in the diary of Ferdinand Bellermann. He was a painter at the Prussian court who had been sent to Latin America on the advice of von Humboldt to sketch certain geographical sites. Bellermann met Linden at Puerto Cabello in Venezuela in 1844. The artist records the latter's receipt of a letter from Ghiesbreght informing him that he had settled in Teapa and that Carmencita was still in love with her "Juan". Seeing her in a state of despair and almost mad with grief, her father had offered her in marriage with a dowry of some 30,000 thalers and no less than three haciendas. Linden was clearly angered by this report.

In the small town of Tabasco, I saw some of these "Creole beauties" strutting around the *zócalo* in their jeans under the shade of the laurels. I smiled as I imagined what the life of Jean Linden might have been like had he stayed there. Perhaps he would have been found every morning on the terrace of the church café sharing *desayuno* (breakfast) with the other *rancheros* and discussing banana growing and cattle raising ...

*Jean Linden, *Rapport... op. cit.*

Zócalo in Teapa. El zócalo is the central square of each Mexican town. December 2003.

Palizada, December 2003.

As early as 31 July 1839, immediately after the French blockade and the attack on Veracruz, the Minister of the Interior was intending to bring the expedition to an end, judging it a waste of time. In two years the government had expended 26,380 francs (115,882 euros), yet only one collection of living plants, seeds, preserved crustaceans and fish had been received. The contract for the expedition basically reserved the right of the government to implement premature termination, while assuring the naturalists reimbursement of their costs for travel back to Europe. Baron Félix de Norman was given the confidential task of contacting the team, obtaining a report on their work and enquiring into the disappearance of certain crates. Off the record he was to decide whether "there was any purpose in making further sacrifices on their behalf".[42] De Norman, though, a keen amateur botanist and explorer, took up the naturalists' cause. He defended the team in the matter of the lost crates[43] and even advanced them monies to meet their needs, the government funds having proved insufficient.

Yet the matter was not closed. On 29 June 1840, the Minister of the Interior, B. de Theux de Meylandt, decided that, once the expedition was over, his department would no longer contribute towards the maintenance of "a mission whose commercial value to the country has been negligible ... In this respect at least, it will have achieved nothing and the money allotted to it from funds earmarked for trade and industry will thus have been totally wasted."[44]

42. Brussels, Archives of the Ministry of Foreign Affairs, dossier 2014.

43. *Ibid.*

44. Letter from the Ministry of Foreign Affairs, 25 June 1839.

The dispute was to continue beyond the team's return. In a letter of 29 January 1841 addressed to the three explorers, the minister informed them that, having fulfilled its obligations to them as laid down in the decree of 7 September 1837, "the government requires them to fulfil their own, that is, to produce, besides the specimens of flora and fauna already handed over, notes and reports on anything of interest to industry and commerce, as well as Mr Funck's sketches, which become the ministry's property under the terms of the above-mentioned contract".[45] On 4 February 1841, Linden and Funck issued a protest against this interpretation of the terms of the royal decree, by which they would become responsible for the expenses of the return voyage. Receiving no reply to their demands for the payment to be reinstated, "they engaged themselves elsewhere", though agreeing to supply the requested notes and dried flower collection in a reasonable time.[46] On 12 May, an act of trade was drawn up declaring that, despite huge financial investment, the ministry had received "a mere ten-page paper on trade with Mexico".[47] Four months later, the same ministry confirmed its refusal to participate in such expeditions in the future, and the two explorers' succinct report ended in the wastepaper basket.

"Of all the regions in the two Americas, Mexico is undoubtedly the best outlet for Belgium's industrial products."[48] Such was the opinion of Nicolas Funck, the expedition's official reporter, as it appeared in his *Comments or General Considerations with Regard to Trade with Mexico*. Ignored by the minister, the document in fact contained, in its ten pages, a wealth of useful information concerning navigation and the extension of trade with the countries of Central America. It urged the government to apprise manufacturers of consumer demand, the companies to deal with and the best commercial ports. Funck also suggested establishing Belgian concerns linked to businesses in the Americas and placing government funds at their disposal. Veracruz and Tampico were identified as the most favourably located ports and, finally, the document proposed following the example of the British, who ran contraband to modern Belize.

For his part, de Norman had advised the government to purchase the island of Pinos near Cuba and another, Cozumel, off Yucatán. The suggestion was never followed. Funck wanted to turn these islands into floating warehouses for goods bought cheaply in order to speculate: "Antwerp could have a monopoly on the wood from Campeche and set the prices for all the European markets."[49] He provided the names of trading establishments in Laguna de Términos, Tabasco and Campeche. In conclusion, he promised a

45. Letter dated 29 January 1841. Brussels, Archives générales du Royaume.

46. Letter dated 4 February 1841. Brussels, Archives générales du Royaume.

47. "Acte de commerce" dated 12 May 1841. Brussels, Archives of the Ministry of Foreign Affairs, dossier 2014.

48. Report by Nicolas Funck, nd. Brussels, Archives of the Ministry of Foreign Affairs, dossier 2014.

49. *Ibid.*

description of Yucatán in the near future, with a brief summary of Cozumel. Curiously, this promised document does not exist in the archives of the Ministry of Foreign Affairs. Basically, Funck remained opposed to the second mission assigned them in 1837: "The principal aim of our expedition was scientific, and the funds allotted us by the government made it impossible to stay in the towns. There was no way under those conditions to obtain the requisite commercial information, such as details of prices; it would have been a simple task for anyone sent out expressly for this purpose and with sufficient funding to stay for a period in each town."[50]

50. *Ibid.*

Growing orchids under glass, circa 1840

View of the greenhouses of L'Horticulture internationale, 1880s.

The information brought back by the explorers proved crucial, revolutionising the culture of tropical plants in the years around 1840. At this time, every plant was grown in an oven-like atmosphere. Europeans held that all that was necessary was to adjust the temperature but, without ventilation, these "stove houses" were no more than heated rooms. As a result, most attempts at introducing new species into Europe failed due to bad cultural methods. Linden then realised that not all tropical plants have the same requirements: plants from the Brazilian mountains – like those belonging to the genus *Cattleya* – require different growing conditions compared to those from the Amazon Basin. The species of the genera *Masdevallia* and *Odontoglossum*, though both tropical in origin, prefer cooler temperatures. Linden did in fact report that he collected some plants in areas where there was a nightly frost.

His discovery led to changes in greenhouse procedures. Plants would now be grown in different types of house, depending on the climatic conditions of their native habitats. Other measures, such as the provision of ventilation, were also implemented. In the case of an orchid like *Gudrunia tuerckheimii,* the growth of the leaves is directed downwards, preventing water from remaining between them overnight and thus precluding the formation of ice which would effectively destroy the plant. The same is true of *Encyclia citrina* (formerly *Cattleya citrina*), a fine illustration of which is to be found in the *Pescatorea.*

Linden also made improvements in the packing of plants for transport and we have learned that certain plants were themselves used as packaging material. An instance of this was the first *Cattleya* to arrive in Europe: the Brazilians had used orchid pseudobulbs to wrap the plants dispatched to William Cattley. The Englishman had the bright idea of potting up some of these pseudobulbs, resulting in the surprise discovery of a new plant that now bears his name: *Cattleya labiata.*

Packing techniques were far more important in those days than today. Now, a shipment from Mexico reaches Europe the next day; in the 1800s, the crates spent weeks, even months, in transit. At Kew Gardens, an herbarium sheet of *Odontoglossum grande* (renamed *Rossioglossum grande*) records a shipment of 10,000 living specimens. It has been annotated by hand with this terse comment: "All devoured by rats." [GUIDO BRAEM]

THE SCIENTIFIC BENEFITS OF THE EXPEDITION

Unlike the government, the press hailed the expedition as a triumph. "The scientific results of this mission have been considerable. Not since Humboldt's time has an expedition been undertaken so successfully, despite the modest material resources and difficult conditions. War, disease, ceaseless privations great and small, bad roads, countless dangers – no obstacle could withstand the indefatigable perseverance of these pioneers of science in the New World."[51]

This matched the enthusiastic mood in Brussels: the Chevalier du Bus de Gisignies, President of the Société royale d'Horticulture, was effusive in his expressions of admiration. His correspondence with the minister refers to the particular care taken with the plant specimens by Jean Linden and the need to alter "the previous practices that resulted in the loss of large numbers of plants".[52]

As can be seen, the pointed exchanges between the ministries of the Interior and Trade failed to dampen scientific enthusiasm. Even while discussions were in progress on whether to fund similar research in the future, plans for a new expedition were being hatched elsewhere. By royal decree, Linden was in effect engaged for a new mission.[53] By now, it was no longer the taste for adventure that motivated him. The naturalist knew there were treasures still to be discovered and that his future now lay in the meticulous observation of the plants he collected. A skilful diplomat, he manoeuvred to obtain the funding that would allow him to return to America in search of more interesting and lucrative prizes.

Senecio cfr. roseus/helodes
on the slopes of Mount Orizaba.

51. *The Garden,* 1867.
52. Report by the Chevalier du Bus de Gisignies,
20 December 1840. Brussels,
Archives générales du Royaume.
53. Report dated 21 May 1841. Brussels,
Archives générales du Royaume.

The arrival of shipments in Belgium

The specimens crated up in Mexico did not always arrive at the explorers' intended destinations. A large amount of correspondence testifies to the confusion over shipments and the attempts to sort this out on the team's return to Brussels. Linden did however manage to recover his personal dried plant collection, which had been sent in error to Professor Jean Kickx in Ghent together with two crates of living plants intended for the greenhouses of King Leopold.

The contents of the crates were sometimes quite astonishing, as we see from this notice of 26 May 1841: one of them contained "several skeletons, including that of an Indian" — a note in the margin describes him as of red race — "a tiger, several monkeys, etc, brought back from Mexico by Mr Ghysbreght [sic] and his companions. As all these items, with the exception of the Indian skeleton, were incomplete, I think, Minister, I had better give you the details."*
Readers will note a certain Western condescension in the wording, not to mention the vagueness of the descriptions: there were (and are) no tigers in the Americas, for instance.

* Ghent, 26 May 1841. Brussels, Archives générales du Royaume.

COLOMBIE
ET
GUYANES
PAR
TH. DUVOTENAY
Géographe

ECHELLES

THE THIRD EXPEDITION

Venezuela and New Granada 1841-1844

View of Puerto Cabello. Painting by Ferdinand Bellermann, 1842.

‹ Map of Venezuela and New Granada with Jean Linden's itinerary from 1841 to 1844.

All records relating to this third voyage make it clear: Jean Linden was sent by the Belgian government. As such, it is interesting to consider that, in January 1841, shortly after his return from his second expedition, Linden made a hasty trip to Paris and signed a "treaty" with the Muséum national d'Histoire naturelle.[54] This document was dated 7 March, thereby preceding the commission from Belgium, which was signed on 21 May. As for the expenses covered by these two official papers, they amounted to 3,000 francs on the French side and 4,000 francs (17,571 euros) on the Belgian.

Thus, Linden revealed his cunning. After the disappointment expressed by his government sponsors, he went directly to Paris to strike a deal that could not fail to pique the authorities in Belgium, for the fledgling state could not possibly permit such an eminent citizen to serve its French neighbour. We can only wonder, however, exactly how Linden thought he could handle this double-dealing sponsorship arrangement without being discovered. The contract of 7 March 1841 clearly specifies French expectations: "(The museum) undertakes to receive and acquire in accordance with the conditions stipulated below the collections Mr Linden sends [and] it is clearly understood that all the species found by Mr Linden will be dispatched to the museum".[55] Two months later, the Belgian government imposed more or less the same conditions.

This was not the first time, however, that France had intervened in this story. Back in 1839, while still in Mexico, Linden had astutely sent three unsolicited crates to the Muséum national d'Histoire naturelle in Paris, with Adolphe Brongniart acting as intermediary. Once Linden was back in Belgium, the French museum informed him that "these

54. Paris, Archives of the Muséum national d'Histoire naturelle, P³, 23 March 1841.

55. *Ibid.*

shipments do not reflect any regular agreement since the museum's administration no longer feels it owes you any commitment, as it [knows] that you were travelling specifically on behalf of the Belgian government; nevertheless, having accepted your shipments, it [is obliged] to reimburse you for the expenses incurred and acknowledges the interest of the plants therein, of which several were new to our garden".[56] Does this letter, dated 7 January 1841, imply that some agreement had already been reached at the time of the second voyage? The museum compensated Linden with a sum of 500 francs (2,196 euros), making clear, moreover, that this amount was "higher than that which any commercial establishment would pay on [the shipment's] arrival in Paris".[57] The concern for exclusivity that would be apparent in the official agreement two months later can already be glimpsed here.

Cattleya chocoensis, a species introduced on a large scale by Linden from 1873, discovered near the Choco river in Venezuela. Plate from *L'Illustration horticole*, 1873.

It remains for us to explain the Belgian ministers' change of heart with respect to a new expedition. All the evidence suggests that certain individuals or organisations put pressure on the government – the Société royale d'Horticulture, for example, which would later invest in the third voyage (although there is no record of this backing before 31 January 1843).[58] The Belgian commission was published in the *Moniteur belge* on 21 May 1841.

A comparison with the commission for the second voyage in 1837 proves instructive, as several notable differences bear witness to changes in the mentality of the authorities. Three aspects are particularly striking. This time, Linden was given sole responsibility for the mission, thus being the only person to receive payment; there is no mention of his former companions, who would eventually accompany him to South America. Secondly, the terms specified an expedition of an entirely scientific nature, financed by universities. Finally, the financial support was substantially less than before. There was no longer any talk of trade or industry, and one single man would be allotted an amount equivalent to 17,500 euros – a paltry sum if we consider that the equivalent of around 27,000 euros was offered in 1837, and the fact that two-thirds of the money was earmarked for the dispatch of natural history collections to Europe.

56. Paris, Archives of the Muséum national d'Histoire naturelle, AM P[1], 7 January 1841.
57. *Ibid.*
58. Meise, Archives of the National Botanic Garden of Belgium.

Jean Linden was not complaining, however, as he undoubtedly had a freer hand in the organisation of this project than was given him in the previous ones. The young naturalist also saw his mission in a different light. While in Mexico, he had discovered a line of enquiry that would later bring him success and wealth: orchid growing. In effect, he would exploit the emerging passion for these exceptional plants in the privileged circles that could afford to acquire them. While keeping his cards close to his chest, therefore, Linden was putting into place all the elements of his future success and, in the short term, needed a third voyage in order to lay the foundations for new research. He had "picked the brains" of his colleagues in Mexico and was familiar with von Humboldt's reports from Colombia and Venezuela.[59] Linden therefore set his sights on this region. It is interesting to consider whether he was once again trying to hide his intentions when he mentioned other countries like Nicaragua and Ecuador before his departure.[60]

Through the examination of documents and old photographs, I have gradually formed an impression of my ancestor's personality. His manner of combining a passion for botany with the prospect of material gain is one of his distinguishing characteristics – it is apparent in every stage of his life. His assiduous research and determination to break new ground with his findings were the drivers of his business enterprises.

Linden began to take advantage of his contacts in preparation for his third expedition. His diplomatic skills and social expertise led him as far as England, where meetings with collectors like Lord Cavendish, the Duke of Devonshire, the Reverend John Clowes and Sigismund Rucker, a German businessman based in London, resulted in numerous orders that guaranteed him considerable earnings. There is no record of any agreements or sponsorship emanating from the Royal Botanic Gardens at Kew, although we know that Linden exchanged many letters with this institution and sent it important shipments.[61]

His first concern, however, was to attract additional funding that would allow him to take companions on his mission, as before. Although Ghiesbreght did not accompany him on this third adventure, Linden was

Oncidium lanceanum var. *superbum*.
Plate from the *Lindenia*.

59. Jean Linden, *Rapport...*, op. cit.

60. Paris, Archives of the Muséum national d'Histoire naturelle, AM P ², 18 January 1841.

61. Correspondence preserved at the Royal Botanic Gardens, Kew.

able to recruit men who had grown up in his immediate circle – a choice perhaps determined by the limited financial backing from the government. It was Louis-Joseph Schlim – Linden's half-brother by their mother's second marriage – who replaced Ghiesbreght. As for Nicolas Funck, he travelled on behalf of Jacob-Mackoy of Liège and would make only part of the journey with them. It could be said, with hindsight, that the expedition was entirely a family affair, as some years later Funck would marry Linden's sister-in-law.

This time, the young explorer, supported by Belgian, French and British sponsorship – as well as by numerous letters of recommendation (particularly from English sources) – was confident that he had means at his disposal that had previously lain beyond his grasp.[62]

One further formality delayed Linden's departure from Brussels, however: his request to the new Minister of the Interior, Jean-Baptiste Nothomb, for "a passport as a traveller of the Belgian State". In the light of his earlier bad experiences, he waited for letters of recommendation addressed to the Belgian consuls installed in the countries he was going to visit, asking them to take charge of the shipment of crates of natural specimens. The composition of these letters required Linden to outline his itinerary, which he described as follows: "I shall land in La Guayrá, from where I will undertake excursions via Caracas into different parts of the republic of Venezuela, and these excursions will take up roughly the first year of my voyage. The second year will be devoted to the exploration of Colombia and the republic of Ecuador."[63] The minister's staff observed, however, that, as "no official Belgian agent has been established in the places that this naturalist proposes to visit",[64] it was impossible to issue the documents Linden had requested. Nevertheless, a promise was made to brief the consuls in New York, Liverpool, London, Le Havre, Bordeaux, Hamburg and Bremen to do all that was required in case of need.

More documentation is available to us with respect to this third voyage than there is for the two previous ones. The commission stipulated that Linden should draw up a report on his return to Belgium, and that this should be published in the *Moniteur belge*.[65] The following duly appeared in the *Moniteur belge* of 10 May 1846: "Account of a scientific voyage undertaken by Mr J. Linden, under the auspices of the Belgian government, in the inter-tropical regions of the New World: in Venezuela, in New Granada and in the Greater Antilles, from the years 1841 to 1844; report presented to Mr Sylvain Van de Weyer, the Minister of the Interior."[66]

62. Jean Linden, *Rapport...*, *op. cit.*

63. Letter dated 14 August 1841. Luxembourg, Archives of the Ministry of Foreign Affairs.

64. Note dated 24 August 1841. *Ibid.*

65. Jean Linden, *Rapport...*, *op. cit.*

66. *Ibid.*

Cattleyas in the trees. Venezuela, 1998.

As in the case of Mexico, I shall combine Linden's documents with the fruits of my own research in Venezuela, along with my personal impressions of the country gained during a trip in 1998. My notes will attempt to put my ancestor's lively, sometimes touchingly poetic, record into perspective. For the moment, however, I will yield the floor to Jean Linden.

Palmar sugar factory, Venezuela, 1998.

"My earlier travels, in the southern provinces of Brazil, in Mexico and to the island of Cuba, undertaken on behalf of the Belgian government, allowed me to become acquainted with areas bounded by the torrid zone and so filled me with the desire, even before my return to Europe, to visit regions located more immediately under the influence of the equatorial line."[67] There follows a geographical and historical description of the areas explored in what are now Colombia, Venezuela and Ecuador.

It should be noted in passing that for a long time Venezuela was of little interest to the conquistadores. Spain soon realised that this humid, sparsely populated country was lacking in resources such as gold and silver. It was not until the discovery of its oil wealth in 1914 that Venezuela became the richest country in South America and the world's biggest exporter of oil up to 1970. In the nineteenth century, however, it attracted barely a handful of colonialists, who went on to establish large farms.[68]

In order to present a clearer picture, I will list some of the stopovers made by Linden and his companions, partly based on the correspondence that accompanied the shipments of specimens to Brussels and Paris (although such missives should be read with a degree of scepticism, as

67. *Ibid.*
68. Different historical sources and conversations.

vagueness in respect to their actual itinerary guaranteed naturalists a degree of autonomy to pursue lucrative opportunities).[69] Nevertheless, I have been able to reconstruct it as follows: Bordeaux, La Guayrá, Caracas, Valle de Aragua and Valle del Tuy, La Vittoria, Barquísimeto, Trujillo, Páramo de Mucuchies, Mérida, San Cristóbal, Río Tachire. Then, in Colombia: Honda, Guaduas, Tunja, Pamplona, Bogotá. Return via Mérida, Barinas los Llanos del Orinoco, Carabobo, Caracas, La Guayrà, Puerto Cabello and Río Hacha, with a detour in the Sierra Nevada de Santa Marta before going on to Jamaica and Cuba.

Realising that his departure would be postponed for some months,[70] Linden was obliged to remain in Paris from August to October. This enforced delay was far from unpleasant, however. He gathered information necessary to his journey and examined the specimens from Colombia on display in the botanical galleries of the Jardin des Plantes. He also used this time to make contact with many prominent figures, including some who would become his protectors or sponsors. Jean Linden's official report allows us to identify these "celebrities", with whom he remained in close touch after his return, taking advantage of their support to launch further projects and publish his work. They included Alexander von Humboldt, Adrien de Jussieu, Adolphe Brongniart, Joseph Decaisne, Ramón Díaz, Colonel Agostino Codazzi (the Colombian geographer who had produced detailed maps of Colombia and Venezuela), Jean-Pierre Pescatore (who did not feature in the report) and the banker and philanthropist Benjamin Delessert.

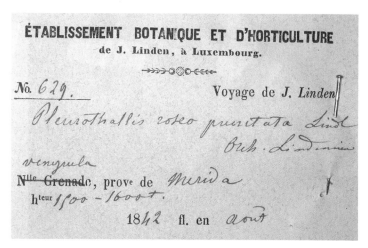

Label accompanying a specimen of *Pleurothallis roseo-punctata*, collected by Jean Linden in Venezuela, August 1842. Herbarium of Benjamin Delessert, Geneva.

We should also note that Linden does not deny his French backing in his report, although he implies that it was only given to him during this enforced delay.[71] It was also during this period that the young explorer declared his intention to discover the sources of the Orinoco, which were still unknown. This ambition seemed to camouflage another, more specific goal. In this respect, we can only rely on a document written by Linden himself at the request of the Belgian government in 1846, a year after his return to Belgium.

Linden set sail from Bordeaux aboard the *Lovely,* then docked in Cádiz to collect plants in Andalusía and the isle of León, before finally dropping anchor in La Guayrá on 27 December.

69. In this respect, see the box on espionage page 161.

70. Jean Linden, *Rapport...*, op. cit.

71. *Ibid.*

View of La Guayrá. Lithograph by August C. Haun, 1833.

My own arrival in Caracas in 1998 undoubtedly lacked much of the charm experienced by Jean Linden in 1841. Today's traveller is not greeted by a stunning view from the sea of La Guayrá bounded by high mountains, but has to confront an overcrowded urban sprawl in which heat and dust reinforce the overriding impression of aridity. I did, however, have one thing in common with my forefather, though 150 years separate us – I, too, was carrying letters of introduction that proved to be a useful precaution. On his arrival, Linden found that no rooms were available in the only two hotels in town, so he used his diplomatic skills and influence to find accommodation – the Prussian consul, Otto Harrassowitz, invited the Belgian team to stay in his outlying villa in Maiquetía.

After spending a few days visiting the beach and town of La Guayrá (still showing severe signs of the devastation wreaked by an earthquake in

Study of the forest near La Vittoria cordillera and the Tovar colony.
Oil on card, Ferdinand Bellermann, 1844.

1812), Linden resolved to explore the temperate slopes of the Cerro de Ávila, in the Caracas Cordillera. He left La Guayrá in February 1842, having first sent off a preliminary batch of 36 species of orchids.

To whom were they sent? Such a shipment would have been coveted by the Belgian authorities, as well as by numerous horticulturists and collectors. Organisations such as the Société royale d'Horticulture, or respected horticulturists like Van Houtte in Gentbrugge, may privately have given support to the young explorer, whose public stock had risen immeasurably after his first voyages. Leading figures from the political sphere had also expressed a special interest in exotic plants. Linden had, for example, maintained a regular correspondence with the Minister of the Interior, Jean-Baptiste Nothomb, who had signed his commission on 21 May 1841 and was effectively his intermediary in Belgium.[72] Without revealing any official information – diplomacy often requires discretion – Nothomb told his immediate circles about Linden's research, from his setbacks to his triumphs, on the basis of the frequent letters he received.

At the same time, Linden was still cultivating the contacts he had made in England. As soon as he arrived in La Guayrá, and before even sending the first crates of specimens to Belgium, he wrote to Sir William Hooker, the head of Kew Gardens, specifying items that could appeal to

72. Brussels, Archives générales du Royaume.

gardens in London. He also stirred his curiosity and desire by insisting on the exclusivity of these dealings. His correspondence furthermore had the freely admitted purpose of obtaining extra financial support to cover the costs of collecting and sending specimens: "The areas I am currently investigating are of great interest to a botanist. [...] The hillsides conceal brilliant orchids [...]. I am not thinking of staying long on these coasts, as my intention is to extend my excursions along the Orinoco and the Apure and penetrate into the high cordillera of Trujillo and Mérida, with their colossal peaks covered with eternal snow. These regions have never been visited by naturalists."[73] Later on, no less than 15 crates left Caracas for Europe: "Various excursions [...] considerably enriched my collection which – three months after my arrival, and notwithstanding the spells I was obliged to spend in La Guayrá and Caracas – already amounted to over 300 species of plants, including 70 species of ferns. The collections of live plants were proportionally more substantial as, during these three months, I had dispatched to Europe fifteen crates and a box of seeds, apart from the zoological collections."[74]

My contacts in Caracas and Mérida revealed a Linden who had entered the country's folklore (although not to the same extent as von Humboldt – there is no Mount Linden!) as part of the collective memory of aficionados of both history and botany. At the mere mention of Jean Linden, Professor Tobias Lasser invited me and my guide to lunch. He was fully aware of Linden's voyage and its value to botany, and put me in touch with the Vollmer family, a powerful dynasty of landowners and bankers. The founding father, Gustave Vollmer, had immigrated to Venezuela from Germany in 1826, and it was his descendant, another Gustave, who referred me to Horacio Becco, who is responsible for the publications of the Fundación Vollmer, based in the Banco Mercantil skyscraper in Caracas. Here, too, Linden was no stranger, and another member of the family, Mrs Vollmer, showed me the earliest photos of El Palmar. I was also received by the administrator of the Fundación de Promoción Cultural de Venezuela, which supports the nation's cultural life by publishing books on its art and history.

Masdevallia davisi [sic].
Plate from the *Lindenia*.

73. Brussels, Archives of the Ministry of Foreign Affairs.
74. *Ibid.*

San Esteban sugar plantation near Puerto Cabello.
Oil on card, Ferdinand Bellermann, 1844.

In contrast to my comings and goings, Linden's expeditions ventured into largely unexplored territory. He did not travel blind, however; even before setting off, he was remarkably well informed about the regions that he hoped to visit. He gleaned useful information from the reports of von Humboldt, who had covered similar ground with Bonpland in January 1800. Linden took up whole pages of his report with descriptions of his route and expressed his deep emotion in the face of the grandeur of nature. At one point he even mentioned the "omnipotence of the Creator".[75]

Nowadays, Linden's route conveys an altogether different impression. I naively thought I could follow his indications, but neglected to take into

75. Jean Linden, *Rapport..., op. cit.*

account the effect of the intervening 150 years. Most difficult was leaving Caracas, a city that is ceaselessly expanding in all directions. After hours of exasperating traffic jams, however, everything suddenly changed. By simply continuing on the route, we found ourselves on a mountain track leading to Los Teques. From there, I followed Linden's tracks to the Hacienda del Palmar, which he described as follows: "I spent several days exploring the surrounding area and went as far as the Hacienda del Palmar (a large coffee and sugar cane plantation belonging to Mr Vollmer, from Caracas)."[76]

Hacienda El Palmar, Caracas, 1998.

The hacienda still belongs to the Vollmer family. Although the plantation has gone from strength to strength, a large modern factory now replaces the old one whose ruins are preserved as an example of industrial archaeology – and despite the ravages of war, pillage and earthquakes, the family has thoughtfully maintained the house in the state in which Linden must have known it. Thanks to the kindness of Mr Vollmer, I was also able to see it for myself. As if time had stood still, I breathed in the atmosphere of another age. The visitors' book contains prestigious signatures, such as those of von Humboldt and Bonpland, dated February 1801, and later that of the painter Ferdinand Bellermann, who produced a splendid picture of the place in 1844. I do not know whether Linden himself slept in the large building now used for Vollmer family reunions. There is no doubt that he was welcomed in the hacienda, but he was probably taken to the house that currently serves as a luxury hotel.

Apart from the Vollmer family, there is a not inconsiderable German presence in Venezuela. Linden enjoyed the hospitality of Colonel Codazzi, one of his Parisian contacts, in the German colony that the latter oversaw in the midst of the Venezuelan mountains. The surrounding landscape is extraordinary. Despite its popularity with tourist coaches, the local road seems to be much as it was when Linden and his team travelled along it. Everything suggests that it follows the path established by the Germans to reach their colony, where Linden stayed twice (in March-April 1842 and September-October 1843).

I went right up to the Tovar colony, in order to see for myself the majesty and wonders described by Linden in his report. This dense, almost impenetrable forest proved valuable hunting ground for Linden. "In the course of these various excursions, I made abundant discoveries in the plant

76. *Ibid.*

kingdom, and my list of new plants grew considerably."[77] One of these discoveries evokes Linden's time in Tovar through its name: *Masdevallia tovarensis.*

On his return to Caracas, Linden took the time to write to the Muséum national d'Histoire naturelle in Paris to announce the arrival of a crate containing live plants. Unfortunately, the crate took four months to cross the Atlantic, to the detriment of its contents, which arrived in Paris totally withered. Sadly, this was not the last experience of this kind – in all, four shipments met a similar fate. On 20 April 1842, another dispatch left Caracas on a French ship (the *Claire*) bound for Bordeaux, where it docked on 1 July. It was sent to Paris a week later, but the museum only acknowledged its receipt on 31 August – by which time not a single plant remained intact.

Linden's disappointment was all the more bitter in that his revenues and subsidies were also affected. His eagerness to send more specimens than anticipated, in order to guarantee the feasibility of his mission, diverted him from his own scientific commitments into the realm of zoology. Botany obviously remained his abiding passion, but he nevertheless sent off collections of insects, arachnids, crustaceans, shells,

77. *Ibid.*

The German colony in Tovar

Venezuela, which was attached to Colombia until 1830, was hard hit by the War of Independence that gave birth to the country in 1821. Whole regions were devastated and there was an acute lack of manpower to work the land. In 1840, the Venezuelan government asked the Italian cartographer Agostino Codazzi – fresh from mapping out the country — to indicate the most suitable place to set up a European agricultural colony. Codazzi investigated the possibilities in Paris with von Humboldt and the German cartographer Alexander Benitz. Ramón Díaz also became involved in the project. Benitz and Codazzi then made a field trip to Venezuela in August 1841, resulting in a list of 11 villages that they presented to the Secretary of State, who was drawn to the first name: Tovar. Situated at a high altitude where the newly arrived European colonists could enjoy a climate and diet resembling those back home, Tovar was surrounded by a majestic forest. Conceded without any charge by Count Martín Tovar y Ponte (1771-1843) — hence its name — the area of eight square leagues (around 24.700 ha.) stretched from the northern ridge of the coastal mountain range to the savannahs of Lagunilla, and from the Cumbre de Palmar to the source of the River Tuy. The colony was built with phenomenal speed. When Jean Linden visited it for the first time in March 1842, the forest had only recently been felled and its huge trees were scattered on the ground, waiting to be used. When he saw it again in September 1843, after his trip to New Granada, he was "astonished by the prodigious changes [...]. Instead of the wild solitude once frequented by tigers and tapirs, I now saw the invigorating image of European civilisation. A pretty German village surrounded by fields with wheat, corn, potatoes and vegetables from Europe stood on the plain where I had previously seen centuries-old trees devoured by fire".* The Tovar colony still exists today, in all its incongruity — a German enclave in the midst of virgin forest, complete with half-timbered houses and signposts written in German.

* Jean Linden, *Rapport ... op. cit.*

The German colony of Tovar.
Oil on canvas, Ferdinand Bellermann, 1844.

Tovar, 1998.

MASDEVALLIA TOVARENSIS, REICH. FILS.

P. De Pannemaeker, ad nat. pinx. in Horto Lind.

J. Linden, publ.

Masdevallia tovarensis

Masdevallia is a magnificent genus of orchids, named in 1794 in honour of José de Masdevall, a doctor and compatriot of the Spanish explorers Hipólito Ruiz and José Pavón. It is indigenous to the neo-tropical regions of South America, particularly the upper Andes.
Masdevallia tovarensis is one of the most beautiful in this large group – around 400 species – of small plants. It was discovered near Tovar in 1842 by Jean Linden (who called it *Masdevallia candida*). In 1849, the young H.G. Reichenbach published a formal description, on the basis of specimens collected by J.W. Moritz in the same area. It was not until several years later, however, that it could be seen blooming in a European garden, when Hermann Wagener sent plants ostensibly collected around Caracas to his employer. The triquetrous inflorescence bears up to five pure white flowers set well above the foliage. *Masdevallia tovarensis* can only be found in the mountains of northern Venezuela, where it still grows in abundance. It is known as the "Christmas flower" in its natural habitat, as its blooms appear around the end of December. [GUIDO BRAEM]

Masdevallia tovarensis.
‹ [idem]. Plate from the *Hortus Lindenianus*.

fish, reptiles and molluscs. The official reaction was not long in coming. On 31 August 1842, the museum wrote to Linden as follows: "We hope that your next shipments will be more extensive and varied, and that zoology will play a part but that, as regards botany, you will not forget the families that were particularly requested before your departure, such as orchids, aroids, bromeliads, dried palms and the same plants in a live state, wood from vines and palms from various species: Also, please make good arrangements for your dispatches of live plants so that at least some of them arrive in good condition."[78] On 8 February 1843, the museum wrote again: "The crate of live plants had suffered so much during the voyage that everything seemed dead. In fact, only one small palm could be saved."[79] Linden would not receive this letter until several months later, as he had already left the coast to explore the interior.

Linden's official report ends with his second stay in Tovar in October 1843. This first part would not be followed by a second written in the same way. We know about the rest of his journey thanks to another document, comprising general observations about the lands he visited, which he published in *Plantae Columbianae* in 1863; we shall return to this account further on.

78. Letter dated 31 August 1842. Paris, Archives of the Muséum national d'Histoire naturelle.
79. Letter dated 8 February 1843. *Ibid.*

› Other collectors had to confront the forces of nature in their expeditions, just as Linden did around 1843. *Critical moment at the Rio Ovéjas.* Drawing by Émile Bayard after sketches by Édouard André, collector for Jean Linden, in *Le Voyage dans les Andes,* circa 1875, p. 285.

Llaneros. Oil on card, Ferdinand Bellermann, 1843.

Río Tocuyo, 1998.

Linden used the next few weeks to prepare for his journey into the regions that the rainy season had hitherto rendered out of bounds: the Llanos. This expedition would take him from Caracas right to the Pacific. Before setting off on this trek, Linden sent various packages to both Brussels and Paris. There is a marked difference in the tone of the letters addressed to Minister Nothomb and those sent to those *"Messieurs de Paris"*. He unwinds more in the missives to his compatriot, unashamed of revealing his emotions and disappointments – as when the turbulent waters of the Tocuyo River swept away the fruit of several days' collecting, as well as half his baggage. This incident also reveals the strength of Linden's enthusiasm, which enabled him to quickly regain control of the situation. "This disaster cost me the best part of my luggage, as well as the few zoological and botanic collections I had laboriously pieced together on this ill-fated excursion. A few days later, I reached Trujillo, where I was happy to be able to

Río Tocuyo, 1998.

assemble a collection of orchids remarkable for the magnificence and novelty of the species that it comprises."[80]

Following the traces of Linden in Venezuela, my husband and I searched for the place where this accident occured on an expedition we nicknamed "Cattleyana". After travelling some thirty kilometres through the mountains, without really knowing where we were, we thought we had found the Quibor road and eventually stumbled across a ghost town, straight out of a Western, lost in a barren landscape. It was then that we understood how we had strayed off course, so we turned round and took the splendid road leading to Humocarabajo. We followed the river tucked into the mountains, the river whose name has a magical ring to me, the river that inspired me to seek out my ancestor: El Tocuyo! There we were, opposite Humocarabajo, by the river, at the point where a suspended footbridge provided a link to the other bank. This was undoubtedly the scene of the disaster in which two mules were carried away by "the impetuosity of the current [...]"[81]. I was deeply moved as I stood on the exact spot where Jean Linden, having passed the point of no return, made the decision to cross the torrential waters. Although the circumstances are very different 150 years on – the water level was fairly low on the day I found the Tocuyo – I suddenly had the impression of being very close to him, of feeling his presence.

Further on, my husband and I made a stop in Guarica. In the square, I had my first encounter with wild cattleyas, as several trees sported thick

80. *Plantae Columbianae, op. cit.*
81. *Ibid.*

clumps that hung down from their trunks. Further afield, I found cattleyas ensconced on hedges and garden fences. The locals did not seem to realise the important place that cattleyas still have in the world; their conservation remains of vital concern to today's botanists.

This same portion of Linden's expedition – although there is no exact date in the documents at our disposal – marked the discovery of the orchid once known as *Uropedium lindenii*. This adventure – for it was an adventure – unfurled on the outskirts of Jaji, near Mérida, between July and September of 1842 or in July 1843 – in other words, before or after his stay in what is now Colombia.

The discovery of *Uropedium lindenii* was not only sensational in itself but was also told in different ways by Jean Linden, Nicolas Funck and Lucien Linden. The story grows slightly longer each time, as if each narrator was eager to outdo his predecessor. Jean Linden's account is the shortest and puts the emphasis on the discovery of the plant, while Funck concentrated on the events after this discovery and the plant's extraordinary attributes – although, in a later version, he viewed the whole saga with amusement and gently made fun of Linden.

Linden was first to tell the tale. When asked by the Comte de Moran which orchids had made the greatest impression on discovery, he replied, after a short reflection: "As regards a great, powerful impression, I could mention the discovery of *Uropedium lindeni [sic]*. It was a bear that made me discover it, and this circumstance, coupled with my astonishment at the sight of this flower, hitherto unknown, with such a strange form, will always prevent me from forgetting such an encounter. I was out hunting hummingbirds, with nothing but a gun loaded with dust shot for a weapon. I was going down a narrow path between the rocks when I arrived at the mouth of a cave, in front of which was standing a fairly large bear. Any fight was out of the question; I threw myself to one side, with the idea of going back to my camp to get a rifle loaded with bullets. I had barely made a few steps back up the trail when I noticed the *Uropedium,* forming a magnificent clump in full bloom, with filaments 70 centimetre long [...]; I was

Cattleyas growing in a tree. Venezuela, 1998.

1.2. Uropedium Lindenii. Lindl. 3_8. Sollya Drummundi.

filled with wonder and, faced with this spectacle, I forgot about my bear and my rifle."[82]

Later on, Nicolas Funck, who did not go on this part of the journey with Linden, gave his version of the incident. "One day, while Mr Linden was on a solitary excursion on the outskirts of Jaji and Mr Schlim was exploring in the company of their servant don José on a hill opposite, the former arrived at the entrance of a superb grotto whose stalactites attracted him from afar. He could not resist venturing inside, but he had barely gone a hundred paces when, to his great stupefaction, he noticed a black bear (*Ursus americanus*) suddenly emerging from the depths of the grotto, advancing intently towards him on its hind legs. As chance would have it, Mr Linden — who had not taken the precaution to carry any firearm at all — fortunately found himself close to a narrow fissure that opened up on to the other side of the rock. As he was young, quick-witted and lean at the time [sic], he leapt into the crevice and came out on the other side, in

‹ *Uropedium lindenii* (now *Phragmipedium lindenii*). Plate from *La Belgique horticole*, 1854.

82. *JO*, 1891-92, p. 316.

Uropedium lindenii

This species was first noted by John Lindley in *Plantae Lindenianae* in 1846, but his description of it is very brief. The Parisian Adolphe Brongniart subsequently made a much more detailed study of the plant, which is currently classified within the genus *Phragmipedium* Rolfe and has received the following taxonomy: *Phragmipedium lindenii* (Lindley) Dressler & N.H. Williams. It is an autogamous form (that is, self-pollinating). Some consider it a variety of *Phragmipedium caudatum*. This is what the *Pescatorea* (1856, pl 2) has to say on the subject: "Although its discovery dates back to 1843, this remarkable cypripediioid was barely indicated to botanists by a short description, which passed over the structural peculiarities subsequently so well conveyed by Mr A. Brongniart. The plant was merely seen as a species of *Cypripedium* with a flat, linear labellum. This error is easy to comprehend, if one bears in mind the resemblance of our *Uropedium* with *Cypripedium caudatum*, and this theory could well have been taken for fact, if it had been proven that the *Uropedium lindenii*, instead of being a normal, constant form, represented the monstrous state of some unknown *Cypripedium*. Whatever the substance of this ingenious hypothesis, put forward with prudent reservations by A. Brongniart and suggested, it must be said, by the strange metamorphoses of certain proteiform orchids

(*Catasetum, Myanthus, Monacanthus*), it seems to us that the *Uropedium* could not be conspecific with *Cypripedium caudatum*, which is distinguished by the lesser [sic] development and colouring of its petals. These petals of *Uropedium lindenii* appear as long narrow ribbons, analogous in appearance to those of various Aristolochiae (*Aristolochia trilobata*), the *Strophanthus* and certain Buttneriaceae (*Herrania*, Goudot), not to mention numerous orchids, such as *Brassia, Habenaria, Cirrhopetalum,* etc. In no other case, however, do the floral parts extend in length to such a degree. Taking into account that these ribbon-like vermiform [sic] appendices, as shown in reduced proportions in the black vignette in the background of the colour plate, measure not less than 55 centimetres, this means that the entire flower, when spread out, would span more than 1 metre.

Furthermore, in this plant, as in *Cypripedium caudatum,* the elongation of the petals occurs almost entirely after the opening of the flower, and proceeds gradually. Twelve days are roughly sufficient for this development, from the moment when the flower begins to open. The flowering lasts five or six weeks. The *Uropedium* is one of the strangest forms in an already highly paradoxical family." [GUIDO BRAEM]

Lulu on the bearskin brought back
by Nicolas Funck.

the open air, some ten minutes later, without the bear being able to follow
him, and he started to run as fast as his legs could carry him through the
nearby forest. Finally, out of breath and worn out, he fell to the ground,
almost unconscious. When he came to again and was able to breathe freely
and look around him, he saw, a short distance away, under a thicket of
trees, an orchid in bloom, over two feet long, with its lower sepals [*sic*]
twisted in a spiral, with their ends resting on the ground. The sight of this
wonder, which he recognised as belonging to the genus *Cypripedium*, made
him forget about the bear and the grotto. He set about investigating and
ended up gathering a half-dozen specimens and rejoining his travelling
companion safe and sound in Jaji."[83]

Funck followed this anecdote with an account of his own adventures.
In October 1845, Linden sent Schlim and Funck back to collect numerous orchids, including the famous *Uropedium lindenii,* thus named by John
Lindley two years previously when it first arrived in Europe. (It had not
survived its Atlantic crossing, however, so it was therefore vital to make up
for this loss with new specimens.) Funck took up the story again from
this trip:

"After three weeks we had collected at least a hundred *Uropedium.* I had
not overlooked a visit to the celebrated grotto where the bear had appeared
in front of Mr Linden [...]. On the eve of our departure [...], I decided to
make one last excursion in the area of our isolated accommodation, in the
company of our guide, don José. No longer having the slightest fear of

83. Nicolas Funck, *Op. cit.*

encountering the bear in question, I left my gun in our hut. We had barely reached a distance of a quarter-league from the hut [...], when I saw our Bariba bear perched on a tree just above us. I ordered my guide, José, to stand watch under the tree and attempt to prevent the bear from escaping through the fields; I myself rushed towards our hut to grab my gun. When I arrived back a quarter of an hour later, my guide was still standing peacefully under the tree and the black bear was quietly perched in its branches. I had loaded my gun with several bullets, and while the bear watched me curiously, I aimed, fired... and saw it fall lifeless to the ground, from where we carried it back to our hut [...]. "[84]

It was Lucien Linden himself who handed down this anecdote, revealing all of Uncle Nicolas' affection for Jean. At family meals in the late nineteenth century, the story was told and retold with a mixture of tearful emotion and peals of laughter. On one occasion, Funck embellished it as follows: "The indications that Mr Linden gave me were so clear that I found the famous cavern without any difficulty [...]. I walked carefully, haunted by the thought of the gigantic bear with its "bloodcurdling howls", my finger on the trigger of my loaded gun, ready for any eventuality, when I suddenly found myself in front of a formidable bear sitting on its rump at the entrance to the grotto. As soon as it saw me, it held out its paw and asked: "Well, Mr Funck, how is dear Mr Linden? Has he recovered from the terrible fright I gave him when he discovered *Uropedium lindenii* ?"[85]

Uropedium lindenii (now *Phragmipedium lindenii*).

In 1854, Charles Morren described this episode in more serious terms in *La Belgique horticole*: "Mr Linden discovered this unusual plant in 1843 in New Granada, on the territory of the Chiguara Indians, in the shady parts of a small wood on a savannah reaching up to 1,650 metres in altitude, overlooking the forests of Lake Maracaibo. Mr Linden wrote to us that, since his discovery, Mr Schlim has found *Uropedium lindeni* [*sic*] in the provinces of Soto and Ocaña in the province of New Granada, where it often grows as an epiphyte on the old trunks of *Weinmannia*."[86]

The *Uropedium lindenii* episode may make us smile, but it proved a turning point for Linden, as it marked the beginning of his veritable passion for growing orchids. At this point in the journey, Mérida, a large town at the foot of the Andes, became Linden's new base for his various excursions into virgin territory. I set out to find any traces of his long stay on my own trip to Mérida. I asked for information from various sources, particularly the

84. *Ibid.*

85. Lucien Linden, in *JO*, 1896-97.

86. Charles Morren, in *La Belgique horticole*, 1854.

Espeletia cfr. *grandiflora*. Venezuela, 1998.

library, which has no lack of archives. By chance, I crossed the path of Gabriel Pilonieta, an historian and photographer with a keen interest in the history of the town. He showed me published accounts of Linden's time in Mérida, as well as a picture of the house where he stayed, painted by Ferdinand Bellermann, who at one point also lived in the very same building. Linden does not appear, however, among the portraits on display in the Museo de la Gobernación of various travellers and explorers who passed through Mérida.

Having installed himself in a large town, Linden wrote once more to his Belgian and French sponsors. The differences in the tone he used to his correspondents were even more marked. For Paris, his style remained concise, with no effusions, focusing strictly on business. In contrast, he unveiled some of his recent discoveries to Minister Nothomb and did not hesitate to specify the sites of these findings. His letter offered more than just mere information: it contained revelations that would substantially influence the world of science – particularly the essential declaration of the existence of orchids at higher altitude in cold regions, which led to a comprehensive reconsideration of the system of stiflingly hot greenhouses. The correspondence between the minister and the scientist bears witness to a mutual trust and esteem. This letter from Mérida was accompanied by a crate containing some 242 specimens of orchids from the cold region of the Andes. Other shipments of similar significance were sent from Mérida, via the port of Maracaibo.[87]

87. Brussels, Archives générales du Royaume.

Linden's letters to the two European institutions allow us to reconstruct the route that he was planning. He planned on taking two months to reach Bogotá from Mérida, via the provinces of Pamplona, Velez and Tunja, crossing the formidable *páramos* and stopping for a few weeks near Cucuta. From Bogotá, he would return to Caracas along the Apure and the Orinoco. This was an incredible undertaking in such an unforgiving climate, involving hundreds of kilometres of dirt tracks through mountains and jungle, covered on foot with mules carrying the baggage. Some of Linden's letters indicate the extent of this baggage. "I have also managed to assemble a small ornithological collection consisting of 170 birds belonging to 70 different species, as well as a young spider monkey. Some of the birds were bought from the Indians in the various regions I have just visited, and the rest I obtained myself. The plant collection comprises 1,517 specimens from 553 species."[88] These figures give some idea of the scope of Linden's expedition.

Cattleyas decorating a garden hedge. Venezuela, 1998.

Our young explorer was increasingly driven by a passionate enthusiasm. A gradual evolution is clearly apparent in the parallel correspondences that he maintained with Jean-Baptiste Nothomb, the Belgian Minister of the Interior, and the directors of the Muséum national d'Histoire naturelle in Paris. This was especially true in the latter case.

So, his reply to the museum's famous letter of 8 February 1843, which was awaiting him on his return to Mérida in July of that year, was reassuring and optimistic. Without the slightest complaint, Linden not only committed himself to replacing everything but also promised to add some extra treats.[89] He displayed a similar approach to Brussels (which had also written to him along the same lines), although he stressed to both that the question of financial support was becoming more and more crucial to the completion of his mission. In the same way, there was a more reconciliatory note in the letters sent by the museum. Its somewhat dictatorial and reproachful stance had softened into a friendlier attitude and this in its turn rekindled the interest of Parisian scientists, who reiterated that Linden's collections should be shared out (while granting the museum's exclusive right to new discoveries) and offered specific solutions for the efficient replacement of the plants that had reached Europe in a desiccated state.[90]

88. *Ibid.*

89. Paris, Archives of the Muséum national d'Histoire naturelle.

90. *Ibid.*

These reassurances on the part of Linden – which clearly transformed his relationships with Europe – are astonishing in these circles, as many scientific explorers lost all hope at the first setback they encountered.[91] Linden had already glimpsed the possibilities of future benefits that, being *in situ,* only he could imagine.

From autumn 1843 to the following spring, Linden investigated the high plateaus around the frontier between Venezuela and Colombia. On 16 November, in La Guayrá, he boarded the American ship *Orion* bound for Puerto Cabello, where he stayed six weeks. Like many ports the world over, Puerto Cabello was a magnet for merchants and diplomats of all kinds, as well as a meeting place for European expatriates. It now offered the chance for Linden to be reunited with his friend and colleague Nicolas Funck, who had left him in May 1842 to continue his research around Caracas on behalf of Jacob-Mackoy from Liège. It was also in Puerto Cabello that the two met Ferdinand Bellermann for the first time, on 9 January 1844.[92]

Funck persuaded Linden to venture into the largely unexplored region of Sierra Nevada de Santa Marta. Linden duly set off, escorted by an armed guard provided by the governor of the province, who was anxious not only to protect him from the fierce, free-spirited Arahuaco Indians but also to throw some light on the strange stories about this territory. (Later on, the British explorer William Purdie, following Linden's indications, did not dare to fully penetrate the region.) The Sierra Nevada also proved singularly lacking in plant life: "four to five new and brilliant orchids"[93] was the sum total of Linden's findings.

By January 1844, Funck had fallen ill, and Linden saw him off to Europe before setting sail for Jamaica. In a letter addressed to Minister Nothomb, Linden expressed the desire to visit Guatemala – one of the stopovers planned for his second voyage in 1837 – and "maybe do a tour of our colony in Vera Paz", which Belgium was trying to establish in this Central American country. There were murky deeds afoot in this settlement, however, and it seems there was little inclination in Belgium to send a potentially embarrassing witness to see them.[94] In the end, Linden headed for Kingston, Jamaica, on 15 March 1844, on board a small schooner loaded with turtles. The following month, he informed his Belgian protector that he was renouncing his plans to advance in the direction of the Honduran coast in order to save what little money he had left for the exploration of the southern part of Cuba. (Linden had been wait-

91. In this respect, see the chapter on collectors page 133.

92. As we have already seen, the German community had a strong presence in Venezuela. Bellermann's arrival in Puerto Cabello preceded by six months that of Karl Moritz, a botanist sent by William IV of Prussia to assemble natural history collections. Moritz had met Funck, 20 years his junior, in Caracas, and they went on to explore the Silla de Caracas together in March 1843. Moritz, who died in 1866, spent the last period of his life in the Tovar colony, which we have already discussed. This circle of naturalists was regularly received by the Vollmers, a wealthy business family that often organized balls in honour of these men from their homeland.

93. *Plantae Columbianae, op. cit.*

94. The attempt to colonize Santo Tomás proved a failure and sparked a scandal that put Belgium to shame. See Carlo Bronne, *Léopold Ier et son temps,* Brussels, Paul Legrain, 1971, and Marc Lafontaine, *L'Enfer belge de Santo Tomas,* Brussels, Quorum, 1997.

Rue de La Guayrá, with figures and oxen.
Oil on card, Ferdinand Bellermann, 1844.

ing in vain for a subsidy that would have allowed him to stay an extra year in Central America.)

Once in Cuba, Linden spent six months making various excursions that yielded several hundred new plant species. Shortly after the passing of a terrible hurricane in October 1844, he left Cuba for the United States, before returning to Europe in December that same year. He was by now extremely weak, and was to pay the toll of ten years of exhaustion and deprivation for some time to come.

Nevertheless, there was plenty to do once he was back home. To fulfil the commission signed four years previously, Linden set about writing a

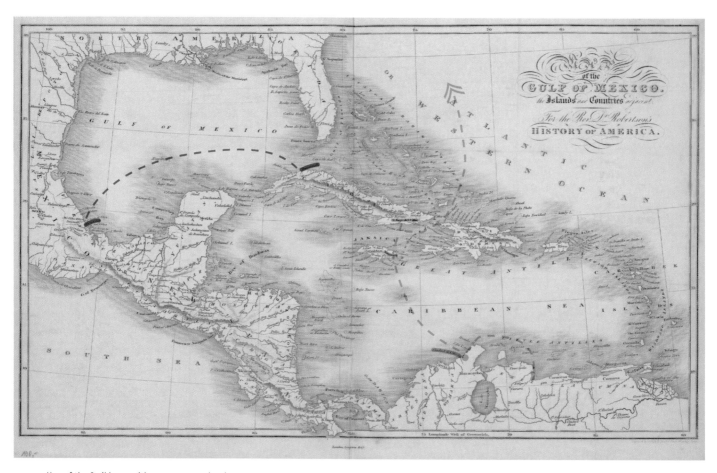

Map of the Caribbean, with return route taken by
Jean Linden via Jamaica and Cuba.

report of his adventures, which was sent to the minister in January 1846.
In fact, the 73 hand-written pages preserved in Belgium at the Archives
générales du Royaume were only the first part of his account, which
comes to a halt after "General considerations on the province of
Caracas"[95].

When published in the *Annales de la Société d'Horticulture de Gand,* the
report served as an advertisement for this type of scientific expedition.
The Belgian government would never again subsidise such missions,
however. Seventeen years later, in *Plantae Columbianae,* Linden added to a
new, abridged edition of his report a brief account of the remainder of
his journey across Colombia and his return via Venezuela, Jamaica and
Cuba. The tone, however, was markedly different and far more imper-
sonal.

No follow-up would appear in the *Moniteur belge.* Linden had undoubtedly satisfied the urgent demands of his sponsors by handing in the first
part of an unfinished report in 1845, and he went back to Luxembourg that
same year. The fact that the text re-emerged nearly 20 years after his return

95. This part would be published in the *Moniteur
belge* on 10 May 1846, before appearing later
that year in the *Annales de la Société d'Horticulture de
Gand,* in the *Plantae Columbianae* in 1863 and in
La Belgique horticole in 1867.

from America is surely due to the significant reputation he had acquired in the meantime. The following chapters explore this rise in his social standing, while an examination of the *Plantae Columbianae* explains the resurgence of interest in Linden during his later career.

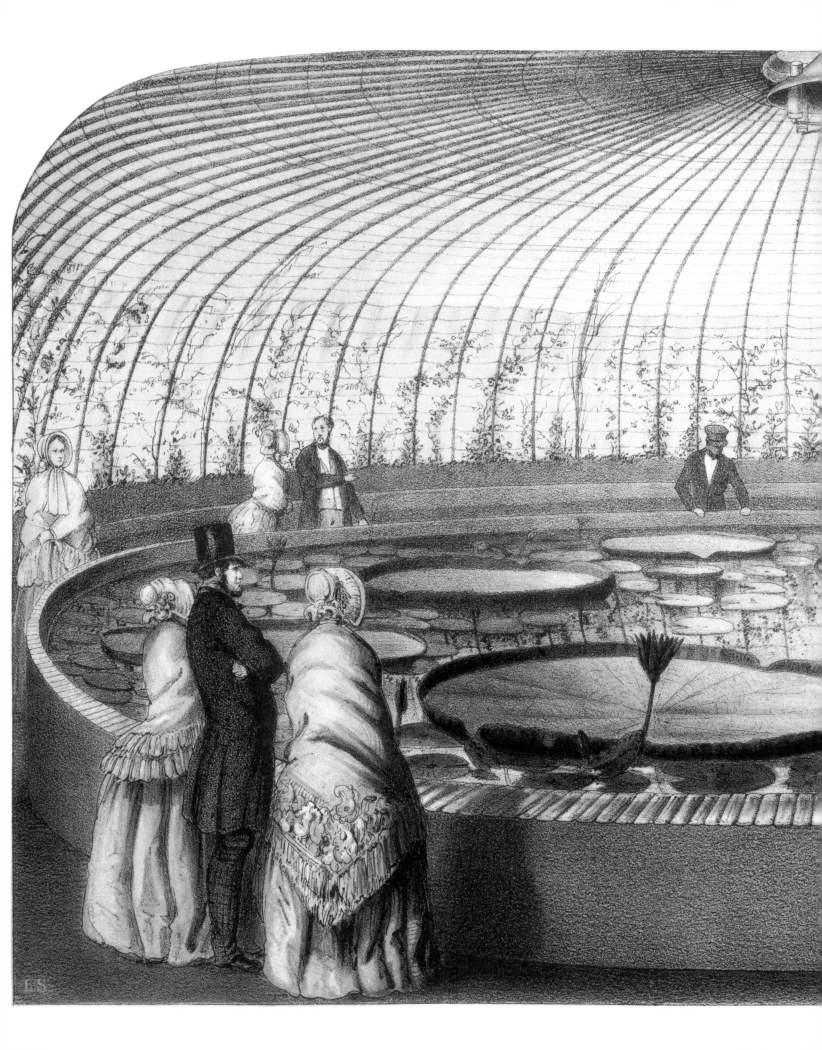

BACK IN
EUROPE

n the early winter of 1844-1845, Jean Linden returned to the Belgian capital after an absence of more than three years. In fact, he had resided there for only a few months altogether, in 1834-1835, 1837 and 1841. Once again, his stay would prove temporary. A decade of exhausting travel had left its mark on the once youthful explorer, now aged 28: Linden had matured, and his dreams of exotic discoveries had given way to more concrete ambitions that would occupy all his energies.

In the meantime he was pondering the lessons of his expeditions. First and foremost, his fascination with travel had crystallised into a passion for orchid collecting. In addition, the government's intentions had become far more specific with regard to scientific and botanical matters. The order for the second expedition (Mexico and Cuba, 1837) was primarily concerned with the search for commercial openings to foster the economic security of the infant state. On the 1837 mission, the trio of explorers had played fast and loose with the terms of their contract in order to concentrate on botany, but the third expedition (Venezuela, Colombia) was conceived from the start on purely scientific lines: possibly the origin of the subsidies influenced this distinct change in emphasis.

Jean Linden's preparatory moves in other directions also reveal to us much about this future horticulturist's ambitions. His contacts with the Muséum national d'Histoire naturelle in Paris had confirmed a determination to become involved with professional botanical institutions. Did he dream of becoming the museum's supplier, or even its future director? In 1845, the young Linden possessed no more than a practical knowledge of botany and zoology, acquired on his expeditions rather than by formal study.

Two letters from early in the same year further demonstrate Linden's indecision as to his future course. In the first, dated 6 January and addressed to Adolphe Brongniart, then in charge of the Muséum national d'Histoire naturelle de Paris,[1] he relates his recent adventures in Venezuela and Colombia, his difficulties in retrieving consignments held up in Ostend and, in particular, his disappointment on realising that most of the plants he had brought back had died at the end of an arduous sea crossing. Linden's concern with maintaining privileged relations with the museum is revealed by the precise enumeration of the sites visited, his mention of substantial sums spent and the constant reiteration of his regret at the losses. He plans to send a dried plant collection to Paris, but is still waiting to lay

Anna Reuter.

« *Interior view of the Victoria House on the premises of Van Houtte*. Colour lithograph from the *Hortus Van Houtteanus*.

hands on the shipment. He hopes that the management of the museum will take all this into account and remember the many setbacks he has suffered.

This letter also makes plain that Linden was dealing actively with the Société d'Horticulture de Belgique; the winter of 1844-1845 was particularly harsh and Linden lost so many plants that barely enough remained to meet the society's orders, for which he had received advance payments. It is not possible to determine whether the advances mentioned in the correspondence were included in the Belgian government's subsidies or whether the society was following a similar but independent track, thus providing Linden with a secondary resource.

The second letter is dated 8 February and is addressed to the board of directors of the Botanical Gardens in Brussels. Linden has learned that the search is on for a curator to run the institution. He presents himself as a candidate, unveiling his "ambition [...] to fill this post, not only because it is most appropriate to my vocation, but because it offers the means to give you practical proof of my devotion and gratitude, and above all the chance to bestow on my country's leading botanical and horticultural establishment all the benefits of my lengthy expeditions in the tropics."[2] Plainly, both these ambitions – as plant supplier and director of a scientific institution – were taking shape in his mind from the moment he returned from Latin America. I could find no reply to this second letter in the various archives I have investigated, but it is a matter of historical record that he did not get the position.[3] The alternative path now engaged his whole attention.

We could describe the second half of the 1840s as an experimental period in Jean Linden's life. The explorer was obliged to readapt to life in Europe. Settling down became one of his priorities, and he was growing increasingly aware of the importance of studying the social and professional circles in which he aspired to move. In short, his plan was to marry, raise a family and establish a business with men of note as his clients. The rapid sequence of events makes clear that he had a head start in this ambition. Less than nine months after he addressed his letter to the Botanical Gardens, he was sending Funck and Schlim back to Latin America – at his own expense – for yet more specimens. A few days earlier, on 13 October 1845, he had married Anna Reuter in Luxembourg. In early 1846, within the space of one week, he both forwarded the report he had promised the Belgian government (20 January) and founded his first company (27 January) in Limpertsberg, a suburb of his native city. The following

Alice Linden with her husband, Victor Alesch.

Auguste Linden.

1. Letter to Adolphe Brongniart dated 6 January 1845. Paris, Archives of the Muséum national d'Histoire naturelle.

2. Letter dated 8 February 1845. Meise, Archives of the National Botanic Garden of Belgium.

3. The post went to Barthélemy Dumortier.

summer, Jean and Anna moved into their new dwelling next to "three hand-somely large greenhouses",[4] which was to be home to the growing family. The birth of Adrienne Linden on 17 August 1846 was swiftly followed by that of five other children: Alice (9 February 1848) and Auguste (9 December 1849), born in Luxembourg; Valérie, born in Schaerbeek (7 September 1851); Lucien (12 November 1853), born in Brussels; and Gaston, the youngest, also born in Brussels (22 April 1860).

In November 1846, the young horticulturist received from John Lindley what would become his first promotional material: the preface of the *Orchidaceae Lindenianae*. In the next chapter we examine in depth the economic strategy orchestrated by Jean Linden, and the origins of his first business. Here, it seems relevant to place things in their European and historical contexts, as they hold the key to the crucial question facing him: where to set up his first establishment?

Was it to be Luxembourg, scene of his birth, his boyhood and his marriage? Or Brussels, from where he set off on his expeditions? Or Paris, where he enjoyed numerous privileged relations? We might also add London – or Ghent, a sort of botanical capital where powerful companies owned by Louis Van Houtte and Ambroise Verschaffelt enjoyed considerable success long before the city's first flower shows ... Despite a few good contacts developed in London among the great collectors associated with Kew Gardens, Linden does not seem to have had any particular desire to set up in England. In the end, fate was to tip the scales in another direction.

Initially, as noted above, Linden started up his plant business in his native Luxembourg. In the summer of 1846, he wrote to Joseph Decaisne: "The countryside is superb and the area where I live one of the most pictur-esque, so though you will not find my establishment as grandiose as the Van Houtte premises, you will be compensated by the beauty of the loca-tion ... I do hope you will come and spend a few days with me ..."[5]

A glance back at the history of Belgian independence as summarised in the first chapter will remind us of the tenuous attachment of the Kingdom of Belgium to Luxembourg. What is today the Grand Duchy ceased to be dependent on the Belgian crown when King William of Orange ratified the Treaty of XXIV Articles in 1838. Leopold I had to withdraw his troops from the provinces he had retained after 1831 and thus, when Jean Linden returned from his expeditions, he found himself once again a subject of the King of the Netherlands. This significantly distanced him from several

Lucien Linden.

Valérie Linden.

4. Letter to Joseph Decaisne.
Paris, Institut de France.

5. *Loc. cit.*

potential commercial opportunities: not just in Brussels, but also Antwerp
and Ostend and the exotic countries accessible from those two ports. Given
his international ambitions, Jean Linden was not particularly concerned
about remaining a Luxembourg citizen, and the Belgian capital appeared the
most inviting destination. It would doubtless have seemed the only possible
place, had Paris not offered so many opportunities.

It would appear that Linden had hopes of major financial gain in the
French capital. In 1850, he wrote twice to Joseph Decaisne, explaining:
"I had toyed with the idea of setting up a combined botanical, zoological
and horticultural business in Paris ... but I was scared off by the February
[1848] revolution. Now, the recent elections in Paris have really got me
worried as to the future, and I hesitate to saddle myself with a business that
cannot prosper until calm returns to Europe."[6]

The wave of revolutions in 1848 had shaken more than one European
nation: France had definitively abandoned its monarchic regime, the
Austrian Emperor and Metternich had been forced to quit Vienna, the
Italian princes were still trembling on their thrones – as was the Prussian
monarchy – and a fresh insurrection had been severely repressed in Warsaw.
In Belgium, however, the 1848 revolts and protests had inflicted no political damage. "Political liberties that people were still clamouring for elsewhere had been written [by the people] into their country's constitution,
and their patriotism was conservative in nature ..."[7] Belgium's difficulties
lay in another direction: the financial panic following the outbreak of
potato blight devastated people's lives more severely than events beyond
their frontiers. On an international level, Belgium – the only monarchy on
the continent not to be overthrown – gained a new legitimacy in the
European stakes, facilitating the forging of new diplomatic links with its
neighbours and the Great Powers. This comparative stability probably confirmed Linden in his decision to settle in Brussels and set aside his Parisian
ambitions, despite the fact that they were based on strong connections in
that city. The following decades bore testimony to his tenacity in that
respect, however, with Luxembourg, Brussels, Ghent and Paris all ultimately
having their own horticultural businesses run by the former explorer. In the
following chapter, we discuss the inexorable rise of Linden in the world of
commerce.

An early portrait of the artist, Gaston Linden,
the youngest of the family.

6. Letter to Joseph Decaisne dated 1 May 1850.
Paris, Institut de France.

7. Comte Louis de Lichtervelde, *Léopold Ier et la
formation de la Belgique contemporaine*, Brussels,
Librairie Albert Dewit, 1929, p. 247.

FINANCIAL SUCCESS

1845-1875

I t would be a bold author who attempted to retrace the history of a company, or rather several successive companies, without access to a single balance sheet and working only from a miscellaneous array of archives consisting of letters and magazine articles. My aim, in any case, is not to quantify the mounting success of Linden's businesses or pass judgement on how he managed his companies. No account of our horticulturist's remarkable career would be complete, however, without a chapter examining his commercial strategies or some attempt to record the various stages of his meteoric rise. Admittedly, we shall discover that Linden benefited from numerous acts of generosity and helping hands in times of crisis; but the fact is that he possessed a trump card of his own – a lucid and calculating mind with a thorough understanding of both the social circles in which he moved and his clientele.

The Zoological Gardens in the Parc Léopold. The director's house. Engraving by Cannelle for an album published by Jules Géruzet, circa 1856.

THE LAUNCH IN LUXEMBOURG

After his brief stay in Brussels, where he nurtured the hope of becoming curator of the Botanical Gardens (see previous chapter), Jean Linden settled in Luxembourg and was soon focusing on the task of introducing new plants. With Nicolas Funck, his lifelong partner, he founded the Établissement d'Introduction de Plantes. The company name leaves no room for doubt as to its ambitions and purpose: the sending out of a new group of collectors to import rare specimens into Europe. These would be acclimatised in greenhouses at various temperatures according to species before gracing the drawing rooms of rich collectors. Linden was one of the very few European growers to make a proper study of the natural habitat and environment of plants and was thus able to exploit his acquisitions to the

‹ Poster for the Linden company in Paris.
L'Illustration horticole, 1879.

full. He clearly learned a great deal from his disappointment on seeing his imports destroyed by the freezing European winter. Thereafter he made every effort to reproduce the original growing conditions, a revolutionary technique unknown to other botanists and horticulturists of the period and which Linden developed clandestinely, at first. Toiling away in his secret garden, he laid down a rational basis for orchid cultivation, ensuring a high level of survival.

The expeditions over, Linden's first move was to draw up an inventory of the plants remaining after losses during shipment. A hundred crates had arrived, only a quarter of which were of any use. From this small remnant he still had to supply the Société horticole and the Muséum national d'Histoire naturelle in Paris. There can be little doubt that he retained for himself a first-rate collection of interesting specimens, including the 250 orchids that formed the basis of his stock. The expedition orders for 1841 in no way forbade him to establish his own collection.[1] A number of these plants, incidentally, survived in the hands of famous collectors in England and Belgium; the rest, 70 or 80 species, went to the Brussels grower, de Jonghe.

Linden's original stock is not, of course, sufficient to explain how he acquired his wealth. Ever conscious of the enormous botanical reserves of Latin America, he was impatient to dispatch his plant hunters before others got the same idea. No later than October 1845 – he had been home only 11 months – he entrusted his old travelling companions, Nicolas Funck and Louis-Joseph Schlim, with a mission to Venezuela and Colombia. Both men were immensely experienced in these countries, so Linden could direct them from a distance. He supplied the funds and called upon his prodigious memory for places to form an itinerary for the journey, together with a list of priority species for collection.

The expedition was undertaken in the name of the Établissement de Botanique et d'Horticulture de Jean Linden, Luxembourg. Such a venture would be incredibly expensive. In a letter of 6 January, Linden mentions the sum of 45,000 francs (212,500 euros) for the third expedition alone. At the time, the government had contributed 12,000 francs and the Paris museum 9,000 francs, both amounts spread over three years. This left a shortfall of 24,000 francs. As Linden certainly had no savings or family means, he had to look elsewhere. On several occasions, he alludes to England as a source of finance. A number of documents also refer to the involvement of the Société horticole de Belgique, a flight of fancy to say the

1. Commission for the expedition. Royal decree dated 21 May 1841, *Moniteur belge,* same date.

least as this organization was not exactly wealthy. Maybe we should search for backers among the ranks of wealthy individuals; could there perhaps have been a partnership with Leopold I, himself an aficionado of things exotic? For many years Linden had been building relationships with bankers and big businessmen such as Jean-Pierre Pescatore and Baron Benjamin Delessert. It is also conceivable that Nothomb, the government minister, contributed a share; like other members of his family he was personally interested in botany in general and, no doubt, orchids in particular.

Apart from the financing of the latest expedition, there is also the question of the source of the capital needed to construct the new premises opened in 1846 in Limpertsberg. Anna Reuter, whom Linden married in 1845, came from a well-to-do family: they owned a large house in the Breitenweg district, two more in Grund and some agricultural land outside the town, and may therefore have offered assistance. We do, however, have two independant sources giving the name of a most prestigious patron: "[Linden] had created a botanical garden in Limpertsberg with the financial aid of the king, Grand Duke William II, but for reasons that escape us, he sold the establishment in 1853."[2] Without other clues and no solid documentation – deliberate, perhaps, for reasons of discretion – the problem of who paid for the expedition and the launch of the new business remains a mystery.

What is beyond doubt is that the venture took off rapidly. Linden had a stock of plants for capital, a reliable supply of new shipments in the proposed expeditions and a secure source of finance from various partnerships and his plant sales. All that now remained was to promote the company.

A clear-headed, forward-thinking figure, Jean Linden did not leap blindly into the horticultural trade but viewed his career as a long-term proposition. He began with an audacious and clever stroke that proved vital in bringing himself to public attention. He wrote to the eminent English botanist, John Lindley, asking him to draw up a scientific description of the orchids discovered on his recent travels. A professor at the University of London and the Royal Institution of Great Britain, Lindley was then at the height of his botanical fame. He accepted Linden's proposal and began his work on taxonomy which, in November or December 1846, resulted in the publication of *Orchidaceae Lindenianae, or Notes upon a Collection of Orchids Formed in Colombia and Cuba by Mr J. Linden*. This was scarcely a year after Linden's return to Europe.

2. The first consuls of the Grand Duchy. Albert Calmes, in "CD et CC", *Ons Hemecht*, No 3, Luxembourg, 1985.

The work was devoted entirely to orchids: *Epidendrum, Restrepia, Masdevallia, Pleurothallis, Dialissa, Stelis, Evelyna, Odontoglossum, Pachyphyllum, Telipogon, Acraea, Cranichis, Oncidium, Solenidium, Maxillaria, Uropedium lindenii,* etc. Lindley provided the nomenclature and diagnostic descriptions in Latin, along with synonyms, native habitats, and the temperatures and months associated with flowering. Linden's manoeuvre was brilliant. Once the orchids had been classified by Lindley, the horticulturist was assured of what amounted to a patent: his name would forever remain attached to the plants he imported. Further, this scientific recognition gained him entrance to the word of professional botanists as well as winning the confidence of growers and orchid lovers.

The results appear to have been sent by Lindley to Ghent – or maybe via Charles François Morren, then residing in Liège. Morren, also in 1846, published a statement to the effect that this descriptive work was only the forerunner of a much larger, illustrated work "at present on the presses in England".[3] For the moment, I am unable to discover details of this publication: those volumes of the *Pescatorea* that reached completion only began to appear in 1854.

The second element in Linden's promotional campaign was the publication of his catalogues, the first dating to 1846.[4] The second (*Prix-courant numéro 2: pour Printemps 1847*) was issued to coincide with the appearance of the *Orchidaceae Lindenianae*, a ploy to turn the spotlight on everything connected with his affairs. Linden, in his new capacity as businessman, addresses his preface to future customers. He recalls his travels as explorer on behalf of the Belgian government and announces the inauguration of his horticultural and botanical centre for introducing new species. He has collectors working for him in various regions known personally to him; he can supply botanists with dried specimens and plant lovers and horticulturists with rare or previously unknown species, suitable for warm temperate or cold greenhouses as desired. A notice on the back cover adds: "The present catalogue includes only living plants that are either entirely new or recently introduced." He deliberately offered only plants already classified by taxonomists; those still being processed he kept under wraps until such time as they acquired their 'identity cards'.

Linden's adroit tactics illustrate his penetrating insight into capitalist society and current social trends. He swiftly shifted the emphasis from his self-confessed lack of formal training as enjoyed by professional European botanists to the practical assets he had acquired from experience: his knowl-

3. *Annales de la Société royale d'Agriculture et de Botanique*, Ghent, 1846, p. 66.
4. First catalogue from 1846. Bibliography of botanists.

John Lindley: when a plant gets its name...

Centradenia grandifolia.

The British horticulturist and botanist John Lindley (1799-1865) is the perfect example of high society's passion for botany in the 1800s. Originally a library assistant (1818-19) to Joseph Banks, Lindley joined the Horticultural Society of London in 1822 before becoming Professor of Botany at University College, London in 1829, a post he was to hold until 1860. As well as being secretary to The Horticultural Society of London (which in 1861 became the Royal Horticultural Society under a new charter arranged by its then president, Prince Albert), he was co-founder in 1841 with Joseph Paxton of the journal *The Gardeners' Chronicle*; this was the same Paxton who ten years later would be responsible for the groundbreaking Crystal Palace in London, the site of the 1851 Universal Exhibition. Many of the plants from Linden's houses were, as a result, announced in *The Gardeners' Chronicle*. Lindley's fame rests largely on his achievements in the field of botanical taxonomy: the orchid genus *Lindleyella* was named in his honour.

In 1753 Carl von Linné (Carolus Linnaeus) published a set of rules for the Latin nomenclature of plant species. Each plant has a name consisting of two words known jointly as the "binomial". The first, always capitalised, denotes the genus, while the second, in lower case, is the species; both are printed in italics. To these are added (in Roman type) the name of the author publishing the plant and the year this description was published. Thus each plant receives a unique name: *Cattleya labiata* Lindley 1822, for instance. For simplicity's sake [?], however, most publications omit the last two terms.

The plant's name is attributed by the first botanist to publish his scientific description of the plant; the choice of Latin words – for both genus and species – describing one of its characteristics or honouring a particular person is left to his judgment. The genus names *Cattleya* and *Cattleyopsis* were chosen to commemorate William Cattley. The second part of the binomial, the species name, varies according to the number and gender of the individual(s) in question. Thus we find *lindenii* (for Jean Linden), *sanderi* (for Frederick Sander) and *hookeri* (for William Hooker and his son Joseph), but also *hookerae* for the latter's wife and *hookerorum* for William Hooker and his son (i.e., plural, masculine ending). In cases where the species name refers to one of the plant's biological characteristics, its ending will agree with the genus name: *Centradenia grandifolia* describes a plant with particularly large leaves, for example. Without going into too much detail, we should note that with natural hybrids the letter "x" is placed in front of the species name, as in *Cattleya* x *lindenii*.
[GUIDO BRAEM]

edge of habitats, of course, but also his grasp of rarity as an important commercial factor, market values, risk taking, etc. He correctly identified the public's desire for 'designer labels' with instant guarantees of quality, staking everything on a simple but effective premise that would become his leitmotif: people would pay anything for "rare orchids from Linden's". His idea caught on: orchids became commercial products and even status symbols for their owners.

Some writers would stigmatise Linden for his non-academic background; a "mere gardener", they cried – and, in a sense, they were right. Linden had no apparent ambition to join the ranks of the great research botanists, regarding his business rather as an adjunct to their work. None of this detracted from his relationship with academia: he maintained professional and personal links with numerous specialists such as Planchon and Decaisne, whom he met in 1841 in Paris. His awareness and eye for business would keep Linden at the top of his profession throughout his working life.

THE CONQUEST OF BRUSSELS

The census lists for the city of Brussels reveal the presence of the Linden family in the spring of 1850: Jean and Anna had settled with their children at 52, rue des Palais. Jean had entrusted the management of his Luxembourg business to Nicolas Funck, then a teacher of natural history at the city's high school. Linden's horizons were expanding: he had just returned from visits to the greenhouses at Kew Gardens in England and those built by Paxton for the Duke of Devonshire at Chatsworth. The Chatsworth "Great Stove", some 91 m long, 44 m wide and 18 m high, was the model, some months later, for Paxton's Crystal Palace.

Brussels was on a different scale than Luxembourg. The Belgian capital was a veritable beehive of commerce – in part due to the first rail links opened in 1851 with the ports of Ostend and Antwerp. In addition it progressively became the hub of a passenger network, with regular services to and from Paris after 1847. As if this were insufficient attraction for Linden, various individuals worked to convince him to leave his remote Grand Duchy and plunge into the whirlwind activity of the Belgian capital. Henri Galeotti, Linden's companion on the ascent of Mount Orizaba,

The Crystal Palace during the Great Exhibition in London, 1851.

L'HORTICULTURE INTERNATIONALE

(Société Anonyme)

PARC LÉOPOLD

BRUXELLES

Adresse télégraphique
LINDENIA, Bruxelles

Téléphone n° 544.

Le 25 Nov. 1890

Monsieur G. Warocqué

Membre de la Chambre des Représentants.

Château de Mariemont.

Nous avons l'honneur de vous remettre facture des marchandises qui vous ont été expédiées par *grande vitesse* en *paniers.*

marque H. I. N° ——— et dont le montant s'élève à frs. 23.800. ———

payables à BRUXELLES ou par notre traite

L'Administrateur-Directeur,
LUCIEN LINDEN.

FACTURE N°

N°S	NOMBRE				FRANCS	CENT.
	12	Cattleya Warocqueana	extra	fr.	8000	,,
	50	"	"	à 200.-	10000	,,
	50	"	"	à 100.-	5000	,,
	2	"	"	extra	800	,,
		Paniers et emballage			"	,,
				Net fr.	23800	,,
				S. E. ou O.		

The price of orchids

Today, we can pick up a *Phalaenopsis* for around 10 euros in the supermarket, a far cry from the situation in the nineteenth century. The legendary success of these plants resided to a large extent in their rarity, with only the big, wealthy collectors being able to afford such exotic treasures. In his monograph *Les Orchidées exotiques et leur culture en Europe* (Brussels 1894, pp 489-92), Lucien Linden devotes a brief chapter to the prices fetched by these glorious plants. Numerous examples bring home the fact that the price of an orchid represented several years' wages for the average labourer.

For instance: "A white *Cattleya Mendeli [sic]*, bought by Mr Day, was divided by him into two portions, one of which was sold for 2,625 francs (12,800 euros); the other was again split into two, and these two pieces made 7,350 francs (35,800 euros) between them. A sevenfold division of a *Cattleya Trianae* var. *[sic]*, [...] reached a total of 18,375 francs (90,000 euros) in 1887. In the same sale a specimen of *Laelia purpurata* var. *bella* went for 4,725 francs (23,000 euros)." These figures speak volumes when compared with the grants for the first expeditions mentioned earlier.

had set up business there in the rue de la Limite. Unfortunately, he suffered severely in the 1848 economic crisis and was obliged to close down in 1853.

Further, in 1873, Édouard André – one of Linden's former collectors and the editor-in-chief of *L'Illustration horticole* – declared: "The affection in which he [Linden] was held by the late King Leopold I soon encouraged him to move his horticultural business to Brussels."[5] Admittedly, there is no proof of this among documents in the public domain; it is probably mere publicity hype. Yet we do know that the king insisted on being kept informed of the progress of the 1844-45 expeditions and, we recall, of the shipments of specimens. These were destined for the monarch's "colonial garden" at Laeken, forerunner of the famous greenhouses constructed by Alphonse Balat during the reign of Leopold II.

In any case, Linden's reputation had preceded him to Brussels. He had already won medals at plant shows: at Chiswick in England, for example, in 1848, and at the Société royale de Flore. On the occasion of a sale of 194 lots of orchids from Latin America at the Stevens salerooms in 1850, *The Gardeners' Chronicle* described his business as "the leading venue for dealers and collectors".[6] Linden's sixth catalogue (15 February 1851) again speaks in clear terms of commercial links with England. "My ongoing relationships with the principal horticultural dealers in England and on the Continent allow me to complement my collections of newly discovered plants from other parts of the world. I can offer these in addition to my direct imports at the best possible prices and in first-class condition."[7]

All the same, we know little about Linden's first businesses in Brussels. Documents unearthed in the Archives générales du Royaume speak of greenhouses situated "chaussée de Schaerbeek". This thoroughfare no longer exists, but it is known there was a rue de Schaerbeek running through the district that was built over during the recent construction of the Cité administrative de l'État – not far, in fact, from the rue des Palais where Linden and his wife lived or from the Galeotti businesses in the rue de la Limite.

THE PARC LÉOPOLD

On 30 August 1851, a royal decree ratified the appointment of Jean Linden, "former naturalist and explorer in the service of the government, dwelling in the rue des Palais, Schaerbeek, to be director of the scientific section of this new institution".[8] The institution in question was the

5. Édouard André, in the *Bulletin de la Société botanique de France*, 1873-1874, p. CIII.

6. *The Gardeners' Chronicle*, 1850.

7. *Prix-courant* No 6, 15 February 1851.

8. "Statuts", Royal decree, 1851. Archives de la Ville de Bruxelles.

Société royale de Zoologie, d'Horticulture et d'Agrément de la Ville de Bruxelles, whose statutes had been published on 25 August. "The aims of the Society are to create an extensive complex where people can meet and enjoy themselves. In separate areas there will be a pleasant garden, salons and function rooms, zoological and horticultural collections, reading rooms, and facilities for staging exhibitions of the arts and displays of natural history and for holding literary and scientific meetings." The project brought to fruition plans put forward five years previously for a royal society comprising a zoo, a winter garden and a museum of natural history. It had the backing of a number of titled and well-placed figures. The Burgomaster of Brussels, Jules Anspach, was elected honorary president; others involved included the Duke of Brabant – the future Leopold II – the Count of Flanders and members of the aristocracy and the Chamber of Representatives. It was an ambitious undertaking, reflecting the spirit of the times by creating a rendezvous for the polite society of Brussels. It was a place where visitors could stroll at leisure, listen to music while admiring the gardens and animals, and tour the greenhouses crammed with specimens from distant lands.

This impressive park was designed as an extension to the city. It was sited on a fine, eight-hectare estate covered with old trees, which once

The Zoological Gardens in the Parc Léopold.
Pelican enclosure with the Vittoria Regia *greenhouse*
in the background. Engraving by Cannelle for an
album published by Jules Géruzet, circa 1856.

formed part of the forest of Soignes and was named after its patron, King Leopold I. It even included a country house and its dependent buildings. The park was also adjacent to the embankments of a railway terminus (the Gare de Luxembourg) – an invaluable asset for the future development of Linden's business.

As head of this royal establishment, he could now launch himself wholeheartedly into his commercial activities. The director was unconstrained by any strict policies and given carte blanche to run the park as he saw fit. Linden planned huge additions, setting about the cultivation of thousands of varieties of new plants, particularly palms and orchids.

The Zoological Gardens in the Parc Léopold.
The Lake. Engraving by Cannelle for an album published by Jules Géruzet, circa 1856.

The year 1853 marked a decisive turning point. Linden abandoned his premises in Limpertsberg and transferred his stock to Brussels, where he began to construct new greenhouses using the latest technique of supporting the glass on iron frames. He organised the enormous area at his disposal in such a way as to satisfy the park's shareholders while deriving maximum personal benefit. Doubtless, and not for the first time, the state had handed him a free gift: all the well-to-do city dwellers flocked to the Parc Léopold, which offered a prestigious setting for his business. He exploited it to the full. Contemporary engravings give a clear idea of the scale of the buildings and greenhouses, which stretched right up to the present rue Wiertz. Other pictures published by Jules Géruzet provide a fascinating glimpse of the park, showing gentlemen in top hats and ladies with pretty parasols promenading among pens of exotic creatures such as camels, elephants, monkeys and pelicans. These pictures often served as a backdrop to the famous *Victoria* House, surmounted by its crown.

Away from the centre stage of the *Victoria* House, Linden was not content merely to satisfy the exotic tastes of visitors from the city. Five large greenhouses contained 600 species of orchid raised in conditions matching their native environment. Some areas were not open to the public: in these, behind locked doors, secret experiments took place with growing and propagating methods. These experimental areas proved crucial to the making of Linden's fortune. Monetary values have changed so much that any sums quoted would be meaningless; a better indication of the scale of things can be obtained from the progressive enlargement of the park: 6.5 hectares in 1853; 9 hectares in 1856; and 11 hectares by 1860. Linden's increasing success was deservedly rewarded with the title of Commander of the Order of Leopold bestowed on him by the king on 9 October 1852; in addition to this honour, he had managed to enlarge still further his circle of contacts. Some months later, Colombia named him as its consul, a status that guaranteed him reliable opportunities in South America and much greater control over his imports.

The Zoological Gardens in the Parc Léopold.
Engraving by Cannelle for an album published by
Jules Géruzet, circa 1856.

Ever the strategist, Linden still had his eye fixed on the botanical institutions among his regular clients. Can we read into his correspondence with William Hooker a regret that he was not a trained botanist? Was he being sincere when he informed the curator of Kew Gardens that, as director of the Brussels Jardin royal de Zoologie et d'Horticulture and consul for New Granada (Colombia), selling plants was for him a secondary affair and of no personal significance? The only interest it holds for him, he adds, is a scientific one, since the proceeds go entirely to maintaining his plant hunters worldwide. He goes on to reiterate his passion for these distant expeditions with all the sacrifices they entail. At the same time, he is happy and proud to say that his import business has rendered signal services to

The *Victoria* House

Victoria regia (now *Victoria amazonica*), photographed in its natural habitat at Manaus-Huamita, Amazonas, Brazil.

A coquettish little building designed to house a single species – hence the name – this immediately became the centre of attraction. It included a huge pool on which floated an extraordinary water lily, *Victoria amazonica*, which was able to support the weight of a grown man. Linden may have seen a similar building at Chatsworth, the seat of the Duke of Devonshire, himself an avid plant collector. This eight-sided "miniature theatre" as it was described was commissioned to be designed by Alphonse Balat, the architect later responsible for the royal greenhouses at Laeken.

The *Victoria* House was constructed in 1853 and suffered a kinder fate than the park's other greenhouses. In 1877 it was ceded to the state and re-erected in the Botanical Gardens, only to be dismantled once more during work on the junction of the north-south rail lines. It was finally transferred to the Botanic Garden in Meise, where it can still be admired as "Balat's Greenhouse"; it was restored to all its former glory in 1983.

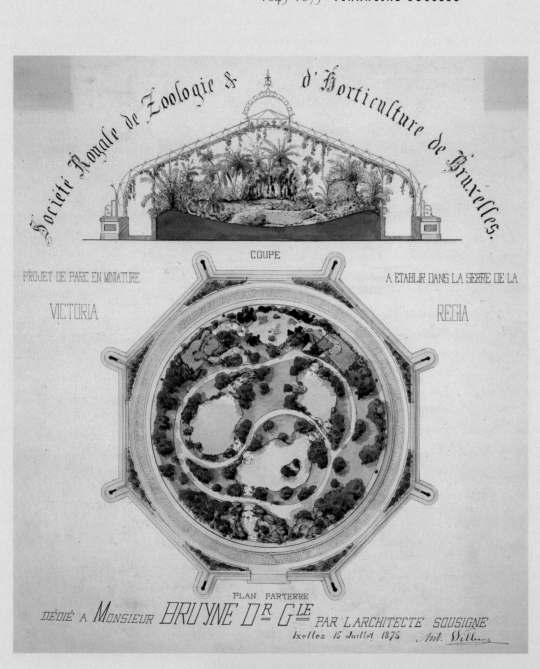

Plans for the refurbishment of the *Victoria* House before its move to Saint-Josse-ten-Noode, 1875.

The *Victoria* House today, in the National Botanic Garden in Meise.

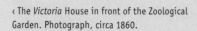

‹ The *Victoria* House in front of the Zoological Garden. Photograph, circa 1860.

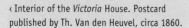

‹ Interior of the *Victoria* House. Postcard published by Th. Van den Heuvel, circa 1860.

The Zoological Gardens in the Parc Léopold.
The bandstand. Engraving by Cannelle for an album
published by Jules Géruzet, circa 1856.

botany and horticulture and that he has succeeded in acquiring a Europe-wide reputation.[9]

What are we to believe? Can we really believe Linden was so disinterested? As the head of a major zoological and horticultural institution, he was taking more and more liberties in developing his own enterprises; the conflict of interests here appears total, and would not in fact be resolved until 1873 when he would purchase from the Belgian State those lots he wanted to exploit on his own account.

On another occasion we find him indignantly refuting statements made by Thomas Moore, Director of the Chelsea Botanical Gardens, who had come over from England to visit the Parc Léopold. Moore repeated his sentiments in *The Gardeners' Chronicle* of 20 March 1858, tactlessly criticising the Brussels park for resembling the Surrey Zoological Gardens in their early days: principally a place for "amusements and pleasure". On 2 April Linden reacted with a letter, complaining he was being slandered by the comparison: the king would never have extended his royal patronage to a mere amusement park, and he himself would never have undertaken the management of such an establishment. A fortnight later, Moore retracted, recognising the efforts made by Linden to introduce a wide variety of new species and the success of his propagation techniques. This anecdote gives us an insight into how Linden turned such arguments to his own advantage: the quarrel, in fact, acted as a fresh piece of publicity for the horticulturist, especially since Moore's article described his set-up as minutely as any tourist guide.

9. Kew archives, vol. 47, 23 November 1853.

In the meantime, probably from 1856, Linden had gradually been making changes in the way he ran the park. Four years later, he drew up a scathing report on the zoological facilities. He had become more and more dissatisfied with the running of these, which led to his resigning his post as scientific director of the Société royale in 1861. Linden was succeeded by his brother-in-law Nicolas Funck but retained the title of honorary director.

THE AGE OF THE INTERNATIONAL CONFERENCES

Linden's resignation left him time to indulge another interest: the organisation of scientific gatherings. In the mid-1800s, international conferences and exhibitions exercised an enormous influence on the way in which plants were introduced and sold on the European market. From these events emerged tales of fortunes invested in orchids, palms and other tropical plants. Backed by the Société linéenne et de Flore and the Fédération des Sociétés d'Horticulture de Belgique, the conferences, beginning in Brussels in 1864, attained a success that had eluded similar attempts in England, France and Germany. Linden, as organiser, invited all the famous names in botany: von Siebold, Brongniart, Planchon, the younger Reichenbach, Regel, etc. The following year, an International Horticultural Exhibition was held from 7 to 12 April to mark the inauguration of the Paleis voor de Volksvlijt in Amsterdam. On this occasion, Linden was to accompany King Leopold.

Two years later, the 1867 Universal Exposition in Paris was the focus of European attention. Once again Linden won several prizes and medals. It was a similar story at an event in Ghent in 1868 and at the horticultural and botanical exhibition in St Petersburg in May 1869. Such triumphs established Linden as the first name in orchid growing. Originally sceptical, even the English were forced to admit his superiority. As we shall discover in a later chapter, his regular role as organiser of conferences and exhibitions went hand in hand with the part he played in the establishment of numerous societies and clubs for enthusiasts and collectors.

THE CONQUEST OF GHENT

The year 1868 marks the start of a spectacular development in Jean Linden's business career. From the society responsible for the Parc Léopold he bought the land on which he had been conducting his private horticultural activities, that is to say 2,700 m² bordering the rue Wiertz, together

with a dwelling house and greenhouses. This appears a wise move, allowing him to concentrate fully on his role as importer and grower of exotic plants, without the encumbrance of the failing zoo.[10] The main development took place elsewhere, however, for in October 1869 Linden set up a business in Ghent.

Two reasons impelled the Brussels-based horticulturist to set up branches in Ghent: lack of space and commercial rivalry. On the one hand, there was insufficient room in the Parc Léopold for all his plants under cultivation. This was really an excuse, however, concealing his main intention of short-circuiting his principal competitors. According to the botanist Regel, Linden had only two rivals in Belgium, both of whom traded from Ghent: Ambroise Verschaffelt and Louis Van Houtte. Every year those two horticulturists brought out a range of new, direct introductions, though on a lesser scale than Linden. At the Paris Exposition, it was Verschaffelt who came closest to Linden in the number of prizes won. In order to neutralise this competition, Linden bought him out in 1869. The purchase was not limited to a handful of greenhouses: founded in 1825, the Verschaffelt firm had launched the periodical *L'Illustration horticole* in 1854. Linden took it over as well, renaming the company "Établissements Jean Linden à Gand".

10. *Le Journal du parc Léopold*, Committee for the Park Centenary.

‹ New entrance to the garden of the Compagnie continentale d'Horticulture in Ghent, after 1869.

Partial view of the nurseries of Ambroise Verschaffelt in Ghent. *L'Illustration horticole*, 1854.

At that time, the premises were situated between the Coupure and the Stoppelstraat, on land that once belonged to the old Abbey of Waarschoot. The price of the transaction was fixed at 425,000 francs (2 million euros). Linden paid some 14,000 francs on account, the rest to follow over twenty years at an annual interest of 5 percent.

Where did he obtain such sums? The archives of the Musée Mundaneum provide an amazing and unique piece of information. Two years earlier in London, on 30 June and 27 August 1866, Linden sold his share of two propeties in South America – which he had apparently owned since the 1841 expedition – totalling 300,000 hectares: El Tocuyo (again!) and Agua Viva.[11] It is clear that he owned a half-share in these, along with Próspero Durand, a Venezuelan landowner. On the other hand, there is no mention in the records of how the horticulturist came to own this important piece of real estate. Family legend speaks of "services rendered to the country"; is there a hint of confirmation in this transaction? Doubtless the properties were connected in some way with the capital Linden needed as early as 1845 to achieve his entrepreneurial dreams.

As the new owner of the Verschaffelt premises in Ghent, Linden undertook a management shake-up. Édouard André replaced Charles Lemaire as editor of *L'Illustration horticole* while Prosper Gloner took over as general manager at the Ghent branch. A 25-year-old native of Luxembourg with a doctorate in law, he would become Linden's son-in-law by his marriage to Adrienne Linden on 4 August 1870.

The buyout of Verschaffelt lent added impetus to Linden's success right up until 1881, with his fame rapidly spreading worldwide as he piled up prizes and awards at exhibitions. He also added to his orchid collection by further purchases. On the death of Schiller, former vice-consul of Venezuela in Hamburg, Linden wasted no time in acquiring over 800 species from his estate. The diplomat had long feared that on his demise the collection he had spent more than 40 years assembling, would be scattered to the four corners of the globe. Édouard André, viewing it in 1869, had declared it without equal in Europe.

Another way in which Linden stamped his mark on Ghent was by his ubiquitous presence at the flower shows held every five years, the

Gloneria jasminiflora, named in honour of Prosper Gloner. *L'Illustration horticole*, 1876.

› *Cattleya schilleriana* var. *Amaliana*, after the collector Consul Schiller of Hamburg. Plate from the *Lindenia*.

11. *IH*, 1873, p. 82.

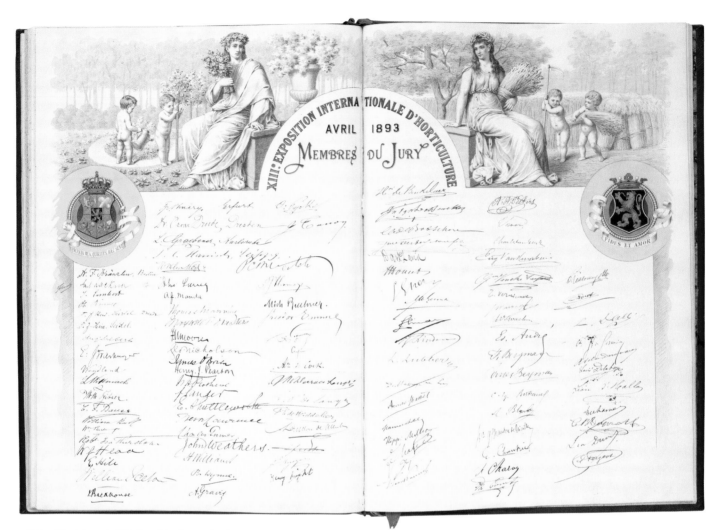

Visitors' book from the XIIIᵉ Exposition internationale d'Horticulture, April 1893. Signatures of the judges. On the right-hand page, in the middle of the first column, are the signatures of Lucien and Jean Linden. Several collectors (such as É. André and C. Ellner) have also signed, as have clients of the Linden businesses.

Floralies, staged by the Société royale d'Agriculture et de Botanique de Gand. On 30 March 1873, the ninth Floralies was opened under the aegis of the Belgian government and once again the event was honoured by a royal visit: this time the king and queen were accompanied by Princess Louise. They were anxious not to leave Ghent without showing their appreciation of and affection for Mr Linden by visiting his splendid horticultural business. The royal party toured the greenhouses in the company of Linden and his son-in-law Gloner; this was the first public appearance of the delightful young Princess Louise. King Leopold II revealed himself as much a lover and connoisseur of plants as his late father. On their arrival, the queen and the princess were presented with a magnificent bouquet of orchids. As he prepared to leave, the king, who had just conferred the rank of Commander of the Order of Leopold on

Linden, turned towards his host. "I have intended this visit", he declared, "as a public mark of appreciation for the services you have rendered not only to horticulture but also to our country."[12] That same year, in August, the *Journal de Gand* announced that the Emperor of Austria had appointed Jean Linden a Commander of the Order of Franz Joseph. I do not know whether Linden travelled to Austria for the investiture, but at that period he was on a business trip in southern Europe and Italy, including Venice and Lake Maggiore. He was astonished to discover carpets of Mondo grass perfectly green at the height of the dry season, and recommended the species for southern gardens.

Autumn 1873 was a tumultuous season for Linden, as he focused on the reorganisation of the premises in Brussels and Ghent. He promoted his second son Lucien to the position of general manager of the company. At

Rhododendron Princesse Louise, named to commemorate the first official engagement of the daughter of Leopold II. *L'Illustration horticole*, 1873.

12. *La Semaine horticole*, 1899, p. 342.

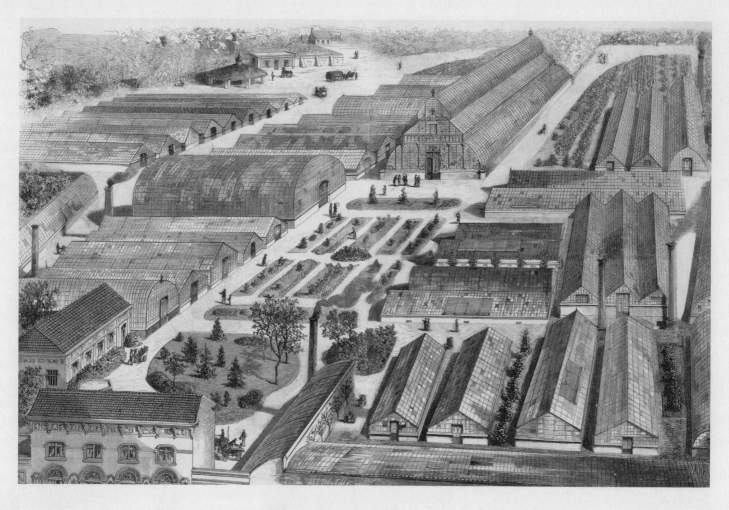

The botanical and horticultural establishment of Jean Linden
in Ghent. Engraving, circa 1880.

Interior view of the Linden greenhouses in Ghent.
L'Illustration horticole, 1881.

first Lucien shared his duties with Prosper Gloner, but the latter eventually left to work for the wealthy Berlin banker Baron Gerson von Bleichröder. Two years later, Lucien was promoted to chief executive at the age of 22. Fritz Pringiers, a contemporary, has left us a brief portrait of the young man. "When only 12, he was already passionate about plants, with his own small self-constructed greenhouse where he grew splendid specimens that won prizes in the exhibitions of the Société royale de Flore in the Botanical Gardens in Brussels [...] His father took the view that he lacked the professionalism to make a good horticulturist, and did all he could to deter him from this career. Thus it was that he began his business life learning the principles of finance as private secretary to an important Belgian banker. He didn't stay long. Missing his plants, he left for England to learn everything he could about them, in the face of his father's opposition."[13] By placing Lucien in charge of his establishments, Jean Linden freed himself of day-to-day business tasks, allowing him to concentrate on his "hobby" in Brussels, where he was seen more and more as indulging his love of orchids.

Lucien Linden.

Was it on the initiative of the youthful team of Prosper Gloner and his brother-in-law Lucien that this complete reorganisation took place? The new arrangements consisted of extending the size of the greenhouses in Ghent to accommodate more specimens and free up space in Brussels. The two directors constructed a huge winter garden that before the end of the year was home to palms, tree ferns and the 1,200 orchid species filling five greenhouses – the world's finest collection at the time. From the heart of his family business, Jean Linden devoted himself to the scientific side of his activities, organising conferences and visiting exhibitions all over Europe, receiving visitors and overseeing his various publications.[14] In 1878, the premises in Brussels were further enlarged by the purchase of a plot of land off the rue du Remorqueur. This extension, however, was soon overshadowed by another investment orchestrated by Jean and Lucien.

ANOTHER STEP UP: PARIS

At an international level, Ghent and Brussels could not rival the other European capitals. The truly great fortunes were made in Paris. In 1879 Linden opened a branch, complete with warehouses, at No 5, rue de la Paix in the French capital. Three years later we come across this announcement: "The Compagnie continentale d'Horticulture has just added to its outlet

13. *IH, passim.*
14. *IH,* 1882, p. 8.

Poster advertising the Linden business in Paris; detail. *L'Illustration horticole*, 1879.

in Paris an information service and a reading room stocking the principal horticultural journals of every nation."[15] Linden followed his usual tactic of advertising his plants with inserts in his publications. "The Compagnie continentale d'Horticulture", typically declares *L'Illustration horticole* of 1882, "formerly trading as J. Linden of Ghent [...] acquires by purchase or exchange prime specimens of orchids, palms, cycads and other ornamental plants." And, for the benefit of the colonies: "We have pleasure in advising connoisseurs, directors of botanical gardens, collectors and growers from all over the world that we purchase or exchange seeds and rare or newly discovered plants."[16]

During this period, Jean Linden struck up a friendship with Édouard Otlet, with whom he would pursue a number of projects. Otlet married Valérie, Linden's youngest daughter, on 27 September 1876. In the South of France the two men were involved in the purchase of Levant Island and the introduction of palms to the Mediterranean coast.[17] Linden also stayed on the shores of Lake Garda at the home of the Marquis della Valle di Casanova in Pallanza, where they appear to have formulated a collaborative project to grow plants under glass. The Otlets and the Lindens, it seems, enjoyed very firm bonds of friendship with the Casanova family. Unfortunately, a lack of documentation has prevented me from researching this matter any further.

The entry into the business by Auguste Linden, Jean's eldest son, was the signal, around 1885, for the launch of a new wave of collecting expeditions in the tropics and Édouard Otlet's collaboration in his father-in-

15. *Ibid.*, p. 4.

16. *Biographie nationale*, vol. 41; supplement to vol. 13 (purchase of the isle of Levant 1880); *IH*, 1882, p. 101 (article in the journal *La Méditerranée*).

17. *IH*, 1888, p. 37.

The San Remigio estate belonging
to the Marquis della Valle
di Casanova at Pallanza.

law's activities. In the meantime, the publication of Henry Hamilton
Johnston's travel account (*The River Congo*) had revived the idea of exotic
lands in the popular imagination in Belgium – and the Congo, still an
independent state, concealed too many treasures for Linden and Otlet to
risk others getting there first. As we shall see in the next chapter, the
expedition under Auguste Linden and Fernand Demeuse did not bring
the anticipated results, while nonetheless being of some use in respect to
horticulture.

Édouard Otlet.

Valérie Linden-Otlet.

H.H. Johnston, *The River Congo*, 1884.

THE BIG COMPANIES

From 1881, the expansion of the Linden businesses demanded the establishment of a more solid base. The difficulties they encountered led the Lindens to set up a limited liability company that year, the Compagnie continentale d'Horticulture à Gand. The board consisted of Jean Linden (managing director), Maloux, Nicolas Funck, Charles Weber and Baron de Brière (chairman). The description "Continental" possibly reflects the ongoing rivalry of Belgian, French and German growers with their British counterparts.

The company underwent a further expansion six years later (1887), an event marked in reviews, since *L'Illustration horticole* was henceforth to be issued in large format, complete with sumptuous colour lithographs. At around this time, the Brussels authorities sold the company a number of plots bordering the Parc Léopold for yet further development. Once again the business was restructured, resulting in the founding, on 17 March, of the limited liability company L'Horticulture internationale. As usual, the board included eminent personalities: Johan Willem van Lansberge (chairman), Count Adrien d'Oultremont, Baron Gerson von Bleichröder and the celebrated lawyer Gustave Joris. Simultaneously, the Compagnie continentale d'Horticulture à Gand was dissolved; any plants not transferred to Brussels were sold off beginning on 16 May 1887. The new premises were opened on 10 May 1888 in the presence of the royal family and numerous ministers and diplomats; 17,433 members of the public came to sightsee. In *Gardening World*, the botanist James O'Brien described the advantages of L'Horticulture internationale's new premises in the Parc Léopold, praising the site for its uncluttered design that enjoyed optimum light and air. He also drew attention to the ingenious layout of the greenhouses "which allow the visitor to see the whole establishment in detail without having to step outside." Today, it is impossible not to feel a twinge of regret when contemplating the European Parliament building – that tower above the former site of the greenhouses.

In the same year, 1888, a sister company was formed to exploit openings in the South of France: the Compagnie méridionale d'Horticulture.

SEMI-RETIREMENT

With his businesses in excellent shape and his succession assured, Jean Linden felt this was the moment to hand over the reins. From now on he would be glimpsed only in his "secret" greenhouse where he watched over

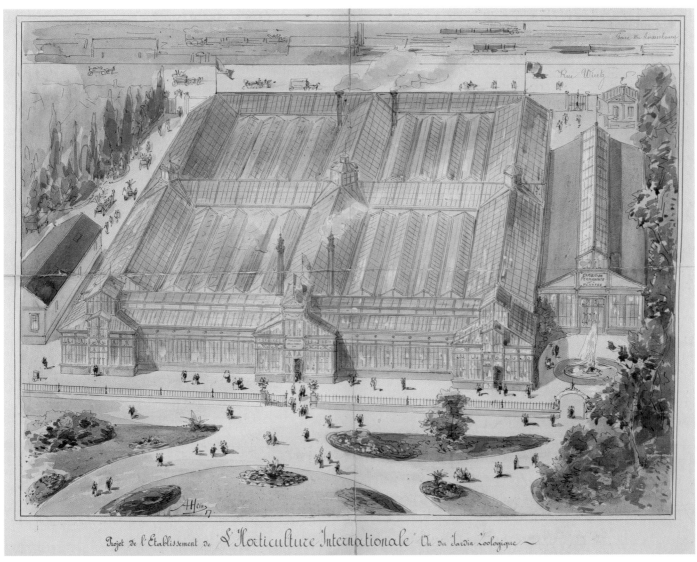

Projet de l'Etablissement de L'Horticulture Internationale Vu du Jardin Zoologique

Plans for L'Horticulture internationale at the Zoological Gardens. Drawing by A. Heinz, 1881.

his large family of "darling daughters" or *danseuses* as he sometimes called his plants. His commercial activities behind him, he nevertheless continued to play an active role in the scientific side of the business, maintaining his links with the various institutions and sending collectors abroad.

Other official roles came to occupy the ageing Linden during the last decade of his life. In 1887 he was appointed *commissaire international* and a member of the Government Advisory Board set up to organise an international exhibition in Brussels for 1888, an initiative for which the government, the king and the Brussels authorities had pledged their support. Linden was also one of the 70 founding members of L'Orchidéenne (created 15 October 1888 in Brussels), an association of orchid lovers eager to share their knowledge, advice and experiences. In the years leading up to his death, the old horticulturist liked to recall his travels and discoveries. "My memories of my first trip to America and my time in Brazil, two years at the least, are those of a visit to an enchanted land. It all seems so far away now, but in my mind it remains so wonderful! You cannot imagine the enthusiasm, the mixture of sheer fright and courage that possessed my companions and me as we arrived at the edge of the virgin forests. When I think back to those moments, I am still filled with joy and trembling. For months on end we travelled under the tall trees, never seeing the sky, the light around us so soft, filtered by the thick foliage. We could only guess at the sun. At night, lying in our tents, we were often assailed by gloomy thoughts. But how different everything was the next morning!"

In 1894, while L'Orchidéenne was devoting its fiftieth meeting to honouring Linden's achievements, seven expeditions were making their way through distant regions at his direction. No doubt the deaths at close inter-

Odontoglossum lucienianum, named after Lucien Linden. *L'Illustration horticole.*

L'ILLUSTRATION HORTICOLE   PL. VII

ODONTOGLOSSUM LUCIANIANUM RCHB. F.

vals of his old travelling companions – Ghiesbreght in Mexico in 1893, Funck in 1896, but also his son Auguste, 1894 – induced Linden to recall how he had begun his active life far away across the Atlantic. He had spent ten years hunting exotic plants, though this was a mere episode compared with his career in Europe. For the rest of his life Jean Linden continued to travel in his imagination with the aid of his memories and the regular arrivals of tropical specimens. The following chapter looks in more detail at the later expeditions organised by the Lindens, of which little is generally known.

A MEMORY FOR PLACES

An explorer by proxy

"How many times did our friend and director Linden mention this magnetic attraction that drew him ceaselessly towards the exotic regions he had spent ten years of his life exploring!"[1]

In 1844, Jean Linden returned to Belgium after a decade of exploration in Latin America; he was never to leave Europe again. Nevertheless, he did not sever his ties with the region; while attending to his personal affairs, he continued his adventures by proxy. Anxious for a regular supply of plants, he sent out a series of collectors to America and later to South East Asia; he guided their activities, advising them on itineraries and other more practical aspects such as unpacking crates. Organising these collections became his major preoccupation as a horticulturist. After 1875, Jean Linden left his son Lucien in charge of his businesses in order to direct his collectors in person, never losing his passionate interest in orchids and travel. Even at the age of 76 and older he was devoting all his energies to the task, leading the younger Reichenbach to comment: "Jean Linden would sooner eat dry bread then give up directing expeditions."[2] His copious notes and correspondence certainly bear witness to his incredible memory for places: his knowledge, born of experience, proved invaluable in advising on expeditions that, for a long time to come, remained perilous undertakings.

PLANT COLLECTING: THE RAPID EXPANSION OF A NEW PHENOMENON
The overwhelming majority of professional plant collectors belonged to the nineteenth century. Their emergence was contemporaneous with the establishment of large-scale horticultural businesses – chiefly in Belgium and Great Britain – and their disappearance likewise coincided with the

Jean Linden. Portrait in *La Semaine horticole*.

‹ The occupation of plant hunter was no sinecure. The equipment carried by Fritz De Scherff – portrayed in this engraving from *Le Voyage dans les Andes* by Édouard André – underlines the many dangers these explorers had to face. Background: detail from plate of *Laelia purpurata* in the *Pescatorea*.

1. É. André in *IH*, 1871, p. 91.
2. Reichenbach Jr, in *JO*, 1893, p. 381.

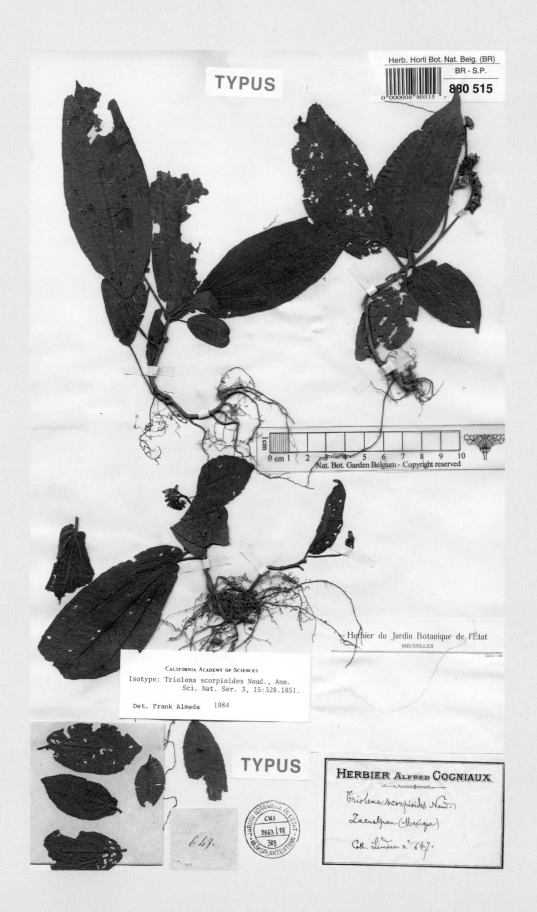

TYPUS

1cm

0 cm 1 2 3 4 5 6 7 8 9 10
Nat. Bot. Garden Belgium - Copyright reserved

Herbier du Jardin Botanique de l'État
BRUXELLES

CALIFORNIA ACADEMY OF SCIENCES
Isotype: Triolena scorpioides Naud., Ann.
Sci. Nat. Ser. 3, 15:328.1851.

Det. Frank Almeda   1984

TYPUS

HERBIER ALFRED COGNIAUX

Triolena scorpioides Naud.
Zacualpan (Mexique)
Coll. Linden n° 647.

647.

decline of these concerns. Other plants were, of course, introduced before and after this "golden age" of plant hunting. Conrad Loddiges, founder of the well-known Loddiges nursery, began his activities in England before 1760: he was already successfully growing tropical orchids, among them *Paphiopedilum purpuratum* from Hong Kong. Nevertheless, the majority of plants introduced before 1830 were shipped back by missionaries, soldiers and other standard-bearers of the British Empire, such as naval officers and ships' captains. We should of course also mention the collections assembled by Joseph Banks during his voyage with James Cook, and the vast numbers of Australian specimens gathered by Robert Brown.

On the other hand, the number of specimens brought home by vessels on cartographic or exploratory missions to distant regions is in no way comparable with the mass collections destined for commercial purposes. In fact, plants garnered by naturalists invariably ended up as dried specimens in the herbariums of London and other European capitals.

One of Jean Linden's most brilliant insights was the realisation that the plants he collected during his ten years of exploration in the Tropics could form the basis of a business. When he finally settled in Europe, he employed several collectors, including two old travelling companions, Schlim and Funck. The other major nurserymen worked in a similar manner. The result was that an army of professional collectors set out to explore every corner of the world where new plants might be lurking — that is, plants unknown to European markets. Given the prices these fetched, it is easy to understand the rivalry and competition among collectors and why they behaved as they did. Some formed independent businesses, selling their finest specimens to the highest bidder and the rest to anyone who would pay. Others retained their association with the same nursery throughout their careers.

These collectors shipped a phenomenal number of plants to Europe. Linden, Sander, Veitch and the rest crammed their greenhouses with thousands of commercially valuable specimens. Every new discovery was worth its weight in gold, with many a speculator supplying horticultural firms in the hope of making a fortune. In this chapter we look at the collectors who worked for Linden; we could easily have written another about Sander or Veitch.

The decline of the great horticultural businesses (Linden, Veitch, Sander, Low) around the start of the twentieth century sounded the

Specimen from the herbarium of Jean Linden. Collection of the National Botanic Garden, Meise.

‹ Specimen from the herbarium of Alfred Cogniaux. Collection of the National Botanic Garden, Meise.

P. De Pannemaeker, ad nat. pinx in Horto Lind.

Étab. Lith. de P. De Pannemaeker à Gand.

death-knell for plant hunters. Now, barely a century later, it is quite normal to buy an orchid in the local supermarket. Who now spares a thought for the men who explored the virgin forests at great risk – sometimes even of their lives? Times have indeed changed. These vast, unexploited regions where the horticultural trade sourced its exotic plants have all but disappeared. In certain regions of Brazil, 95 percent of forests were felled during the last century. Today, with techniques available for the mass breeding of plants under laboratory conditions, plants can be manufactured virtually to order. And the Rothschilds of this world who could pay a fortune for a single rare plant – with the reward, of course, of having one or more orchids named after them, like *Paphiopedilum rothschildianum* – have vanished for ever. Professional growers are no longer invited to accompany monarchs around horticultural exhibitions.

Cattleya trianae, named in honour of José Triana.

In our present society, the consumer demands affordable plants with compact foliage and big red flowers, which are easy to grow indoors. Some exotic specimen that used to sell for the equivalent of 50 years' wages for a gardener can now be bought for a derisory 15 euros. The great private collections of the late nineteenth century are but a vague memory: horticulturists now earn their living much more easily by selling plants produced by the million in the Netherlands rather than by risking all the perils and complications of introducing new species from the wild. In the words of one such professional: "There is no way I can send a collector out to Borneo for three or four plants." Botanists are no longer allowed to collect plants freely, and taxonomists, trained to describe and classify new species, risk prosecution for exercising their talents.

Benedict Roezl, whose contribution to European horticulture is celebrated in plant names like *Phragmipedium (*formerly *Cypripedium) roezlii* (left).

We have come full circle. New plants are imported by missionaries, tourists and employees of firms with interests in faraway countries. The old ships' captains have been replaced by captains of aircraft. Contraband plants are smuggled through Customs in hand luggage, wrapped in dirty laundry or attached to the carrier's body. Limitations on the import of wild species have finally been adopted, yet the destruction of natural habitats is still permitted, or impossible to halt. The few nurseries willing to introduce new wild species find themselves constantly harassed by misguided bureaucrats. Our century has no further need of plant collectors: a sad ending for those who once tramped through those timeless forests.

Dendrobium macrophyllum, collected by Auguste Linden in Indonesia. Plate from *L'Illustration horticole.*

› *The bridge of Chucunès,* Venezuela. Drawing by Riou after the sketches of Édouard André, published in his *Voyage dans les Andes,* circa 1875.

3. "La Recherche du *Cattleya rex*", *IH,* 1891, p. 18.

FIFTY YEARS OF ORGANISING EXPEDITIONS

Linden lost no time in organising his first expeditions from a distance. Having established his business in Luxembourg in 1845, he rapidly realised his stock of plants was insufficient to meet the huge projected demand. He was equally impatient to dispatch his collectors to search for quality specimens before others beat him to it. He was aware too that his success would derive in large measure from his customers' ceaseless demand for the unusual, necessitating continuous explorations of areas rich in new species.

Quantity, novelty and exclusivity were the watchwords in this constant commercial battle.

All the same, it was Linden's heart and razor-sharp memory that were to guide his collectors. "In 1841, Linden discovered an orchid (*Cattleya rex*) of unique beauty", we read in *L'Illustration horticole* of 1891. "Its image remained engraved on the memory of a man who was an orchid lover as well as a botanist. From that moment on, he never passed up a chance, sending one collector after another to seek out the habitat of this splendid orchid with its large, white flowers and its exquisite crimson, pink and purple labellum. But all his efforts were in vain – until finally one of his collectors had the good luck to find the plant and was able to introduce a number of perfect specimens to the business."[3]

Though he sometimes accepted specimens from freelancers, Linden relied in the main on collectors who had already gained his professional confidence. In his dealings with them and organising his expeditions he could be direct and authoritarian. His itineraries were highly detailed: journey planners before their time.

All his pains, however, could not prevent the occasional upset, as certain collectors failed to heed his expert advice. One, for instance, became overzealous during his explorations: covering a larger number of regions than his instructions demanded, he assembled a great number of plants which he was eager to ship back to Ghent as quickly as possible. He failed to take the precaution of opening his crates at sea, however, and on disembarking in Europe found that the entire contents had been reduced to a rotted mass. Another collector took it into his head to alter his itinerary and visit areas already scoured by Linden and his collectors and where nothing new was left to discover: he ignored fine, new specimens in favour of the old ones, and Linden was forced to send out a replacement. Then there was a man who went to a rival firm and showed them his itinerary,

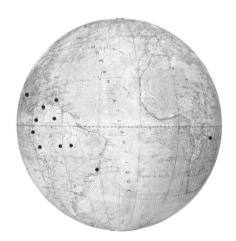

Jean Linden dispatched plant hunters to the four corners
of the globe, including Latin America,
Africa and the South Seas.

selling himself to them for a higher fee. And finally a collector who, having arrived in his designated area, immediately stole the expedition's funds and made off with bag and baggage. After spending the thousands of francs entrusted to him, he wrote that he liked the place, and had settled there!

The list of collectors engaged by Linden allows us to make a clear identification of three distinct periods in his scientific and business enterprises. His first wave of appointments on his return to Luxembourg brought together men with personal ties to him, who he assigned to familiar areas. He acquired the services, for instance, of two former companions in Venezuela – Funck and Schlim – and sent them back to areas he knew had high potential.

The second phase was more experimental. Its beginning corresponds to the period when Linden quit his post at the Zoological Gardens in the Parc Léopold to devote his entire time to his horticultural business. During this period he engaged various collectors from France and England; the regions they explored included not only Latin America, but also places as far afield as New Caledonia and the Fiji Islands. This was also when he suffered most of his staff problems, a few of which have already been cited.

Then there was a third and final phase covering the last ten years of Jean Linden's life. Following a somewhat fallow period of just under a decade, activities during this period revolved around the personality of Auguste Linden, Jean's son. The following table gives a clearer picture of the three phases, while underlining the relative continuity of the expeditions that assured Linden of a prosperity long coveted by rivals.

During the 1800s, "plant hunting" gradually became a professional activity. The word conjures up a very romantic image, but in reality it was an arduous business. Often pitchforked into these adventures with little awareness of the risks, under-equipped and with scant information on the places and peoples they would encounter, a considerable number of collectors lost their lives. Even some of Linden's envoys died in the attempt. Édouard Klaboch – who worked principally for Sander but also supplied Linden – was killed in Mexico; his brother Arnold disappeared in the Orinoco Basin; Digance was murdered by natives in Brazil; Falkenberg perished in Panama; Hendres at Río Hacha; Brown in Madagascar; Libon in Brazil; and Isidore Pancher in New Caledonia. Other collectors escaped injury, but were forced to abandon the fruit of several weeks' work in hos-

EXPEDITION FUNDED BY LINDEN	COUNTRIES AND REGIONS EXPLORED	IRREGULAR SHIPMENTS
Funck & Schlim (1845-1846)	**Venezuela and Colombia**	
Schlim (1846-1851)	**Colombia**	
Schlim (1852-1857)	**Colombia**	
	Mexico	Ghiesbreght (1849-1860)
	Colombia	Triana (1853-1854)
Wallis (1858-1871)	**Amazonia**	
	Colombia	Triana (1859)
Libon (1859-1861)	**Minas Gerais (Brazil)**	
Wallis (1865)	**Eastern Peru**	
	Amazonia	Baraquin (1868)
	Merida and Pamplona provinces (Venezuela)	Wagener (1870-1871)
Wallis (1871-1877)	**Rio Puyocatengo, Mexico**	
Roezl (1871-1877)	**New Granada**	
	Nicaragua, Amazonia, Ecuador, Isthmus of Panama	Seemann (1870-1871)
	Java, Philippines	Porte (1870-1871)
Rodigas (1876)	**Colombia**	
Pancher & De Maerschalk (1875-1877)	**New Caledonia, Solomon and Fiji Islands**	
André (1875-1876)	**Colombia, Ecuador, Peru, Brazil**	
	Borneo, Rajah mountains	Teuscher (1882)
	Borneo, Rajah mountains	van Lansberge (1882)
	New Granada	Lalinde (1883)
	Calcutta (India)	Thattersee (1884)
A. Linden & De Ronne (1885-1886)	**Eastern Malaysia, Papua New Guinea**	
A. Linden & Demeuse (1886-1887)	**Congo**	
Ellner (1890-1892)	**Brazil**	
Bungeroth (1885-1889)	**Colombia, Venezuela, Ecuador, Brazil, Peru**	
Klaboch (1895-1896)	**Colombia, Venezuela, Ecuador, Brazil, Peru**	
Claes (1893-1894)	**Brazil, Pernambuco (Brazil)**	
	Para (Brazil)	Rand (1895-1896)
Three separate expeditions (?)	**Brazil, Peru, Upper Orinoco (Venezuela)**	

tile areas. Schlim and Triana found their collections suddenly scattered when a courier was attacked at the beginning of the troubles in Colombia in 1861.[4] Twenty years previously, we should recall, Linden had lost several crates of specimens in Venezuela when they were swept away by the fierce current of the Tocuyo, together with the two mules carrying them.[5] Many others, however, more experienced, or perhaps just luckier, rapidly acquired towering reputations from their expeditions. Beside Linden, Reinikka also mentions Warszewicz, Roezl, Bateman, Cuming, Wallis, Hartweg, Lobb, Low, Parish and Welwitsch.[6]

THE FIRST WAVE: FUNCK, SCHLIM AND GHIESBREGHT (1845-1858)

Not surprisingly, for the first expeditions conducted in his absence, Linden turned to his old comrades: Nicolas Funck and Auguste Ghiesbreght had accompanied him to Brazil, Mexico and Cuba, the former (with Schlim) having also been on part of the third trip to Venezuela. These initial proxy missions proved extremely profitable, producing a continuous supply of specimens until 1860.

Linden might have returned permanently to Europe at the end of 1844, but for Funck and Schlim their homecoming merely signalled further, imminent departures. In October of the same year, both men left once more for Venezuela and Colombia. Funck returned in 1846, while Schlim stayed on in the New World, apart from a 12 months' spell in

Tomb of Isidore Pancher in New Caledonia.

› *Phragmipedium* (formerly *Selenipedium*) *schlimii*. Plate from the *Lindenia*.

Mexicoa ghiesbreghtiana, named in honour of Auguste Ghiesbreght.

Phragmipedium (formerly *Selenipedium*) *schlimii*, named in honour of Louis-Joseph Schlim, half-brother of Jean Linden.

4. *JO,* 1893-1894, p. 341.

5. Jean Linden lost the collection he had made in the Aroa Mountains, at Urachiche, Yaratigua, Barquísemeto and Quibor just before crossing the Tocuyo. *Ibid.*

6. Merle A Reinikka, *A History of the orchid,* p. 27.

SELENIPEDIUM SCHLIMII. Lind. et Rchb. fil.

Brussels, still dispatching plants to his half-brother Linden until around 1856.[7]

Many of the most celebrated plants brought back by the pair were to be illustrated later in *L'Illustration horticole*. Some had already been introduced to Europe by Linden in the years before. Among other species Funck and Schlim gathered were *Odontoglossum cordatum* (from the Cumbre de Choacas), *Anguloa purpurea* (Venezuelan Andes) and *Odontoglossum pescatorei*, first seen in 1847 in the provinces of Pamplona and Ocaña and dedicated to Jean-Pierre Pescatore[8]. Orchids were not the sole object of these expeditions, however: Linden's two relations also sought out palms like *Acanthorhiza aculeata* and *Thrinax graminifolia*[9] (discovered by Linden in 1840 near Teapa in the state of Tabasco).

Schlim, for his part, was to continue collecting for his half-brother independently of Funck. In particular, he introduced living specimens of *Oncidium cucullatum* from Colombia and Venezuela: Linden was soon selling them by the thousand. He also made a reputation by giving Belgium species such as *Odontoglossum phalaenopsis*, *Maxillaria grandiflora*, *Houlletia tigrina* and notably *Restrepia antennifera*, according to Lucien Linden, named after José E. Restrepa, Director of the Brussels royal theatre La Monnaie. Our recent research, however, shows that this information is wrong (see p. 145). Another of his acquisitions was *Houlletia odoratissima*, which he collected in 1849 in the province of Soto, on the banks of rivers east of the Río Magdalena, "where its presence was betrayed from afar by its scent". Linden's greenhouses in Brussels soon also boasted the odd example of *Themistoclesia coronilla*, *Stenia fimbriata* and *Ada aurantiaca*.[10]

While his former expedition companions were thus occupied, Auguste Ghiesbreght settled in Mexico, from where he sent back plants until 1860. Among his principal shipments were rarities of the time such as *Oncidium tigrinum* and *Oncidium incurvum*. He was also responsible for the reintroduction of *Aristolochia cordiflora*. This plant had originally been spotted by Linden on the banks of the Tabasco River, and was cultivated in the greenhouses in Brussels from 1864. Ghiesbreght is also associated with *Lindenia rivalis*,[11] a native of the same region where its delightful green fringes and white blossoms adorn the banks of the Puyocatengo.

The original trio was joined in 1851 by the Colombian botanist José Triana. His specimens proved invaluable to Linden's business, but the collaboration between the two men soon turned sour following a serious disagreement over a publishing project.[12]

7. *IH*, 1970, p. 176.

8. *Odontoglossum cordatum* [*IH*, 1879, p. 122]; *Anguloa purpurea* [*IH*, 1881, p. 120]; *Odontoglossum pescatorei* [*IH*, 1881, p. 7].

9. *Acanthorhiza aculeata* [*IH*, 1879, p. 185]; *Thrinax graminifolia* [*IH*, 1884, p. 187].

10. *Oncidium cucullatum*, [*IH*, 1878, p. 27]; *Odontoglossum phalaenopsis* [ibid., p. 57]; *Maxillaria grandiflora* [*IH*, 1870, p. 74]; *Houlletia tigrina* [*IH*, 1869, pl. 612]; *Restrepia antennifera* [discovered by von Humboldt and Bonpland in Colombia on old tree trunks and later re-identified by Linden from terrestrial specimens in the province of Mérida at 3,940 m and at Santa Fé de Bogotá, growing on oak trees at 2,500 m. Wagener would also find specimens near Ocaña, as did Schlim in the same period. *IH*, 1869, pl. 601]; *Houlletia odoratissima* [*IH*, 1870, p. 59]; *Themistoclesia coronilla* [ibid., p. 176]; *Stenia fimbriata* [*IH*, 1871, p. 194]; *Ada aurantiaca* [ibid., p. 305].

RESTREPIA ANTENNIFERA. *H.B. & K.*
Colombie (Serre-froide.)
A. Verschaffelt publ.

Restrepia antennifera, named in honour of José Manuel Restrepo, Colombian historian and lawyer, whom von Humboldt and Bonpland met in Bogotá in 1801. Plate from *L'Illustration horticole*, 1869.

THE SECOND WAVE – NEW COLLECTORS, NEW COUNTRIES (1858-1877)

The second phase of explorations was characterised by a marked change in policy. Linden's instructions were being increasingly influenced by the state of the horticultural market: with the burgeoning fashion for exotic plants, the demand for imports increased and customers became more demanding. From this time on, it became essential for collectors to target regions that were totally, or partially, unexplored. A short list of destinations evolved, to be radically revised around 1875. After 30 years spent in exploiting areas of Colombia, Venezuela and Brazil, Jean Linden was to send a new generation of collectors to the Pacific regions, New Caledonia, Indonesia and Malaysia. Funck and Schlim had in the meantime ceased to work for their relative: Funck went into zoology, succeeding, in effect, Jean in the running of the Parc Léopold before assuming a similar post at the Zoological Gardens in Cologne. Schlim completed his last expedition

11. *Oncidium tigrinum*, [*IH*, 1875, p. 155]; *Oncidium incurvum* [*IH*, 1882, p. 31]; *Aristolochia cordiflora* [*IH*, 1870, p. 158]; *Lindenia rivalis* [*IH*, 1871, p. 155].

12. See the chapter on publications by Jean Linden, particularly pp. 193-194.

> *Odontoglossum wallisi [sic]*, named in honour of the collector Gustav Wallis. Plate from *L'Illustration horticole*, 1871.

13. *Masdevallia lindenii* [shipped by Wallis in 1869, *IH*, 1870, pl. XLII, p. 226]; *Odontoglossum nevadense* [shipped by Wallis in 1868 following its discovery in the Sierra Nevada. *IH*, 1870, pl. XLV, p. 243]; *Odontoglossum luteo-purpureum* var. *sceptrum* [discovered by Wallis in New Granada in 1868; standard variety found by Linden in the forests of Quindiu]; *Odontoglossum odoratum* [almost certainly discovered by Wallis in New Granada; received by Linden in 1868; Wagener would rediscover it later. *IH*, 1870, p. 201]; *Odontoglossum bellulum* [*IH*, 1891, p. 49]; *Odontoglossum wallisii* [*IH*, 1871, p. 56].

14. *Calathea (Marantha) lindenii*. A *Calathea* taken by Linden in New Granada received high praise at the World Exhibition in Paris in 1867. Wallis discovered it on the banks of the Río Huallaga in Peru [*IH*, 1871, p. 211].

15. "I found him penniless, unknown, abandoned. When he left me he had a reputation, a small fortune, a virtual museum full of curiosities of every kind. I took him from the Amazon Delta to the Isthmus of Panama, a journey which cost me more than 125,000 francs: an enormous sum compared with the paltry returns resulting from the specimens arriving in poor condition ... He disappeared secretly to South America with a return ticket paid for with my money to collect on his own account and for a certain other individual; these were the very same plants he had just brought me at such cost to myself" [*IH*, 1875, p. 11]. Sander states erroneously that Wallis was murdered during a field trip [*IH*, 1878, p. 118].

in 1856 to return to his old occupation as a clockmaker in Paris. There, he died at a comparatively young age, on 22 May 1863.

Linden, who had his finger firmly on the pulse of the business world, was quick to seek out collaborators with reputation. In 1858, an unidentified German firm engaged the services of a certain Gustav Wallis (1830-78) and sent him to Brazil to establish a horticultural station. When the company went bankrupt, Linden contacted Wallis with an offer of work. Wallis was to spend 18 years plant-hunting in the Amazon Basin, eastern Peru, the Sierra de Parima, at the headwaters of the Rio Branco on the borders of Venezuela and Brazil, and in Ecuador. In 1866 he also explored along the Río Negro, then, two years later, in Antioquia and the mountains of the Sierra Nevada in New Granada. His shipments included a large number of orchids, several of which featured in professional publications: *Masdevallia lindenii, Odontoglossum nevadense, Odontoglossum luteo-pupureum, Odontoglosum odoratum* and *Odontoglosum bellulum*. Several of his discoveries were named after him, one of them being *Odontoglossum wallisii* (1868).[13] *Cattleya, Masdevallia* and *Odontoglossum* were the main genera Wallis sent to Europe. Of course, these plants were not new to Linden, but these genera were still "the boss's favourite".

The "boss" was evidently satisfied with his collector, who made no secret of his emotions during his expeditions. "I have at last found the object of my dreams," he wrote in 1871. "This *Maranta [sic]* with its transparent leaves ... this little gem suddenly appeared before me in all its beauty, right in the depths of the forest ... I was overcome to the point of tears ..."[14] Around this time (the early 1870s), however, relations with Jean Linden became strained. Wallis secretly absented himself and began collecting for James Veitch, an English rival of Linden, before returning to his Belgian employer. In the meantime he scoured the Philippines, Moyobamba, the Fiji Islands, the New Hebrides, New Guinea and New Caledonia. The final quarrel between the two men took place in 1875. In *L'Illustration horticole*, Linden exposed Wallis's behaviour, calling him a cheat and a rogue: he had rescued Wallis from poverty and unemployment and had, he claimed, wasted huge amounts of money supporting his collector, sums he could never have recouped from him. A few years later a penniless Gustav Wallis died in Colombia from the effects of a fever.[15]

Meanwhile, Jean Linden was setting up other collaborations that were to prove extremely profitable, even if only for a short time. As well as

ODONTOGLOSSUM WALLISI *(Reich. fil.)*.

NOUVELLE-GRENADE.   SERRE FROIDE.

J. Linden publ.

Wallis, Joseph Libon (1821-61), a native of Verviers, was working for him from 1858. Trained with Jacob-Mackoy[16] in Liège, he accompanied Claussen[17] on his 1841 expedition to Brazil. He continued to explore the country for de Jonghe[18] whose business in Brussels he later managed for several months. Entrusted with collections in the Minas Gerais region of Brazil by Linden, Libon introduced a number of exclusive plants to Europe, one of which was named after him.[19] He died of exhaustion at Insainna on 2 August 1861.

Linden's warmest relationship, however, was with Benedict Roezl (1823-89). Head gardener with Van Houtte and at the École d'Horticulture in Ghent, Roezl's first attempt in the horticultural business had failed.[20] He then turned his hand to the demanding task of collecting, working for himself and for the London-based Sander. Between 1871 and 1874, *L'Illustration horticole* noted his shipments to Jean Linden, with André devoting an article to his 1871 expedition to the Peruvian and Ecuadorean Andes, along the banks of the Choco River and the Río Dague in Bogotá Province.[21] His name is commemorated by several plants: *Miltonia roezlii, Phragmipedium* (formerly *Cypripedium*) *roezlii, Odontoglossum roezlii* and *Zamia roezlii*.[22] He was also involved in the introduction to Belgium of *Tropaeolum chrysantum, Tydaea pardina, Zamia lindenii* and *Masdevallia polysticta*.[23] He ceased collecting in the mid-1870s. He died in Prague on 14 October 1889 and, three years later, a statue was erected in the city (Karlovo square) to honour him. The Linden family raised a subscription for a photograph in his memory.

After the cessation of Roezl's activities and the rupture with Wallis, Linden formed three new teams between 1875 and 1877. His haste reveals his need for new supplies to replace the countless specimens provided by Wallis over 18 years. Jean Armand Isidore Pancher (1814-77) appears as the most experienced of the three new collectors. An old expedition hand, he had worked in New Caledonia as a gardener-botanist for the French government before joining up with De Maerschalk, Linden's assistant head gardener in 1874. The pair explored New Caledonia, the New Hebrides, the Fiji and Solomon Islands and New Guinea. Linden had obtained for them the status of project leaders for the French government. The mission was short lived, however: Pancher died on 8 March 1877 at the penitentiary farm of Uaraï-Fomwhary in New Caledonia. He was not an orchid specialist: his principal introductions were ferns, conifers and, above all, palms.[24.]

16. *BH*, 1865, p. 46.

17. *Loc. cit.*

18. *Loc. cit.*

19. The name appears to have changed. From the descriptions, it is probably *Cleistes libonii*.

20. M.A. Reinikka, *op. cit.*, p. 219.

21. *IH*, 1871, p. 91.

22. *IH*, *passim*.

23. *IH*, *passim*.

Frederick Sander.
‹ *Phragmipedium wallisii.*

24. Of particular note among the ferns are *Todea wilkesiana, Lomaria gigantea* and *Lomaria ciliata*. Of the palms, the most interesting are *Kentiopsis divaricata*, discovered on Mount Coughi in New Caledonia, *Pritchardia filifera, Kentia lindenii*. He also discovered the verbenaceous *Oxera pulchella*.

Miltonia roezlii.

› *Anthurium andreanum,* named in honour of Édouard André. Plate from *L'Illustration horticole,* 1892.

Édouard André (1840-1911) also collected for Linden. Editor-in-chief of *L'Illustration horticole* during the period 1870-75, he left his post to participate in an expedition with Jean Nötzli, Fritz De Scherff and Jean Clavier, De Scherff's servant.[25] After initially putting in at Martinique where he visited the Saint-Pierre Botanical Gardens, André spent 11 months during 1876 in Colombia, Ecuador, Peru and Brazil. His efforts were concentrated mainly on the Cordillera of the Andes,[26] which he crossed several times. Well aware of his own scientific status, he did not hesitate to describe some of his fellow collectors as "mere garden-ers" whose research was of little value to botany.[27] Among the plants named after him are *Anthurium andreanum* and *Pitcairnia andreana.*

Emile Rodigas was the third figure in this new generation of collec-tors. Director of the École d'Horticulture d'État in Ghent but a novice in the matter of collecting, he made only one short trip for Linden, which is almost undocumented, though we know he was in Bogotá on 16 January 1876.

The death of Pancher marked the end of the second wave of collect-ing directed by Jean Linden. Nevertheless, a number of irregular plant dispatches prolonged this phase into the early 1880s: Teuscher and van Lansberge, for instance, supplied him in 1882, Lalinde in 1883 and Thattersee in 1884.[28] But after seven years without systematic deliveries, Linden needed to broaden his commercial base with the introduction of new plants.

25. Fritz De Scherff could be described here as a "Luxembourg tourist", so under-prepared was he for this type of mission. Further, Jean Clavier was to save him from certain death.

26. André reached the Cordillera by travelling up the Río Magdalena from Barranquilla on the paddle-steamer *Simón Bolívar.*

27. *IH*, 1875, p. 71.

28. Teuscher and van Lansberge explored the Rajah Mountains in Borneo. Lalinde scoured New Granada; Thattersee spent time in Calcutta.

ANTHURIUM ANDREANUM J. LIND. var. WAMBEKEANUM

Region of Peru explored by Édouard André in 1875-76. Map from André, *Le Voyage dans les Andes*.

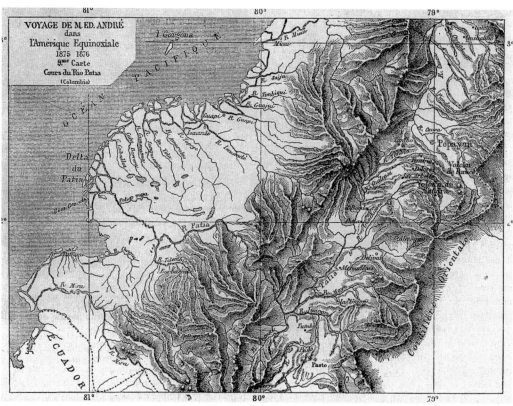

Émile Rodigas.

THE THIRD WAVE – THE FINAL YEARS (1885-95)

Linden's passion for exotic plants thus drove him to mount further expeditions. For his business to remain commercially viable demanded the constant import of rare, beautiful and unusual species.

Age had caught up with Linden, as it had with all the collectors of the first phase, and it was the next generation that now set off in search of exotic specimens. Thus we find Auguste, Linden's eldest son, bitten in his turn by the collecting bug. In 1878, Auguste left the Belgian army in which he was serving as a second lieutenant in the Grenadiers, and became a willing pupil in his father's greenhouses in Brussels. In 1884 his training was complete and he crossed the Indian Ocean to Papouasia, New Guinea, the Celebes archipelago, Malaysia and the Moluccas. The following year he was back in Belgium.

On 17 April 1886, he left Brussels for the Congo, an independent state founded by King Leopold II. The botanical party formed part of a much larger expedition that was also engaged in zoological and ethnographic research and was organised by Jean Linden and Édouard Otlet. Auguste's instructions required him to give priority to completing the collections of the Compagnie continentale d'Horticulture. He was

assisted by a horticulturist from Verviers, Fernand Demeuse (1863-1915), who accompanied him in the role of preparator. After collecting flora and fauna from the Lower Congo, the expedition made its way through the forests of Mayumbe towards Loango, which marked the end of its itinerary. The return route was in the direction of Stanley Pool via the Niara-Kouilou Valley in the Congo Brazza. An outbreak of smallpox caused the desertion of a large number of porters, forcing the party to return to the coast and thence to Europe in December 1886, though in possession of a splendid booty of photographs and specimens of every kind, including orchids.

This was to be Auguste's final expedition. During a visit to Spain, where his brother-in-law Édouard Otlet was in charge of extensive works on the railway line between Torralba and Soria (1887), his life was suddenly shattered by an accident that required the amputation of a leg and left him partially paralysed; he died some years later, on 10 August 1894. He will always be remembered for the many orchids he discovered on his travels.[29] Between 1890 and 1892 the expeditions were taken over by C. Ellner. His work took him to the banks of the Upper Río Negro in Brazil where he collected *Cattleya rex*[30], one of 200 different plants he shipped home after long months of searching.

Florent Claes was also to win fame for his numerous botanical missions between 1890 and 1894. Born in Bevere (Oudenaarde), he was a landscape architect for L'Horticulture internationale who, in 1889, found himself placed in charge of the Brazilian contribution to the World Exhibition in Paris. It was there he met a Brazilian painter, a member of the committee, who was enthusing about a recently imported specimen of *Cattleya warneri*. This unidentified painter then confided to Claes the existence of a similar plant in his native province, Pernambuco, in the vicinity of Belém.[31] Seeing the collector's interest, the Brazilian continued: "I have an oil painting of it that I did myself – and the plant I used as a model. You can have the plant, but I will keep the painting." Claes offered Linden the orchid and asked to be sent on an expedition to its habitat. Some time afterwards he was to return to Belgium with the famous

L'ILLUSTRATION HORTICOLE

PANDANUS AUGUSTIANUS L. LIND. & ROD.

Chrom. P. De Pannemaeker.   J. Linden

Pandanus augustianus, commemorating the contribution of Auguste Linden. Plate from *L'Illustration horticole*, 1886.

29. For instance: *Dendrobium stratiotes, strebloceras* and *inauditum, Spathoglottis augustorum, Vanda lindenii* and *Aerides augustianum*. The last-named he discovered in the Philippines: it flowered for the first time in December 1889. Also ornamental plants, e.g., *Alocasia villeneuvei, A. augustiana* and *A. lindenii, Phrynium variegatum* and *Ansellia congoensis* discovered in the Congo, 1885.

30. The reports concerning the introduction of *C. rex* are contradictory. Was it originally discovered, for instance, by Gustav Wallis? [*IH*, 1891, p. 72]. O'Brien described it for the first time on 13 December 1890 after seeing it in bloom in one of Linden's greenhouses. *Le Journal des orchidées* (1 October 1891) nevertheless states that: "*Cattleya rex*, introduced not long ago to international horticulture by our intrepid collector and collaborator, C. Ellner, has just flowered, attracting a growing crowd of admirers over several days." See also *JO* (pp. 256 and 309) on this particular orchid. Others, however, attribute its discovery to another of Linden's collectors, Édouard Bungeroth [G. Braem: *The Unifoliate Cattleyas*, 1986].

31. Flowering from November to February, the plant was known as "Quaresma" (Lent) in the province in question.

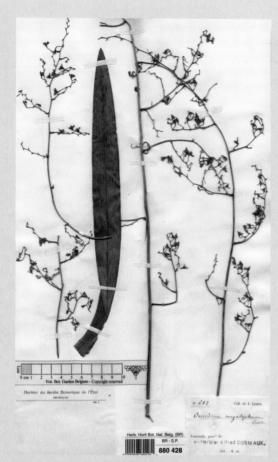

Specimen from the herbarium of Alfred Cogniaux.
Collection of the National Botanic Garden, Meise.

The packing and transport of imported plants

The pillages often mounted by collectors on certain regions were also partly motivated by the prospect of major financial gain. The organisers also had to take account of considerable losses in the course of shipment. For instance, writing in *Le Journal des orchidées,* Florent Claes explains: "The ocean crossing and railway transport to the destination takes a month, sometimes two. But this lengthy journey is perhaps less fatal to *Odontoglossum* than the transit from Honda to Barranquilla, during which the specimens are almost constantly subjected to intense heat; this is when they suffer most, and many plants are already in a state of putrefaction on arriving at the coast.*

Like his father, Lucien Linden constantly reiterated the care needed in packing plants for the crossing to Europe. "The crates must be made of thick, really solid planks that will not break when knocked around during transport; this will keep the rats out too ... Before the journey, all insects must be removed. It is also vital to support the plants inside the crates so that the pseudobulbs, leaves and stems are not damaged, otherwise rot will set in ... On board ship, the crates must be stored away from high temperatures, not in the sun or close to the boilers." In the same passage, Lucien lists the most suitable ports for unloading such fragile merchandise: "Antwerp, Liverpool or London, where there will be someone to oversee things ..."**

The unpacking of the crates – a highly secretive affair – was described by Max Garnier (1890), Charles Van Wambeke (1893) and Lucien Linden himself (1894). Garnier recalled a particular delivery of botanical materials.*** The 50 cases (each about one cubic metre) had travelled for two months. He was astonished to find that less than a hundred of the plants were seriously damaged. Some had produced buds and two or three had even flowered in the cases. The collections were sorted under the watchful eye of the Lindens – father and son were always ready to give a hand with the unpacking – and next day they were cleaned and potted up. In less than a year the orchids had recovered their healthy, flourishing appearance and would soon be ready to leave the greenhouses for the drawing room of some rich plant lover.

Van Wambeke also describes the reception of shipments in Brussels.**** He tells how a fascinating solution was found to the discovery of insects when the crates were opened. When a new delivery was announced, the management of the Musée d'Histoire naturelle, close to the Parc Léopold, would send two specialists to examine the contents. As well as removing parasites from the orchids, they would retrieve any insects worth adding to the state entomology collections. Nothing was to be wasted: a policy that in those days satisfied all the government-run scientific departments!

*　　Florent Claes, in *JO,* 1 February 1890, p. 348.
**　　Lucien Linden, "L'Importation des orchidées", in *JO,* 1893-94, p. 345.
***　Max Garnier, in *JO,* 1890, p. 141.
****　Van Wambeke, in *JO,* 1893, p. 135.

Cattleya labiata, just beating Frederick Sander's plant hunters to it. No less than three collectors were working in 1892 for L'Horticulture internationale to ensure the safe transportation of 25,000 plants of this species: P. Silver, Claes himself and a certain Van der Ley, who was based at the port of embarkation.

As yet, we know little about the other collectors who worked for Linden's business during the three phases, the reason being that their shipments were sporadic. For the sake of completeness, here is a brief resumé of their names and spheres of operation.

At the same time as Wallis was conducting his searches, i.e., in 1868, Baraquin was active along the course of the Amazon. From 1870 to 1871, a man named Wagener worked the Venezuelan provinces of Mérida and Pamplona, while Seemann was in Nicaragua and Marius Porte in the Philippines. Teuscher, van Lansberge, Lalinde and Thattersee supplied irregular deliveries to Linden between 1882 and 1884. Finally, during the third phase, Linden benefited from the highly successful expeditions of Erich Bungeroth (1885-89) and Édouard Klaboch (1895-96). Working in areas already explored, these collectors, among their other achievements, contributed to the reintroduction to European greenhouses species originally identified by Jean on his own travels but which he had been unable to bring home as living specimens. [32]

COLLECTOR, A PROFESSION FOR THE DISCRETE

There was another side to the successful spread of horticulture in Europe, as collectors began to reveal the experiences of their hair-raising missions. Gradually, they wove a colourful and exotic web around the whole business, while their accounts of habitats provided valuable information on the best means of cultivation of the various species.

Nicolas Funck had been the first to document his procedures, accompanying all his shipments with meticulous notes on habitats and advice on cultivation. Ellner followed suit, recording, for instance, the collection of *Cattleya eldorado*[33]. Under the heading "Orchids in their native habitats" in *L'Illustration horticole*

32. Jean Linden, in *IH,* 1891, p. 150.

33. *Cattleya eldorado* was discovered by Linden and introduced by him to Europe in 1866. Ellner mentions it in *JO* of 15 October 1891, pp. 243-244.

Notylia bungerothii, named in memory of Erich Bungeroth.

> *Psychopsis* (formerly *Oncidium*) *kramerianum*, a species collected in Ecuador by Warszewicz in 1852 and dedicated to Kramer, gardener to the collector Jenisch. Plate from the *Lindenia*.

Auguste Linden revealed how he discovered *Vanda batemanii* and *V. lindenii* in Malaysia.[34] Claes, in turn, filled several pages of the *Le Journal des orchidées* with accounts of his trips: his comments shed useful light on the circumstances in which certain species were found. On his return from New Granada he relates: "The discovery of *Odontoglossum alexandrae* dates from 1842 and was due to Carl Theodor Hartweg and Jean Linden. It was also subsequently documented by Warszewicz and Schlim, the latter succeeding in importing the first living specimens ... Alas, the greed and selfishness of some collectors, or maybe their desire to corner the market, has gradually led to the almost complete disappearance of *O. alexandrae* from these regions. Around Pacho, where [this species] used to be found by the thousand, there are only a few specimens left, and I fear that in many places they will not return due to the vandalism of certain speculators who burned all the plants they could not carry away ... *O. alexandrae* is usually found in clearings where an old tree has fallen and let in the light and air; the plant prefers to grow on the trunks of trees, rarely on the branches, and even then only the thickest. It is difficult to collect, as the natives have a horror of climbing trees because of the scorpions and the thousand-and-one insects hiding there, especially ants, which have an extremely painful sting. Normally the only way is to cut down the tree, which is not always easy: sometimes it takes four or five men working together for a whole day, and then, when the job is done and you think the treasure is within reach, you can sometimes find that your precious orchid is not on that tree after all ..."[35]

Some passages in these articles reveal interesting facts about the daily lives of collectors working in arduous conditions. "Each expedition lasts on average a fortnight, and provisions have to be carried for the whole trip ... It is very hard to preserve a proper notion of time on the march. The Indians cannot tell the time of day from the state of the sky or the height of the sun like our country folk at home and, if you ask them, they will stare at their shadow and then the sun for ages, only to reply that they really have no idea. They are the same with distances: they give random estimates that must never be taken seriously. I made a point of noting each passing day on a calendar – without this precaution I would soon have forgotten what month it was."[36]

Through their botanical reports and accounts of their journeys, terse as they were, these men enhanced their contribution beyond that of mere

34. *IH*, 15 November 1890, p. 270.
35. *JO*, 1 February 1891, p. 348.
36. *Loc. cit.*

ONCIDIUM KRAMERIANUM RCHB. F.

Adiantum tetraphyllum var. *obtusum*, fern discovered by Auguste Linden in the Congo. Plate from *L'Illustration horticole*.

collection agents. Their "business shipments" assisted the development of botanical and horticultural knowledge, which was then disseminated through specialist books and periodicals for the practical grower. Professor Guido Braem makes a detailed examination of these publications on pages 191-213.

Horticulture and commercial espionage*

When in 1881 Lucien Linden announced the departure of his expeditions, he made it clear he could not divulge the target regions. "It would not be the first time that 'pirates' have followed collectors whom they know to be on to a good thing."** His reference was to the bitter rivalry between horticultural businesses. In this great era of discovery, which was characterised by a relentless race that was not only scientific but also, and more particularly, commercial, what counted was discovering unexplored regions where orchids and other exotic species abounded. Indeed, it was not unusual for pitched battles to be fought between rival collectors.

In consequence, collectors and their patrons regularly circulated false itineraries and ambiguous information. Sometimes, though, this misinformation was the result of genuine errors arising from itineraries that became extended or were broken by frequent halts. *Cattleya granulosa,* for example, associated with Guatemala until the mid-twentieth century after its discovery by Hartweg and classification by Lindley, actually comes from Brazil. For almost a hundred years the eminent London scientist's writings were trusted implicitly; the orchid did not exist in Central America, but the specimens brought back by Hartweg had formerly been shipped via Guatemala, causing it to be linked with that country. Similarly, *Paphiopedilum rothschildianum* (or Linden's *Paphiopedilum neoguineense*), which grows on the flanks of Mount Kinabalu in Borneo, was long held to be a native of New Guinea before it was realised that the only justification for the attribution was that it was trans-shipped at Port Moresby.

A formidable opponent of Linden in this eternal rivalry was Frederick Sander, the "Orchid King", who employed numerous stratagems to pin down many new locations. Sometimes, spotting an incredibly rare specimen in a plant-lover's greenhouse, he would worm the truth out of him; on other occasions, he would have rival collectors trailed by his own men if he could not buy their services outright. Lucien Linden recounts the case of Erich Bungeroth, a brilliant collector working for him, who was followed far and wide by Sander's "pirates" in southern Peru.*** Armed with an illustration of *Cattleya rex,* this gang scoured the area around Belém in the province of Pernambuco where they came across Florent Claes, who was also working for Linden. Claes mentioned Bungeroth. On hearing of this conversation, Sander instantly dispatched two other sleuths, Oversluys and Perthuis, in a vain attempt to track down Bungeroth.

So it was that the laws of silence and secrecy reigned supreme in the world of the major collectors, the four greatest of which were Linden, Low, Sander and Veitch. To this day, far too many unscrupulous plant hunters have gotten away with shockingly radical tactics. Some, for example, have been quite happy to torch the habitats of rare plants after taking what they wanted, thus threatening a large number of species with extinction. [GUIDO BRAEM]

---

*   For further details of this scientific espionage, see Guido Braem and Guy Chiron, *Paphiopedilum,* Saint-Genis Laval, Tropicalia, 2003.
** Lucien Linden, in *IH,* 1881, p. 152.
*** Lucien Linden, in *JO,* 1895, p. 19.

CATTLEYA GUTTATA VAR. LEOPOLDII, Hort.

JEAN LINDEN

and his networks

As we have already seen, Linden had the lifelong knack of winning the confidence of people in different spheres, whether scientific, political, diplomatic or financial. Most of them warmed to his thirst for discovery, his desire to succeed and his infectious enthusiasm. This passion for horticulture took hold of even the greatest in the land – starting with the Belgian kings, Leopold I and Leopold II – and saw many of them acquiring their own greenhouses and becoming major collectors of plants.

In this chapter we attempt a brief overview of the network of relationships that Linden established as his career progressed, analysing the way he frequently turned these to his advantage, in particular by developing partnerships or obtaining strong backing from eminent figures.

In the light of our present knowledge we can discern a number of distinct threads:[1] relationships in differing directions that connected him as much to leading Belgian industrialists as to professional botanists at the Muséum d'Histoire naturelle in Paris. While Linden almost certainly was not a personal friend of the Belgian royals, he did on the other hand embark on a diplomatic career for his native country, Luxembourg. Let us examine, in chronological order, the various circles in which he moved.

THE FIRST CIRCLE – TINANT, NOTHOMB, DUMORTIER

Three persons can be seen as firing Linden's original passion for botany. Indeed, we could probably attribute to them his move to Brussels to study science. Nothomb and Dumortier also used their influence to launch the young Linden into the cycle of Latin American expeditions: he was familiar with the trio from the somewhat limited social circles in Luxembourg, and

Letter from the Brussels authorities to Count Oswald de Kerchove de Denterghem confirming arrangements for the subscription to erect a bust in Jean Linden's honour, 17 March 1899.

‹ *Cattleya guttata* var. *leopoldii* Plate from the *Lindenia*.

1. Letters that could provide information about these relationships are undoubtedly dispersed among the numerous archives that remain unknown, or simply inaccessible, to me.

François Auguste Tinant,
Flore luxembourgeoise, 1836.

Édouard Martens.

2. Worthy of mention here are *Bijdragen tot de natuurkundige wetenschappen* (1850), *Flore luxembourgeoise* (1836), *Orchideen Luxemburgs*. Tinant corresponded with the Vandermaelen brothers in Brussels, with Decaisne in Paris and with Professor Kickx in Ghent. He also left behind a sizeable collection of dried plants, spread over 28 albums and collected under the title, printed in gold: *Herbier du Luxembourg recueilli par F.A. Tinant,* 1857.

3. Paris, Archives of the Muséum national d'Histoire naturelle.

we know he was already making botanical forays with Tinant before arriving in the Belgian capital in 1834.

Born in the city of Luxembourg in 1803, François Auguste Tinant had helped set up the Société de Botanique and published works in French, Dutch and German.[2] Three plant genera have been named in his honour: *Tinantia* Martens & Galeotti, *Tinantia* Dumortier and *Tinantia* Scheidweiler.[3] The names give vital clues to the botanist's relationships: Martens, Scheidweiler and Galeotti were themselves distinguished specialists and collectors. Tinant died in January 1853.

The Athénée royale de Luxembourg once boasted among its pupils the lawyer Jean-Baptiste Nothomb (1805-1881), one of the leading figures in the formation of the 1830 Belgian constitution. He was to hold various administrative and political posts, some of which would prove very useful to Linden's commercial progress. After his tenure as Minister of Public Works in the de Theux government, where he masterminded the enlargement of the rail network and improvements in coalmining, he joined the Académie in 1840; the following year, he would sign the orders for Linden's third expedition. Nothomb retired from Belgium's internal politics in 1845 to take up a diplomatic post in Berlin, where he spent the remainder of his life.

It was possibly through Alphonse Nothomb, the lawyer's younger brother who was also born in 1817, that Linden came into contact with Jean-Baptiste. The correspondence between Linden and the minister during the third expedition reveals more than merely official correspondence: the two men appear to have had a deep admiration for each other. Linden confided his most recent discoveries and sincere gratitude to the politician, who in return insisted on the very real contribution of the third expedition (to Venezuela) in the face of scepticism on the part of other ministers.

The third pivotal figure in Linden's Luxembourg circle was Barthélemy Dumortier (1797-1878), who also collected plants with him in the province's countryside. Dumortier, a professional botanist, was born in Tournai; by 1831 he had won a seat in the Chamber of Representatives where he proved to be one of the Catholic Party's most distinguished orators. At the same time he was appointed the first President of the Société royale de Botanique and was involved in 1824 in the establishment of the Botanical Gardens in Brussels. He became its president in 1837, and was elected a member of the Société royale d'Horticulture de Paris in 1841.

In contrast to the reports addressed to Nothomb during Linden's expeditions, there remains today little documentary evidence of sustained

Jean-Pierre Pescatore (1793-1855)

Many question marks still hang over the connection between Jean Linden and the wealthy businessman Jean-Pierre Pescatore. In Luxembourg, the Lindens and Pescatores were near neighbours, the Lindens' house bordering the latter's property. When Jean Linden went to study in Brussels in 1834, Jean-Pierre Pescatore was already established in Paris and on the verge of a glittering social and financial career.

The fourth of six children, he grew up in a troubled era of progressive financial insecurity in which education appeared not to be among life's priorities. At 16, the young Pescatore joined the Napoleonic forces. On his return to Luxembourg, he went into partnership with his brother Antoine, processing imported Cuban tobacco. By 1817, after some clever manoeuvring, he had obtained exclusive rights with the Régie française for the import of tobacco from Havana, the firm of J.P. Pescatore Bankers and Tobacco Manufacturers remaining in existence until 1841. The income generated was enormous, allowing the banker to purchase a magnificent private mansion in Paris that became the scene of many memorable social occasions.

As a businessman, Pescatore was also to play a role in organising the first World Exhibition in London in 1851. The following year, he was appointed consul-general of the Netherlands in Paris, before assuming the post of director-general of the 1855 World Exhibition, also in the French capital, where he died a few months later. At the time, he was one of the principal shareholders of the Banque de Paris et des Pays-Bas, banker to the King of Greece and a member of the Luxembourg Masonic Lodge.

In Paris, Jean-Pierre Pescatore soon displayed a keen interest in horticulture. By 1840 he had founded the Société d'Horticulture de Seine-et-Oise, before becoming president of the Société de Flore at Versailles. Purchasing a royal estate at La Celle-Saint-Cloud*, which once was owned by Mme de Pompadour, he proceeded to equip it with an orangery and greenhouses. These acquired a reputation as home to the world's finest orchid collection, which its owner entrusted to the care of head gardener G. Lüddemann.

In contrast to Tinant, Nothomb and Dumortier, Pescatore's influence on the young Linden does not appear to have enlarged the latter's network of contacts. It did, however, widen both his market and reputation.

Pescatore's contribution could be summarised in three words: buying, publicising, subsidising. Linden was, in fact, supplying the Paris banker with exotic specimens for his greenhouses at La Celle-Saint-Cloud. Almost certainly he stayed there with Pescatore during the few weeks he spent negotiating with the Paris museum for financial backing for his 1841 expedition and awaiting its departure. There was probably a further stay in 1849, a period when Linden was ill and received a visit from Joseph Decaisne; the banker's home may also have been the scene of Linden's introduction to Benjamin Delessert (1773-1847).

Finally, the name of Jean-Pierre Pescatore will be forever linked with that of Jean Linden through the famed *Pescatorea: Iconographie des Orchidées*.** Only one volume was completed, containing twelve folios of four colour plates with text, but it still remains essential reading for students of Latin American orchids. Pescatore ensured its publication with a series of large subsidies.

Odontoglossum pescatorei.
Plate from *L'Illustration horticole.*

---

*   He was elected Mayor of La Celle-Saint-Cloud on 15 July 1852.

** For a detailed analysis by Professor Guido Braem of this work, see the chapter on Linden's publications.

Barthélemy Dumortier.

relationships between the explorer, Tinant and Dumortier. We do not know, for instance, whether the latter two, bound to Linden by a common love of botany, committed themselves financially on the latter's behalf. Of course, the rules of diplomacy demanded a great deal of discretion in matters of this sort. What we can be sure of is that Tinant, Nothomb and Dumortier played a major role in launching the young naturalist on his horticultural career. His relationship with the three, resulting in a powerful form of protection for a young man in whom they saw great promise, was to open for Linden the doors to Brussels and the Société belge d'Horticulture. Most probably they were also behind Linden's meeting with the Vandermaelen brothers, who developed the large-scale production of detailed maps.

THE PARIS NETWORK

Although the Luxembourg banker had set up his headquarters in Paris, Jean-Pierre Pescatore does not appear to have been the catalyst for Linden's love affair with the French capital. The young naturalist turned to the City of Light very early, immediately after his return from Brazil in 1837 – though our information on the subject relies on a handful of remarks in Linden's report on the expedition.

It was essentially with men of science that he cultivated long-term relationships, though the nature of many of these has proved ambiguous. Despite his scientific interest in the plants he was providing to the museum, it is clear that what he was really seeking from Paris was sufficient backing to launch him on a commercial career. Anxious to gain recognition in the scientific community, he kept up a regular correspondence with Professors Decaisne and Brongniart at the Muséum national d'Histoire naturelle in Paris with the aim of getting his name and plants into a broad spectrum of scientific journals.

Adolphe Théodore Brongniart (1801-76), a graduate in palaeobotany from the University of Paris, is still regarded as the leading French taxonomist of the 1800s. A member of the Institut de France and a professor at the Muséum national d'Histoire naturelle in Paris from 1833, Brongniart first encountered Linden just before he left for Venezuela in 1841. During this third expedition, Brongniart dealt with the correspondence between Linden and the museum's administrators. The collector had, in fact, received subsidies from Paris and had promised the museum several crates of specimens.

Back in Europe, Linden settled in Brussels, continuing his cordial relationship with the Frenchman. The latter asked Linden for a delivery of some 600 dried plants recently shipped from New Granada; Linden replied requesting details of the museum's intentions. Later, when the institution intended to acquire a specimen of *Uropedium lindenii*, Linden stated his opposition, suggesting instead a collection of "new orchids of very high quality, which I can state without exaggeration are among the most thrilling discoveries in this fascinating family". The list contained nearly 40 species. "The high prices I charge for these plants", continued Linden, "would make it difficult or impossible for the museum – or any other scientific body for that matter – to purchase them outright. But in the hope of doing you a favour by enlarging your collection of these novelties, I am prepared to forget their commercial value and let you have the entire collection for the sum of a thousand francs, which is less than a third of their true worth. If your funds for the acquisition of living plants are insufficient to cover this, the payment could be spread over a couple of years. My only condition for this transaction would be that the price is kept secret, otherwise it could have a damaging effect on the value of my stock."[4]

In the end, the shipment of the plants to the musem was announced on 21 February 1852, and they arrived in the course of the year. The crates also contained several drawings, which Linden asked to be forwarded to Joseph Decaisne for publication in leading horticultural magazines.

Joseph Decaisne (1807-82), himself a native of Brussels, was a gardener's assistant at the Muséum who rose to become one of the founders of the Société botanique de France. In 1847 he joined the Académie des Sciences in Paris (rural economy section) and was appointed to its chair of horticulture four years later. In 1865, he became the institution's president. Linden's relationship with him gradually developed from the distant to the friendly, judging by the closing salutations of their abundant correspondence: sometimes "your obedient servant", later on "yours in

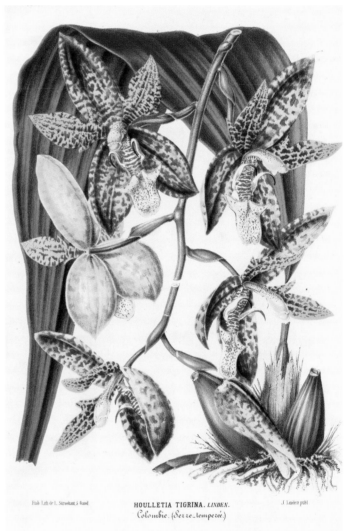

HOULLETIA TIGRINA. *LINDEN.*
Colombie. (Serre tempereé.)

Brongniart contributed to the description of numerous botanical genera and species, including *Houlletia*. This is *Houlletia tigrina*. Plate from *L'Illustration horticole*.

4. Letter from Jean Linden dated 16 December 1851. Paris, Archives of the Muséum national d'Histoire naturelle.

A. de Candolle.

Label accompanying a *Pleurothallis roseo-punctata*, collected by Jean Linden in Venezuela, August 1842. From the herbarium of Benjamin Delessert in the Conservatoire de la Ville de Genève.

great affection" and, in 1872, "from your old friend": Their letters have much to say about botany, of course, in classifying plants, soliciting the services of gardeners, etc. Here and there, however, we find an invitation to stay in Luxembourg, Linden's confidential remarks about Belgian politics and signs of his anti-Prussian sentiments. Decaisne also gave proof of his high estimation of Linden by acting as intermediary in the dispute that brought him into conflict with José Triana and Planchon over the publication of *Plantae Columbianae*.

Baron Benjamin Delessert (1773-1847) was the third major figure linked to Linden in Paris. A French industrialist, financier and philanthropist, he was director of the Banque de France and, in 1818, in partnership with de Candolle, a French botanist, had set up the first savings bank. Delessert himself was a keen amateur scientist with a profound interested in the advancement of the natural sciences – he was an honorary member of the Académie de Sciences in Paris as botanist and conchologist and had succeeded in acclimatising the rarest species in his magnificent park then situated off the rue Raynouard in the capital. At Passy, the Delessert experimental gardens made headlines: under the Empire and encouraged personally by Napoleon, he and his staff had perfected a procedure to extract sugar from sugar beets in response to the allied blockade of the continent, which demanded new solutions to the problem of food supplies. Linden also supplied Delessert with orchids from 1841 and, the following year, he made a sizeable contribution to the baron's dried plant collection – the Delessert Herbarium, now preserved in Geneva – of "196 species, a total of 364 plants".[5]

For the other influential figures Linden met in Paris and who assisted his career in the botanical world and on his earlier mission to Venezuela, the only sources we have are his expedition reports. In these notes we find the names of von Humboldt, de Jussieu, Ramón Díaz and Colonel Agostino Codazzi: we have already mentioned the career of Friedrich Wilhelm Alexander, Baron von Humboldt (1769-1859), in the first chapter. This German naturalist and explorer had won a reputation for his expeditions with the Frenchman Aimé Bonpland in South America (1799-1804); he also made important contributions in the field of biogeography.[6] In addition, he furnished the German government with a great deal of advice on extending the country's presence on this continent, including the establishment of the Tovar colony, Ferdinand Bellermann's mandate for recording local topography and customs, etc. Linden's meeting with von Humboldt may well have had an influence on the route the former adopted for his third expedition: although, strictly speaking, he did not follow the German's itinerary, we know that the information he obtained from him proved invaluable.

Adrien Henri Laurent de Jussieu (1797-1853) occupied a chair in botany at the Muséum national d'Histoire naturelle in Paris (1826-53); in 1839 he was present at the reception of Linden's shipments to the institution. Ramón Díaz, for his part, had acquired a certain celebrity for his history of Colombia and Venezuela;[7] he and Linden were later to meet up again in Caracas. In addition, Díaz had contributed to the *magnum opus* of Agostino Codazzi (1792-1859). An Italian and a former volunteer in the French artillery, Codazzi traded in Constantinople before joining up with Simon Bolivar in Colombia (1817). There, he was appointed lieutenant colonel of artillery and given the task of mapping Lake Maracaibo and its sandbar. From 1831 to 1838 he was engaged on a topographical survey of Venezuela; he then explored the Guyana Desert (1838-39), almost reaching the sources of the Orinoco. In 1848 he entered the service of New Granada, again as cartographer and visiting the Isthmus of Panama to study the possibility of a canal linking the Atlantic and Pacific Oceans.

Following these numerous meetings and having returned from his expeditions, it appears that Linden had high hopes of making his fortune in Paris.

His letter to Joseph Decaisne dated 1 May 1850 shows these ambitions before the political situation decided otherwise.[8] Before examining the networks he forged in the Belgian capital, however, we need to take a brief look at Linden's relations with his fellow growers and botanists across the English Channel, where greenhouse culture had undergone important developments around the beginning of the nineteenth century.

THE ENGLISH CONNECTION

While he was cultivating his links in Paris, Jean Linden was also furthering connections with England that would prove of immeasurable importance. In fact, as early as 1841 he had approached William Hooker, the director of Kew Gardens, offering to undertake expeditions and collect for him. Hooker had refused at the time, but this did not prevent Linden sharing with him the news of his finds in a letter of 29 November 1841 from

Portrait of Jean Linden, alongside those of Agostino Codazzi, Jules Émile Planchon, Joseph Decaisne and Hermann Karsten on the cover of a biography of José Triana.

5. Letter dated 3 May 1842. Paris, Archives of the Muséum national d'Histoire naturelle. According to A. Lasègue [*Le Musée botanique de M Benjamin Delessert*, Librairie de Fortin, Masson & Cie, 1845, p. 43], the Delessert family was on friendly terms with Jean-Jacques Rousseau. "Mr Benjamin Delessert had acquired the taste that led him towards the study of plants in Jean-Jacques Rousseau's letters on botany. These letters were addressed to his mother, Mme Delessert, whom Rousseau delighted in calling his "cousin" as a sign of friendship. "La petite", the young girl referred to in the first letter and for whom he wrote out his lessons, was the sister of Mr Benjamin Delessert [...]. The Delessert family has carefully guarded a collection of dried plants that J.-J. Rousseau had made for Mme Gautier (la petite) [...]. In the last part of Rousseau's life, botany became his favourite occupation."

6. Furthermore, a sea current that bathes the west coast of South America bears his name.

7. Ramón Díaz, Rafael Baralt and Agostino Codazzi, *Resumen de la historia de Venezuela en 3 volúmenes,* Paris, 1841.

8. Letter to Joseph Decaisne dated 1 May 1850. Paris, Insitut de France.

La Guayrá (Venezuela). Ten years or so later, the two men were to begin a regular correspondence.

Meanwhile, Linden had derived enormous benefit from the openings created through his deliveries of orchids to Kew. It was, as we recall, in 1846 that he asked John Lindley to classify the plants shipped from Latin America; Lindley eagerly accepted this invitation, lured by the possible fame he might acquire in the scientific world. The exchange worked in both directions, since Lindley was no stranger to the great collectors with whom Linden established commercial relations: Lord Cavendish, Sigismund Rucker and the Reverend Clowes. In 1853, Linden was constantly on the move, meeting with eminent specialists and soliciting favours. In particular, he travelled to London, where he announced the transfer of his collections to the greenhouses of the Parc Léopold.

When in 1853 Linden resumed contact with William Hooker, the main subjects of his correspondence were his plant deliveries and the activities of his collectors – the quantities of seeds collected by Triana for him since 1853 in New Granada; the plants (1,286 species) that Schlim gathered in the same year and shipped on 9 January 1854; and the death of his collector Joseph Libon at Insainna (Brazil). He also sent Hooker the catalogues he published from his nurseries in Brussels, hoping to see some colour plates reproduced in the London-based *Botanical Magazine*, even offering to produce these at his own expense.

As with his relationships in France, Linden proffered the scientific bait to lure his clients. With his arguments concerning the advancement of science, he aroused the interest of British specialists and skilfully enmeshed them in a system of supply and demand. Extracts from this correspondence are very revealing. In one such letter to William Hooker (12 January 1856) we read: "As science knows no frontiers, I permit myself to hope that you will grant these a place in the collection."[9] Elsewhere, he regrets his English correspondent's refusal, indicating *en passant* that he has not received the "modest subsidies" he had been promised.[10] Linden also continued to solicit the assistance of Kew in classifying new plants from America or even Malaysia.[11] On another occasion, he recommends the employment at Kew of an ex-trainee called Drenthmann, whom he had taken on at one of his sites. From the fragments of Linden's correspondence with Hooker up to October 1861,[12] it appears he never obtained a satisfactory reply.

This cool relationship reflects the tensions that tended to plague relationships between Kew and the horticultural business. William Hooker and

9. Letter from Jean Linden dated 12 January 1856. Kew Archives, vol. 47 (237).

10. Letter from Jean Linden dated 23 November 1853. Kew Archives, vol. 47 (234).

11. On 16 October 1861, Linden announced the first flowering of a plant he had previously admired in Mexico, later identified as a non-climbing *Aristolochia*. Kew Archives, vol. 48 (95).

12. *Loc. cit.*

his successors for a long time treated "non-botanists" with scant respect. Lindley, distinguished as a taxonomist but not a trained botanist, never managed to get into print in Kew's publications; he wrote for other periodicals, such as *The Gardeners' Chronicle*, which he himself had founded and whose technical quality Hooker called into question. Another well-respected taxonomist, Heinrich Gustav Reichenbach, apparently refused to bequeath his herbarium of several million specimens to Kew – Joseph Hooker aspired to look after it in person – because of the unfriendly manner in which he was received there.[13] More generally, Linden was several times to experience at first hand the strained relationships between the British and their opposite numbers on the continent, and his rivalry with Sander (a German who had settled in Britain) took on distinctly unhealthy overtones. According to some modern botanists, this cross-Channel rivalry is still alive today ...

FROM BRUSSELS TO GHENT

Finally back in Belgium after ten years of traversing lonely tracks, virgin forests and other uncharted wildernesses, Jean Linden was able to resume in person the contacts he had striven to maintain by correspondence, including those eminent personalities in Belgium and Luxembourg already mentioned. Some of these relationships would, with the course of time, blossom into enduring friendships based on profound mutual respect.

The decade of expeditions had in itself provided Linden with a number of promising encounters. Even before his third departure for South America, he was closely involved with a network of contacts centred on Paris and London; this was now to be developed by connections with distinguished Belgians both in Brussels and across the Atlantic.

In Brussels, Henri Galeotti had perhaps played a role in Linden's rise to fame in the horticultural trade. The two adoptive Belgians had first met at El Mirador hacienda, then again back at home, where different fortunes awaited each. Despite their diverging financial destinies, however, Galeotti, like Linden, was involved in the brave new world of the natural sciences.

The explorer, naturalist and geologist was present at the arrival and unpacking of Linden's specimens. He was not the only one. Founder of the Société royale d'Horticulture de Belgique, Jean-Baptiste Meeûs[14] took on the task of supervising the expeditions' shipments on arrival, ensuring they were unpacked according to a well-established procedure and shared among

13. The collection finally went to Vienna – the only institution that guaranteed the dried plants would remain shut away for 25 years.

14. Jean-Baptiste Meeûs was the uncle of Ferdinand Meeûs, who ran the Société générale de Belgique after 1830.

the three principal universities and the Société horticole. Way back on the eve of Linden's first departure with Funck and Ghiesbreght, Meeûs had entrusted the three volunteers with a quantity of seeds for the Botanic Gardens in Brazil. It is also worth mentioning that Jean-Baptiste Meeûs had married the sister of the brothers Vandermaelen, a family that would be involved in Galeotti's own 1838 mission to Mexico.

In another direction, Linden found favour with Bernard du Bus de Gisignies (1808-74), an ornithologist at the Musée d'Histoire naturelle in Brussels, where he would later become curator (1846-67). The son of Léonard du Bus de Gisignies, Governor-General of the Dutch Indies under William I, he had built up a collection of exotic items which his father regularly sent home. After law school in Leuven, du Bus developed a passion for biology, leading him to collaborate with the Musée d'Histoire naturelle, which opened its doors to the public in 1814. He very quickly forged himself a worldwide reputation for his ornithological collection. A member of the Société royale d'Horticulture from 1840, he was elected its president four years later.

At this juncture we must consider a particular person with whom Linden carried on a casual agreed correspondence from the time of his third trip to Latin America. This was Johan Willem van Lansberge, whom Linden met in Caracas in 1841. Van Lansberge's father, Frans Reinhart, had been Consul-General of the Netherlands in Caracas when Linden arrived in Venezuela. He later held the position of governor of Curaçao and the Dutch Antilles, and then of Surinam. Himself an amateur explorer, he eagerly undertook trips to Venezuela and, until 28 September 1851, sent back his collections to Belgium. Born in Bogotá, Johan Willem was only a lad of 13 when Linden and his companions took him on botanical expeditions in the country around Caracas. His career was to mirror his father's in every respect. Entering the diplomatic service, he was stationed first at St. Petersburg, then Brussels and Paris. From 1871 to 1875 he was Ambassador and Plenipotentiary of the Netherlands in Brussels before reprising his father's role as Governor-General of the Dutch Indies, a post he held until his resignation in 1881. He did much to promote horticulture and was especially fond of orchids, which he collected by the hundred at his château at Duno in the Veluwe district near Arnhem. In fact, his was the largest collection in the Netherlands. In 1887 the Lindens dedicated a new variety of terrestrial orchid to Johan Willem's wife: *Anaectochilus lansbergiae* var. Madame van Lansberge.

Johan Willem van Lansberge. Portrait in *Le Journal des orchidées,* 1895.

From 1851, although now settled in Brussels, Jean Linden was turning his thoughts to the Flemish city of Ghent, which remains to this day Belgium's horticultural capital. The key figure in its rise to this position was Louis Benoît Van Houtte (1810-76).

As early as 1838, all the plants collected by Linden and his companions in Mexico were being directed to the University of Ghent, where the regular shipments were unpacked, sorted and subjected to detailed examination. It was only after this process that the spoils were shared among this university and those of Liège and Leuven. Astonishingly, Brussels University does not appear on the list of institutions that benefited, despite the fact that Linden was a student there when he embarked on his first expedition.

Three years before, Ghent had celebrated the foundation of its Société anonyme d'Horticulture et de Botanique. In due course, under Louis Van Houtte, it was to organise regular plant exhibitions; ten years later, it was issuing its own publication (the *Annales*) as well as another periodical – *La Flore des serres et des jardins de l'Europe* – the first specialist publication of its type in Europe. In 1849 a horticultural

Begonia lansbergeae. Plate from *L'Illustration horticole.*

"What's in a name...?"

As we saw in a previous text box, many plant species bear the name of a person. In the early days, botanists and taxonomists took pleasure in naming newly discovered species after their academic mentors, but it was not long before the nomenclature began to include members of high society. Genera, species or varieties of exotic plants were soon sporting now-famous appellations like *pescatorea, lansbergiae, rothschildianum* and *leopoldii*. The choice of names was more than innocent amusement. The plants were very often offered exclusively to the person concerned: the epitome of flattery, they came with a definite hint of the donor's wish to be accepted into the tightly-knit circle of wealthy patrons.

Remembering that all exotic plants fetched staggering sums in the 1800s, it is obvious that the market was very limited. Growers and botanists seized on every chance of fresh business or a new patron in order to finance their expeditions and publications. "Flattering the great" thus helped to fuel the mechanism of supply and demand, with vanity encouraging many a prosperous fancier to leave his own memento in a way that reflected his lifetime's passion.

Louis Van Houtte

Louis Benoît Van Houtte (1810-76) studied business in Paris and Clermont-Ferrand (1826-28), finding his way into horticulture in much the same way as Jean Linden. A year before the latter, Van Houtte, then a mere amateur botanist, explored Brazil, Guatemala, Honduras and the Cape Verde Islands on account of Parthon de Von, ex-Consul of France, and King Leopold I, though the results failed to match expectations. On his return, he was appointed director of the new Botanical Gardens in Brussels, where he remained in charge for the two years up to 1838. When he left, he took care to preserve the long list of contacts that secured him as a major force in the horticultural business. He settled in Gentbrugge, a suburb of Ghent, running the Société anonyme d'Horticulture et de Botanique de Gand. On 13 April 1849, he founded the city's École moyenne d'Horticulture, becoming its director. That same year he was honoured with the rank of *Chevalier*: the equivalent of a knighthood.

Two botanical genera – *Houttea* and *Vanhouttea* – and several species commemorate him, revealing the tremendous impact of a man whose foresight in business was matched only by his talents as an explorer and horticulturist, and in that respect may very well be compared with Jean Linden.

school – the École moyenne d'Horticulture – was established. In no time, the Society had become a centre for continuous exchanges between horticulturists and botanists across Europe. Many plant fanciers bought there, and it was the alma mater of many a professional collector.[15]

On 5 March 1846, Jean Linden, barely returned from an expedition to Colombia and Venezuela, dispatched a "mass of plants" to Van Houtte. Doubtless he had gained knowledge of the latter's success, recognising in him a slightly older version of himself. In fact, the delivery was only for storage. Linden had been experiencing problems with the horticulturist de Jonghe in Brussels, who had unexpectedly refused to house the large number of specimens resulting from Linden's third expedition, thus breaking an earlier, if tacit, understanding. Though they were keen rivals in the exotic plant market, Linden and Van Houtte would always maintain friendly and respectful relations, with the former addressing the latter on occasions as "my dear friend Van Houtte". In the aftermath, shortly before his move to Brussels, Linden wrote to the knight Frans Heynderycx[16] for permission to exhibit at the Floralies.

The Société royale d'Agriculture et de Botanique de Gand organised frequent shows (Floralies) where prizes and other marks of distinction were awarded. The Floralies were held every five years, the first began on 30 March 1839, without however overshadowing the biennial events for specialist growers.[17] The shows attracted large numbers of horticulturists and connoisseurs from the cream of European society, and even wealthy

15. Planchon, Roezl, Warszewicz and Siesmayer would all spend significant periods there. Rodigas, a collector for Linden from 1875 to 1876, would study at the École moyenne d'Horticulture.

16. The knight Frans Heynderycx was a senator, as well as the chairman of the Société royale d'Agriculture et de Botanique de Gand, which organised the famous Floralies in 1846. Letter from Jean Linden to Frans Heynderycx dated 12 July 1849.

17. These exhibitions were in existence prior to the Floralies. The Vandermaelen brothers had already exhibited 12 orchids in them in March 1837.

Russian amateurs.[18] In 1873, no less a figure than Prince Troubetzkoï was among the visitors. By now, Jean Linden was well in the public eye: that year he won several first prizes and gold medals in various categories, besides making a number of new acquaintances that would lead to business trips to Vienna,[19] the south of France and Italy.

Ghent was also at the origin of a posthumous tribute to Linden: a subscription was raised through the efforts of Count Oswald de Kerchove de Denterghem – President of the Floralies – for a commemorative monument.[20]

THE AGE OF THE HORTICULTURAL SOCIETIES

In the 1800s, the horticultural world made great strides through the societies that brought together connoisseurs, scientists, and amateur botanical collectors. The prolific number of these elite groups once again bears witness

The knight, Frans Heynderycx.

Siesmayer, horticultural director for Louis Van Houtte, was invited to work at the Imperial Gardens in Saint-Petersburg. He is seen here in the grounds of the Taurida Palace in the old Russian capital. *La Semaine horticole*, 1898.

18. In 1851, Siesmayer, who was Van Houtte's head gardener, was asked to provide his valuable services to the Grand Duchess Elena Pawlowna in Saint-Petersburg. In 1866, he became the inspector of the Imperial Gardens in Russia. *La Semaine horticole*, 16 February 1898, p. 103.

19. In the Austrian capital, the jury of the World Exhibition awarded the medal of merit to *L'Illustration horticole*, the magazine published by Linden.

20. This monument is currently located in the Parc Léopold in Brussels. In this respect, see pp. 214, 219-220.

Oswald de Kerchove de Denterghem,
President of the Floralies.

21. Letter dated 8 February 1845. Brussels,
Archives of the Académie royale des Sciences.

22. *Société royale linnéenne et de Flore, Bruxelles. Discours prononcés lors du centenaire de la Société royale linnéenne,* 16-18 May 1936. The origins of this society date back to the eighteenth century, when botany became fashionable thanks to the efforts of Jean-Jacques Rousseau. In 1784, the English doctor, J.E. Smith, bought the dried plants, manuscripts, zoological collections, library and correspondence of Carl von Linné (1707-1778), the Swedish naturalist and writer who was the father of binary nomenclature in botany, from his widow and daughters. The Linnean Society of London was constituted in the same year (1788) as the Parisian Société linnéenne. Further Linnean societies were founded in France (Bordeaux, Lyon, Caen, Saint-Jean d'Angely, Amiens, Le Havre); Belgium (Brussels); the United States (Philadelphia, Boston, New York); and Australia (Sydney). These were devoted to cataloguing the riches of nature in accordance with the methods pioneered by Linné.

to the passion of the *haute bourgeoisie* for such intellectual study, subject of many speculations. Jean Linden was not immune to the lure of this social environment, and speedily made known his ambition to join the social elite.

Shortly before his arrival in Brussels, he became an honorary member of the Société des Sciences naturelles du grand-duché de Luxembourg. In 1851, he was rubbing shoulders with the eminent figures who patronised the institution: Jean-Pierre Pescatore was also an honorary member, as was van Lansberge. Funck, incidentally, was busy managing the Society's ornithological collection.

In Brussels, Linden, no doubt encouraged by his influential friends, adopted a new tactic with the institutions. On 8 February 1845, he applied to the president and board of the Société royale d'Horticulture de Bruxelles for the post of director of the city's Botanical Gardens. Listing his numerous talents and specialist areas of botanical knowledge, he promised, if accepted, to "give proof of his gratitude and loyalty"![21] His application failed, however, and in the end he was appointed to the management of the Parc Léopold.

At a later stage, Linden sat on the committees of numerous horticultural societies: sources make frequent mention of his name in connection with the constitution of various bodies in 1861, for instance. Within the Fédération des Sociétés d'Horticulture, he was horticulturist-administrator (1861) and delegate to the general assemblies, as well as being a member of the steering committee, the secretariat and the board of editors. Among other officials were: Royer, president of the Commission royale de Pomologie; de Cannart d'Hamale, senator and president of the Société royale d'Horticulture de Malines; van den Hecke de Lembeke, president of the Société royale d'Agriculture et de Botanique de Gand; Ronnberg, government representative; Kegeljan, secretary of the Société royale d'Horticulture de Namur; Morren, Professor of Botany at the University of Liège; and De Puydt, a horticulturist from Mons. Most of these men were also members within the central office of the International Horticultural Congress held in Brussels in 1864.

Also in 1861, Linden served on the committee of the Société de Flore alongside Nicolas Funck, as assistant secretary; he would become president in April 1879. This association dated back to 1822 and had doubtless contributed to the growing interest in orchids ever since the Vandermaelen brothers exhibited a specimen imported from Brazil by the collectors Crabbe and Deyrolle. At the same time, Linden is likely to have had a hand in the dramatic enlargement of the collections owned by the Société lin-néenne de Bruxelles.[22]

By the end of the century, orchid fanciers were both more numerous and more demanding. They were anxious to extend their knowledge through regular meetings and conferences, and for this they needed to improve their means of communication. As a result, the society known as L'Orchidéenne was created in Brussels on 15 October 1888. There were 70 inaugural members, with the elected committee consisting of Georges Warocqué (chair), Lucien Linden (secretary) and du Trieu de Terdonck (treasurer). Jean Linden was elected honorary president. The society met at frequent

The British delegation at the Congrès international d'Horticulture of 1864. Standing, left to right: Mr Eyles, A. Murray, B.S. William, W.E. Dixon, D. Cooper, R. Warner. Seated, left to right: T. Moore, G.U. Skinner, J.J. Blandy, C. Wentworth Dilke, J. Lee, Mr Fitz-Gerald and J. Veitch.

The central committee responsible for the organisation of the 1864 Congrès international d'Horticulture de Bruxelles. Standing, left to right: Mr Santo Garovaglio, A. Brongniart, Mr Penzl, J.É. Planchon, H.G. Reichenbach, P.F. von Siebold, Mr Lecoq, Mr Barlet, F. Fischer. Seated, left to right: Mr Wesmael, J. Linden, Mr Van den Hecke, Mr de Cannart, É. Piré, Mr Ronnberg, E. Kegeljan and B. Dumortier.

intervals: on 11 March 1894, Jean and Lucien Linden were honoured on the occasion of the fiftieth official gathering. A few years before, in 1887, Linden had been appointed to the board of directors (commissariat général) charged with organising an international exhibition in Brussels the following year.

Abroad, Jean Linden was a member of the Sociedad de Ciencias Físicas y Naturales de Caracas (Venezuela) alongside personalities already mentioned: Joseph Dalton Hooker, Berthold Seemann, Charles Victor Naudin and José Triana.

PAUL AND ÉDOUARD OTLET

It used to be said that the Linden family once owned Levant Island, the easternmost island of the Hyères archipelago. These were family rumours, somewhat vague in nature – supposedly the rights had lapsed or been lost through negligence – but they were enough to set me one day on a trail leading to the south of France and the Linden-Otlet relationship dating to the last quarter of the 1800s.

The Otlets at the time were among Belgium's leading financial dynasties. Today, Paul Otlet is still famous for initiating the foundations of the Mundaneum (a sort of "universal information centre" based on card indexing) that was originally installed in the Cinquantenaire palace in Brussels. In Brussels, the name of Édouard Otlet remains associated equally firmly with the celebrated private mansion – at the corner of the rue de Livourne and the rue de Florence – that he commissioned from Octave Van Rysselberghe. Édouard, a senator and businessman, joined the Linden family when he took Valérie – Jean's daughter – as his second wife. He had been close to Jean Linden for several years, sharing with him his own network of commercial contacts.

In 1880, Édouard Otlet purchased Levant Island in Valérie Linden's name. The seller was a certain Philipart, who obtained it from the Comte de Pourtalès, the latter having originally planned to turn it into a penal colony for male teenage offenders – "Working in the fields is one of the best ways of teaching wayward young people morality". Levant Island became a sort of holiday resort for the two families. Paul Otlet described their stays on this small fragment of Paradise: "Ah", I used to think, "how on earth can people be silly enough to spend the whole winter shut up in their apartments in foggy Paris instead of in the South?"[23] The passion of his friends and family for botany can be judged from the fact that this young man, then

23. Paul Otlet, *Mon premier voyage. Impressions. Pâques 1881.* Mons, Mundaneum – Centre d'Archives de la Communauté française, private papers of Paul Otlet.

The Otlet family at table.

Jean Linden (seated, extreme right) poses with the Otlets. Also recognisable are: Édouard, Joseph and Paul Otlet (standing: third, fourth and fifth from left), Auguste Linden (seated fourth from left, with hat). Auguste was in poor health, having lost a leg in an accident in Spain.

Map of the Hyères archipelago.
Souvenir album of Paul Otlet.

only 14, kept a complete record of his stay on the island, with detailed accounts of the composition of the soil, the plants he encountered, and the local people and their activities.

For Jean Linden, the purchase of Levant opened up new horticultural perspectives. Now, in fact, he had at his disposal huge, rent-free areas with an ideal climate for growing selected species. It is impossible today to imagine the famous views of the Côte d'Azur without the rows of palm trees imported from warm and semi-tropical regions across the world.

Édouard Otlet was also an active partner of Linden in organising the 1886 Congo expedition led by the latter's son Auguste.

WAROCQUÉ AND HIS CIRCLE

Orchid growing would never have reached the stage it did at Mariemont in the Hainault without the intervention of the Warocqué family, three generations of which toiled in the greenhouses on their estate. In fact, this passion for plants threatened the family with ruin, such were the sums lavished on his obsession by Georges Warocqué (1860-99).[24]

The first of the dynasty to show a growing interest in orchids was Abel Warocqué (1805-64). In 1854, he was one of the subscribers for the publication of the *Pescatorea*. His links with this celebrated orchid book did not end there: in 1862 he began commissioning François de Tollenaere – one of the illustrators of the *Pescatorea* – for a series of at least 277 watercolours. In

Palm tree on Levant Island.
Souvenir album of Paul Otlet.

24. For more on the development of horticulture and the involvement of Mariemont and Warocqué in this field, see Robert Platiau's beautiful book, *L'Orchidée à Mariemont*, Morlanwelz, Musée royal de Mariemont, 2003, pp. 50-85.

the meantime, Nicolas Funck wrote an account of a visit to the greenhouses at Mariemont in the *Journal d'horticulture pratique de Belgique*. Linden's old expedition companion was already able to report the makings of an orchid collection: a series of records proves beyond doubt that Warocqué had started to buy in 1856.[25] Jean Linden was to maintain friendly links with Arthur Warocqué, Abel's second son, with whom he rubbed shoulders on the committee of the Société de Flore.

This friendship continued down the generations: when the orchid-fanciers' society L'Orchidéenne was formed in 1888, it was Lucien Linden who nominated Georges Warocqué as president.[26] By then Jean Linden had largely withdrawn from dealings with the world of big business. It was at this period, too, that the purchases made at Mariemont reached astronomical sums. The number of prizes won by Georges Warocqué gives the impression that he was buying up the majority of new species imported by Linden's collectors. The high point of these investments came with the naming after him of *Cattleya labiata* var. *Warocqueana,* a plant that for two years and more aroused fierce controversy because of its similarity in several respects to *Cattleya "labiata autumnalis",* recently introduced into England.[27] Financial considerations, however, gradually got the better of Georges' massive purchases from Linden and Sons. Obliged to sell to clear his brother's debts, Raoul Warocqué (1870-1917) nevertheless did not sever the links between the two families. Lucien Linden, indeed, invited him to sit on the panel at a meeting of L'Orchidéenne in 1895. The golden age was over, though, with the expenditures at Mariemont slashed to more reasonable proportions.

Georges Warocqué.

LINDEN, PURVEYOR TO THE COURT?

In 1873, Édouard André wrote of Jean Linden in the *Annales de la Société botanique de France*: "The affection in which the late King Leopold I held him quickly induced him to move his horticultural business to Brussels."[28] Fact or fiction? There is no documentary evidence to confirm this. What is, however, undeniable is that Linden did have regular dealings with Belgium's royal family. Properly speaking, of course, we are looking not so much at a personal friendship as at a series of exchanges based on mutual admiration and a shared passion for orchids.

Relations with the king and the royal family went back, in fact, to Linden's return from the first Brazilian expedition. He and his companions were received at the royal palace, where they presented the queen with some

25. Nicolas Funck, in *Journal d'horticulture pratique de Belgique,* 1859, 3, pp. 62-64, quoted in Robert Platiau, *Op. cit.,* p. 54.

26. Robert Platiau, *Op. cit.,* p. 58.

27. *Ibid.,* pp. 64, 81-82.

28. Extraordinary meeting of the Société botanique de France in Belgium, July 1873.

rare tropical birds. The king also honoured the three with a gold medal, in token of his recognition and satisfaction.

Leopold I was to prove a keen follower of the expeditions' progress. On 16 January 1841, the intendant of the Liste civile informed Minister Jean-Baptiste Nothomb that "MM Linden and Funck, during their stay in Mexico, have sent back a crate of living plants ... for His Majesty personally, not for the government .... and [these have been forwarded] to the head gardener at the château of Laeken".[29] On other occasions, the king himself expressed his concern – through Jules van Praet, his private secretary – about the arrival of crates addressed to him in person. Ten years later, on 30 August 1851, the king became patron of the Société royale de Zoologie, d'Horticulure et d'Agrément de la Ville de Bruxelles, of which Jean Linden was appointed scientific director by royal decree. The society was of very recent formation, its statutes having appeared only five days earlier. On its committee were the Burgomaster of Brussels, Jules Anspach, the honorary president; Leopold Duke of Brabant, future king of Belgium (1865); the Count of Flanders; and numerous members of the Chamber of Representatives.

Linden and the king would meet again on many occasions during royal visits to greenhouses and exhibitions. In 1865, they toured the horticultural exhibition in Amsterdam together.[30] The spiralling reputation of Linden's businesses soon transcended international frontiers, such that a visit to his greenhouses became *de rigueur*. When in February 1870, for example, the mayors of leading English cities visited the Belgian king they took the opportunity to admire the flowers in Parc Léopold. Forewarned of the impending visit headed by the king and queen and the Count and Countess of Flanders, Linden organised an exhibition to promote the genus *Cattleya*. Among the 240 plants were the new "Choco" varieties with their rose-like inflorescence *(Cattleya chocoensis)*: seven hundred flowers in full bloom. Contemporary opinion was that such a feast of colour in mid-winter was unparalleled among European collections.[31]

In 1883, Linden had cause to celebrate yet another royal visit. The exhibition inaugurated on 15 April by the queen, Princess Clémentine and the Count and Countess of Flanders, attracted no less than 60,000 visitors in 6 days,[32] Linden personally escorting the royal party. Afterwards he continued to supply plants and orchids for the royal gardens. Lucien, his son and heir, was to carry on this "business relationship" when he took over the family firms. On 10 October 1884, he was commissioned to construct four

‹ *Cattleya warocqueana.* Watercolour no. 105 from the Warocqué collection.

29. Brussels, Archives générales du Royaume, dossier TO15/569.

30. Guido Braem, "The Lindens and their Lindenia", *American Orchid Society Bulletin*, September 1994.

31. *IH,* 1870, p. 27.

32. *IH,* 1883, p. 69.

New greenhouses constructed at the Laeken Royal Estate by the Compagnie continentale d'Horticulture, 1884-85. Engraving from *L'Illustration horticole*.

large, new greenhouses at Laeken.[33] These were of a revolutionary kind especially designed for azaleas and orchids: the plans were drawn up by his architect, a man named Marchand, under Lucien's personal supervision and to his own specifications. The work was completed in January 1885 and the new houses officially opened on the occasion of a garden party on 10 April. By now, horticulture was ranking amongst Belgium's most significant trades, and the two Lindens expressed their delight at seeing the sovereign displaying such an enlightened taste for the products of this flourishing economic sector.

The matter of the *Plantae Columbianae*[34] revealed another aspect of Linden's relationship with King Leopold I. Linden wrote on 4 December 1858 to Joseph Decaisne, whom he was urging to act as arbiter in the dispute over publication: "Mr Planchon, like myself, is committed to the Belgian government; what is more, he knows that the breaking of these agreements would plunge me into a crisis. Already now I am avoiding every chance of meeting the king, who keeps pressing me about this book. Again, the Minister of the Interior has written me several insistent letters."[35] Linden was not bluffing. Publication had been ordered by royal decree in 1852 and his evident disquiet on the subject reveals how seriously the king took horticultural issues.

33. Leopold II had ordered Emiel Vandewoude to build a winter garden in Laeken from 1874 to 1876. *IH*, 1885, p. 79.

34. In this respect, see the chapter on the publications, pp. 193-194.

35. Letter from Jean Linden to Joseph Decaisne dated 4 December 1858. Paris, Institut de France.

Right up to his death, Jean Linden was to be a privileged guest of the royal family. On 10 May 1888, the Count and Countess of Flanders accompanied by Prince Baudouin and the charming young princesses opened the new family business at Moortebeek. An estimated 14,733 persons visited the inaugural exhibition, including government ministers, the aristocracy and members of the diplomatic corps. In July 1898, Leopold II would visit the greenhouses in Anderlecht in person, six months after Linden's death. At the latter's funeral (14 January 1898), the king was represented by Lieutenant-General Bocquet; he even sent the "royal musicians" for the occasion. Two days earlier he had commanded Count J. d'Oultremont, Grand Marshal of the Court, to "express to the family [his] deepest regrets".

However scant the written evidence may be, Linden's relations with the Belgian monarchy went beyond mere commercial dealings. It all started with a few crates of living plants sent to the king after the second (Mexico) expedition and the official reception for the three explorers at the royal palace. Most would have seen this as a simple mark of recognition for three young men who had contributed to the scientific and economic development of their emergent nation; Linden, however, interpreted it as the basis for long-term exchanges. Aware of the interest shown in botany by Leopold I and his successor, Leopold II, Linden turned royal patronage to his advantage both in the management of the Parc Léopold greenhouses and for his publishing projects. This did not go unnoticed by the king. In his own, inimitable fashion, Linden was constructing a personal showcase for Belgium, in which the royal family actively encouraged him by their visits and their orders for new greenhouses.

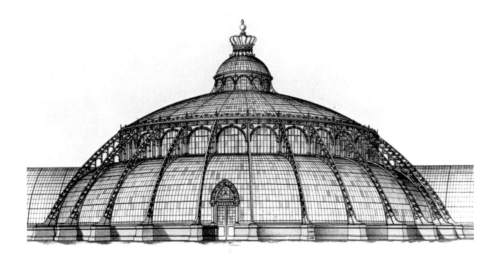

Winter garden by Alphonse Balat
at the Laeken château, 1874.

LINDEN THE DIPLOMAT

A significant number of archives in Luxembourg shed light on another facet of Jean Linden's career: his diplomatic, political, even humanitarian role, albeit sometimes an involuntary one. His correspondence with the Luxembourg government reveals that, in fact, he played two separate parts, both however linked to the same international conflict.

On 18 November 1868, Linden was appointed First Consul in Brussels by the Grand Duchy of Luxembourg. On 4 December of that year Emmanuel Servais, Minister of State and head of the Luxembourg government, congratulated him in these terms: "I am convinced that with your devotion to our native Luxembourg you will not fail to bring the matters entrusted to you to a happy conclusion."[36]

What was expected of Linden was "to procure aid and protection for citizens of Luxembourg who applied for it and to keep the government informed of anything it might find of interest. It might also be his duty, according to the generally accepted protocol of the day, to intervene personally on behalf of his fellow citizens with the appropriate Belgian authorities, should circumstances so demand".[37] This appointment, in itself a signal honour, reveals once again the extent to which Linden had woven about himself a web of wealthy and "useful" contacts.

Diplomatic status, all the same, was not exactly new to him. He had already had a taste of this responsibility at a very early age, when the Belgian authorities required their explorers to research and report on a range of issues concerning the regions they visited. As a result, Linden's appointment as Luxembourg's consul has for a long time overshadowed the fact that, as early as 20 January 1862, he was acting as Colombian representative to the Belgian government in Brussels.

The year 1870 was momentous, to say the least. In addition to Jean Linden's numerous commercial preoccupations,[38] the armed conflict between Prussia and France was a matter of supreme personal concern now that he had joined the diplomatic ranks. His actions as Luxembourg's consul have been variously interpreted by historians; what follows is a résumé of the controversy as it stands.

Having adopted a position of neutrality towards the warring parties, the Luxembourg government requested Linden to investigate Belgium's attitude, with a view to following suit. The Belgians, however, were not adopting any special measures, except that "they would defend themselves in the case of attack, and urged the country's newspapers to exercise the

36. Letter from Emmanuel Servais dated 4 December 1868. Archives nationales de Luxembourg.

37. Letter from Emmanuel Servais dated 12 November 1868. Archives nationales de Luxembourg.

38. He had just taken over the Verschaffelt establishments in Ghent as well as the magazine *L'Illustration horticole*. In this respect, the August/September issue contained a plea against the war, written by Édouard André: "war, which sprays with blood fields that should only be fertilised by labour [...] the union of the inhabitants of the whole world, in which those large, fruitful events like the 1867 Exhibition [in Paris] had been the crowning achievement".

greatest prudence". In the course of innumerable meetings, however, Linden became the recipient of a disconcerting piece of confidential information: Jules Favre, emissary of the French government, privately informed the consul of the instructions he had received regarding peace negotiations with Prussia, warning him of the risk to the Grand Duchy's independence should Luxembourg be offered to France as part of a peace deal. While Belgium's independence at the time was solidly guaranteed by the British, Luxembourg had to rely on a collective guarantee "which merely called upon foreign powers to act in concert". Given that the warring parties were themselves signatories to these agreements, these guarantees appeared of little worth. The historian Vannérus, on the other hand, casts doubt on the matter: in his opinion, it is unlikely Favre would have revealed such information, and Linden was probably misled.

Between 5 and 8 October 1870, Linden travelled to Berlin on a mysterious diplomatic mission under cover of business: a major horticultural exhibition being prepared in the city for the following year. There he met up with his old mentor, Jean-Baptiste Nothomb, now plenipotentiary of Belgium. Numerous European diplomats were also active in Berlin, including a certain Föhr, Luxembourg's chargé d'affaires in Berlin from 1867 to 1875, and Gerson von Bleichröder, Bismarck's banker, Consul-General of Great Britain and a personal friend of Leopold II. Few traces remain of any part Linden played in the Berlin negotiations, but "his revelations caused a certain stir in the chancelleries. At any event, Bismarck knew all about it ... The news was simultaneously confirmed from London".[39] A letter sent to Beaulieu by Auguste Lambermont, Secretary-General to the Ministry of Foreign Affairs, effectively confirms Linden's role as intermediary. The warning was passed on to Jules Van Praet, the king's private secretary, and Devaux, Minister of State, who concluded that the rumour must be scotched, while being kept from Leopold's ears.

While engaged in this undercover role, Linden did not neglect his duty of aiding expatriates. Christian Calmes[40] describes the problems faced by

Jean Linden, First Consul of the Grand Duchy of Luxembourg in Brussels.

39. C. Calmes, *Le Luxembourg dans la guerre de 1870,* pp. 414, 420-421.
40. *Ibid.*

Luxembourg migrants in Paris who were suffering the repercussions of the war and, in so doing, clarifies the impact of Linden's measures. In August, the Luxembourg Legation in the French capital was besieged by "a whole crowd of working men and servants" desperate to return home. Linden became involved in a disagreement with his minister, Servais, who opposed the mass repatriation of Luxembourg nationals fleeing Paris for Brussels. He claimed that a large number of those who would benefit from such assistance had a dubious past.[41] On this, Calmes tell us,[42] Servais was wrong: in many cases the applicants were craftsmen or young families who had sought better training or remunerative employment in Paris – at the time in question, Luxembourg was among the least developed countries of Europe, both industrially and economically.[43] The correspondence between Servais and Linden from September 1870 to May 1871 sheds light on the attitude of the Luxembourg government towards its expatriates in Paris. Linden begged the Minister of State to come to the aid of the numerous refugees from the French capital living without food or shelter around the Gare de Luxembourg in Brussels – the Quartier Léopold, a stone's throw from the Parc Léopold where Linden had his establishments. Linden revealed that he was giving financial assistance to Luxembourg nationals in distress, but urged the government to intervene officially. The absence of relevant official documents prevents us, however, from pursuing the matter any further.

Five years later, on 7 December 1875, Linden was appointed Consul-General of Luxembourg by William III, King of the Netherlands, Prince of Orange-Nassau and Grand Duke of Luxembourg. He retained this post until 23 August 1893, after which he expressed the desire to be relieved of his duties, citing "diplomatic-family" reasons that we have not been able to identify. He nevertheless kept this honorary title until he died.

EXPANDING THE NETWORK

With his imposing presence, Jean Linden left an abiding memory with all who met him. His photograph at the Royal Horticultural Society (page 8) clearly reveals the magnetic personality of a man skilled at exploiting one relationship to form another. He never let discretion get the better of achievement. He knew how to win over men of science, to obtain the collaboration of fellow businessmen and the patronage of the wealthiest collectors, including politicians of the first rank. From 1870 on, he also found himself entrusted with diplomatic missions. Furthermore, when the storm

Baron Gerson von Bleichröder.

clouds of the Franco-Prussian War gathered over Luxembourg, he revealed a selfless and humanitarian side – though it cannot be forgotten that most of his activities appear to have been rooted in financial considerations. Whether dealing with Kew Gardens, the Muséum national d'Histoire naturelle de Paris, his colleague Van Houtte or the king, Jean Linden cease-lessly strove to develop his business among the highest echelons of society, where he found his most rewarding clients.

41. "I did not think that I could authorise you to make advances to Luxembourgians who had come from Paris to Brussels en route for Luxembourg [...] Of the Luxembourgians who reside in Paris, not a few are bad fellows: some have left behind their wife and children, leaving them in the hands of the charity bureau. It would be too convenient for this class of people if, when things are no longer going well for them in Paris, we were to pay them to come back. That type of approach would only be an encouragement for others. Many of them are corrupt [...]. They set the population extremely bad examples, teaching it very bad things, and they are a very real danger [...], these people risk being carriers of the virus of subversion." *Ibid.*

42. *Ibid.*

43. The economic and industrial boom of the Grand Duchy of Luxembourg occurred in the last quarter of the nineteenth century. For more on this subject, see: Arthur Herschen, *Manuel d'histoire nationale*, 9th edition, revised by Nicolas Margue and Joseph Meyers, Luxembourg, P. Linden imprimeur de la Cour, 1972. We should note in passing that Arthur Herschen was the son of Jean Linden's sister, Marie, and thus his nephew.

P. Stroobant, ad nat.pinx.in Horto Versch. **EPIDENDRUM AMBIGUUM.** *LINDL.* Etab. Lith. de L. Stroobant, à Gand.

Mexique (Serre tempérée).

A. Verschaffelt publ.

THE LINDEN PUBLICATIONS

La Semaine horticole, title design, 1898.

The Linden name is associated with a number of important publications. Two of these – *Pescatorea* and *Lindenia* – are commonly ranked amongst the most magnificent and outstanding works in the orchid literature. Beyond a simple listing of the titles of these works, this chapter briefly describes each one, some of which were published over several decades, touching upon their genesis and the context of their development and eventual demise. Through these thousands of printed pages we can also begin to appreciate the motivations that drove the Lindens, both father and son.

ORCHIDACEAE LINDENIANAE (1846)

Although Jean Linden was not the author, we have decided to start our listing with this book, as in a sense it paved the way for future publications. The *Orchidaceae Lindenianae* [or, *Notes upon a Collection of Orchids Formed in Colombia and Cuba, by Mr J. Linden*] was written by John Lindley and published in 1846 in London by Bradbury & Evans.

At that time, Lindley, a self-educated botanist and friend of William Jackson Hooker, was unquestionably the world's leading authority on orchids. It is not surprising, therefore, that Linden should have decided to send him examples from his collection, providing the Englishman with his personal notes and dried specimens of 143 species of orchid. The interest of Linden in so doing is discussed in further detail in a preceding chapter of the present work.

In the preface to his book, Lindley states: "The following plants are part of a large collection made by Mr J. Linden among the mountains which form a curve closing in the Gulf of Maracaybo on the south, and extending

‹ *Epidendrum ambiguum.*
L'Illustration horticole, 1869.

as far as Santa Fé de Bogota *[sic]*: a district inclosed between the parallels of 4° and 10° north latitude. A few species from Cuba that were collected in the same expedition are intermixed with them. They make a very interesting series, of which more than one half was previously undescribed. [...] I have therefore willingly undertaken the agreeable duty of publishing a short account of them at Mr Linden's request. In doing so, that enterprising traveller's own notes have been literally translated, placed between inverted commas, and printed in italics [...]" This last remark suggests that Jean Linden should henceforth be considered as co-author.

There is no doubt today that Jean Linden wished to use this publication as a commercial instrument. Lindley himself indicates that most of the species that survived the voyage back can be purchased at the Brussels premises of Mr de Jonghe, while carefully noting the full address of the latter.

The botanical and horticultural value of this book at its time of publication, however, should not be underestimated. It gives an outstanding overview of the orchids discovered and collected by Linden and his fellow explorers. It also includes a wealth of information on the ecology of these plants. We have to remember that this book appeared at a time when many orchids, having been collected and brought back to what was then known as the civilised world, suffered in the overheated "stove houses" of English and European gentlemen. Furthermore, as Lindley indicates in his preface, a large number of the plants described in the book were, at this time, unknown to science.

Of the 143 plants listed, 11 originated from Cuba. The others were collected from the areas now known as Venezuela and Colombia. Seventy-nine plants were then new to science. Insofar as their description is based on Linden's notes, we should make due acknowledgement of their scientific names and cite them correctly as Linden ex Lindley.

REPORT OF A SCIENTIFIC MISSION

Jean Linden concluded his third expedition, to Venezuela, at the end of December 1844. The commissioning order included a directive that the naturalist should draft a report on the explorers' activities. The handwritten report, which extends to 73 pages, is now kept at the Archives générales du Royaume. The text was published in the *Moniteur belge* on 10 May 1846, before being re-printed that same year in the *Annales de la Société royale d'Agriculture et de Botanique de Gand*.[1] The report was also published in *La Belgique horticole* in 1867 and formed part of Jean Linden's extensive obituary, which was published in *La Semaine horticole* on 12 February 1898.

The report narrates Jean Linden's third voyage, but has very little in common with the publication known as *Troisième voyage de J. Linden* (see below). In fact, only a fraction of the report by Jean Linden was to be incorporated in this latter title.

PRELUDIA FLORAE COLUMBIANAE (1853)

This book was first published in a French periodical, the *Annales des Sciences naturelles*.[2] The text was then reprinted in the *Bulletins de l'Académie royale des Sciences, des Lettres et des Beaux-Arts de Belgique*.[3] It is co-authored by Jules Émile Planchon, who was then professor of botany at the École de Pharmacie in Nancy and assistant professor at the renowned Montpellier University.

Sub-titled "Matériaux pour servir à la partie botanique du voyage de J. Linden, par J.É. Planchon et J. Linden", the *Preludia Florae Columbianae* is limited to a description of four taxa, all belonging to the *Rutaceae* family:
- *Erythrochiton hypophyllanthus* Planchon and Linden
- *Naudinia amabilis* Planchon and Linden
- *Zanthoxylon camphoratum* Planchon and Linden
- the genus *Naudinia*[4] Planchon and Linden

In addition to these, a fourth plant, *Z. melanocantha* Planchon, is also described in a note at the end of the publication.

A more detailed publication on Colombian flora, essentially based on the plants collected by Linden, was expected to follow the *Preludia Florae Columbianae*. The project was supported at the highest levels of the Belgian government, and was planned to consist of at least three volumes in folio, each of about 500 pages. To this end, the authorities made a significant advance payment to Linden.

During a visit to Paris, Linden came to an agreement with Planchon and José Triana, a Columbian doctor, co-opting them as co-authors of this book, which in consequence would incorporate some comments on Triana's collections.

The agreement was not honoured, however. Apparently Triana, a young and wealthy man who enjoyed the best relations with the Colombian government, managed to convince Planchon to work without the collaboration of Jean Linden. It would appear that he explicitly demanded that the Belgian horticulturist be excluded from the collective work.

1. *Annales de la Société royale d'Agriculture et de Botanique de Gand,* 1846, 2, pp. 205-272.

2. *Annales des Sciences naturelles. Botanique.* 1853, 3rd series, 19, 2, pp. 74-82.

3. *Bulletins de l'Académie royale des Sciences, des Lettres et des Beaux-Arts de Belgique,* 1853, 20, 1, pp. 186-196.

4. Charles Victor Naudin (1815-1899), a French botanist and horticulturist, was one of the first scientists to create hybrids of plants. His name was immortalised in three generic designations: *Naudinia* Achille Richard (1845), *Naudinia* Planchon et Linden (1856) and *Naudinia* Descaisne ex Triana (1866). None of these designations is in use today.

Linden was of course very disappointed by Planchon's attitude. The latter had benefited from advance payments over a number of years and had also received part of Linden's collection. Joseph Decaisne, a Belgian botanist who worked for the Muséum national d'Histoire naturelle in Paris, was asked to arbitrate in the dispute, but to no avail. Decaisne's proposal was unacceptable to Linden, and the latter's counter-proposal was in turn rejected by both Planchon and Triana. To date, no other elements of the correspondence between Linden, Decaisne, Planchon and Triana have been discovered. On the other hand, we know how the story ended: Triana published the *Prodomus florae novo-granatensis* in two volumes, in January 1862 and in 1868. Planchon co-authored the first volume of this publication.

PESCATOREA (1854-1860?)

The following announcement appeared in *The Gardeners' Chronicle* of 15 April 1854: "We learn that a work on orchidaceous plants is about to appear in Brussels, under the name of *PESCATOREA*. It is to be published monthly, in folio parts, each containing four coloured plates and as many leaves of letter-press. The gentleman whose name it bears, and by whose munificent support the cost of the work is to be partly provided for, possesses the finest collection of Orchids known upon the continent at his château de La Celle-Saint-Cloud, near Paris; and he is most richly entitled to the compliment paid him in the title of the work. The editors are to be, in the first place, Mr LINDEN, the well-known traveller, now director of the Royal Zoological and Horticultural Gardens of Brussels *[sic]*; 2, Mr LÜDDEMAN *[sic]*, the skilful superintendent of the greenhouses of Mr PESCATORE; 3, Prof. PLANCHON, of Montpellier; and 4, Prof. REICHENBACH the younger, to whom, in intimate knowledge of the order no continental botanist even approaches. These favourite plants are now so largely imported by continental growers, Mr PESCATORE is so extremely rich in fine plants, and Mr LINDEN has such abundant materials, both living and preserved in the Herbarium, that we anticipate the appearance of a work of sterling value. The first number is announced for the 1ˢᵗ of June in Brussels."

What magnificent news this must have been for the insiders of European horticulture! What a project! What a team! A work on orchids, financially secured by the wealthy banker Jean-Pierre Pescatore and authored by Linden, one of the most famous botanical explorers, if not the most famous; together with Jules Émile Planchon, Professor at Montpellier and formerly assistant to William Jackson Hooker at Kew; Heinrich Gustav

› *Paphiopedilum* (formerly *Cypripedium) villosum*.
Plate from *Pescatorea*.

CYPRIPEDIUM VILLOSUM. Lindl.

P.De Pannemaeker, ad nat.pinx in Horto Lind.   Étab.Lith.de P.De Pannemaeker à Gand.

Reichenbach, at the time professor at Leipzig and within a few decades to be regarded as the greatest orchid botanist of all times; and G. Lüddemann, the head gardener of Mr Pescatore at the château de La Celle-Saint-Cloud.

Regrettably, this project was doomed to failure. Pescatore died, without leaving any provisions in his will to secure the publication. His heirs were obviously not interested in continuing with support for the project; in his introduction to the *Pescatorea*, Linden bitterly notes: "This sacrifice, insignificant in view of Mr Pescatore's colossal fortune, has become for us a rather heavy burden, one that will not be lightened by cutting back on the copies printed."

Ultimately, in spite of other intentions indicated by Linden[5], only one volume was published, consisting of 12 instalments of 4 colour plates each and the corresponding text. Obviously, Linden was preparing for a big business set-up, However, for such a venture as was the *Pescatorea,* he was not strong enough. We will see, however, that times would change.

It is difficult even now to obtain detailed and reliable information on the publication of this magnificent volume. The first five sections indicate the precise drafting dates – from June to October 1854 – after each block of text. It is somewhat surprising that, considering the distress Linden had previously been caused by Professor Planchon (in connection with the *Preludia Florae Columbianae*), the latter should be contributing to the *Pescatorea* beyond 1858.

It is obvious – and the first reviewer[6] of the folio confirms this – that Lüddemann drafted the sections related to the cultivation of plants. The extent of the participation of the three other authors remains unknown to us.

Maubert[7] and François De Tollenaere, who was also in charge of the lithographs, drew the plates, the originals of which have never been found.

Maubert had previously worked with H.G. Reichenbach – who was also a fine botanical illustrator – on the *Histoire naturelle des îles Canaries* (1835-1850) by Webb & Berthelot. He had also supplied the drawings and collocations for the *Choix des plus belles roses* (1845) by Redouté and worked on d'Orbigny's *Dictionnaire universel d'histoire naturelle* (1842-1849), *The Floral Register* by Maund (1825-1850), the *Iconographie illustrée des cactées* by Lemaire (1841-1847), the *Illustrationes plantarum Orientalium* by Jaubert & Spach (1842-1857), Francis Boott's *Illustrations of the Genus Carex* (1858-1867) and *L'Horticulteur français* by Hérincq (1851-1872). Evidently, he was one of the best botanical artists of his day, and it is therefore surprising that his

‹ *Cycnoches maculatum.*
L'Illustration horticole, 1873.

5. *The Gardeners' Chronicle,* 1860, 1st series, 20, p. 148: "The 12th and last number of vol. I. of the *Pescatorea* has appeared with the title-page and index. [...] Amateurs will be glad to hear that Mr Linden announces his intention of continuing this attractive work notwithstanding the death of Mr Pescatore; and he expects that his collectors in tropical Asia and America will supply its pages with novelties in abundance."

6. *The Gardeners' Chronicle,* 1854, 1st series, 14, p. 455: "*Pescatorea.* – The first number of this work [...] To each plant Mr Lüddemann has added a detailed statement of the cultivation which he finds most successful."

7. We have not been able to find any indication as to his Christian name.

name has been overlooked in the literature. De Tollenaere (sometimes cited as Detollenaere) worked principally as a lithographer.

The price for a volume was set at 72 francs. This substantial amount would make the *Pescatorea* available only to the wealthiest, or to the customers of Jean Linden's nursery. The clear intent was to produce one of the most splendid works in the orchid literature. In respect to quality, the only comparable works of the time are *Collectanea botanica* (1821-1826) by Lindley, *The Orchidaceae of Mexico and Guatemala* (1843) by Bateman and *A Century of Orchidaceous Plants* (1851) by William Hooker.

A second article in *The Gardeners' Chronicle,* published in April 1855[8], discloses some interesting points of debate concerning this publication: "Could they not, without impropriety, occasionally admit plates of non-introduced species by way of variety and for the purpose of guiding collectors to what is wanted? Suppose three or four species of the beautiful genus *Masdevallia,* such as *sanguinea, rosea,* etc, were put upon one plate; on another, as many of the gigantic Peruvian *Pleurothallids,* very different from the uninviting things occasionally seen in cultivation; a third were occupied by *Chloraeas,* and a fourth by *Telipogons,* the most lovely of occidental orchids, the interest of the *Pescatorea,* would be greatly enhanced. Our friends Linden and Reichenbach could easily find the materials, and Riocreux would do the rest."

These words demonstrate that garden-made hybrid orchids did exist in 1855. The authors and publishers of the *Pescatorea* evidently did not respond to this initiative. Jean Linden was clearly the driving force behind the project following the death of Pescatore. Since he himself commercialised orchids, he concentrated his efforts on the types his customers wanted – those that amateurs could cultivate and show their visitors. This meant plants such as *Cattleya elegans* and *Laelia purpurata,* or the cypripediums and odontoglossums, but not plants with tiny flowers such as the pleurothallids, nor plants that were either difficult (masdevallias) or just about impossible (telipogons) to cultivate. Some of those would later feature in the *Lindenia.*

HORTUS LINDENIANUS (1859-1860)

Hortus Lindenianus – or "Recueil iconographique des plantes nouvelles introduites par l'établissement de J. Linden au Jardin royal de Zoologie et d'Horticulture à Bruxelles" is published in folios and printed by Hayez, the

8. *The Gardeners' Chronicle,* 1855,
1st series, 15, p. 599.

90

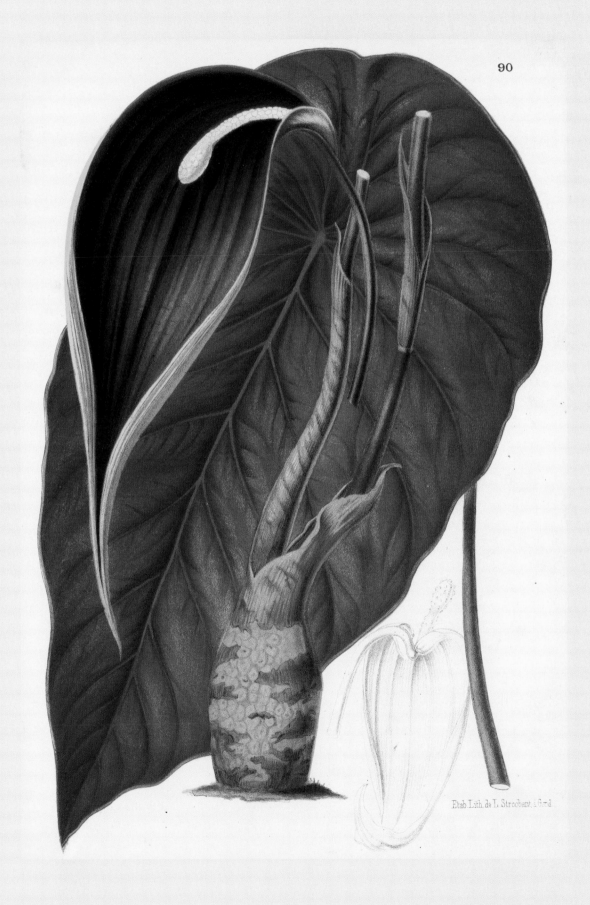

Etab.Lith.de L.Stroobant, à Gand.

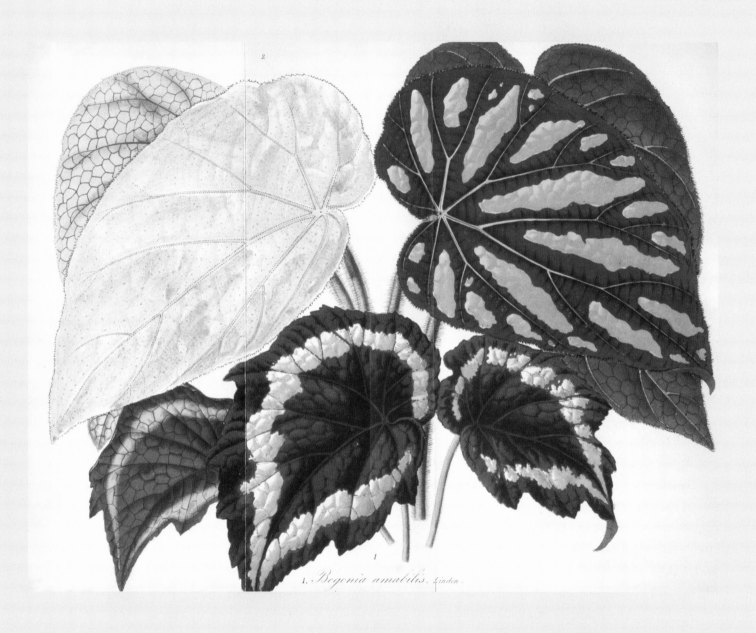

1. *Begonia amabilis*. Linden.

official printer for the Académie royale de Belgique. The book is published in two parts.

The cover of the first volume bears the date of April 1860 at the top, and the year 1859 at the bottom. This section comprises 18 pages and 6 plates. The text mentions a seventh plate, but the latter is not included in the final work. All plates are colour lithographs.

The second section bears the year 1860 on its cover. It consists of 13 pages and 5 colour lithographs. Plate 13 is mentioned, but would not be published.

It is obvious that this publication was intended to double as a sales catalogue. Jean Linden wrote the introduction and François De Tollenaere signed the plates. It appears to us that, from now on, other pages were originally intended to complete the first two folios.

PLANTAE COLUMBIANAE (THIRD VOYAGE OF J LINDEN) [9]

We do not quite know whether Jean Linden personally published this book. According to the date on the title page, this work of 152 pages was written in 1863. According to Stafleu and Cowan, however, it was not published until 1874-1875, when Cogniaux allegedly published five copies from the corrected proofs.

Linden and J.É. Planchon are cited as co-authors of the book, which is based on herbarium specimens prepared by Linden (1840-1844), Funck and Schlim (1845-1847), Funck (1840-1843) and Schlim (1848-1853). Linden states that his collections took shape during a mission for the Belgian government. He makes it clear that other collectors travelled at the expense of the Linden company.

The title page carries the descriptors "Première Partie" and "Tome 1", which indicate that a sequel was intended. The first section of the book (paginated in Roman numerals) describes Colombia's physical features and climate. It also describes the different areas of vegetation. Pages XXXVII to LXIV are devoted to a "Historical Summary of the Voyages of Exploration". Jean Linden cites 2 October 1835 as the date of departure (page XLVIII). Additional information on the geography and climate of the country follows this "travel section". The second section (pages 1-64) is entitled "Plantae Columbianae" and includes descriptions of species belonging to the 21 families and 67 genera of flowering plants. The plants described are without exception dicotyledons. The description also includes 52 species that Linden and Planchon deemed new to science.

9. Although subtitled "Voyage de J. Linden – Partie Botanique – Plantae Columbianae", the work has no clear original title. For reasons of bibliographical coherence, we shall use the title *Plantae Columbianae*.

José Triana.

› *Lindenia. Iconographie des orchidées,*
cover of vol. 4, 1887.

To this day, it is not known why Linden did not publish this work as he intended, or why it was prematurely discontinued. We may hypothesise, however, that he did not wish to exacerbate further his already heated relations with Triana and Planchon.

LINDENIA (1885-1906)

The *Lindenia* is one of the best-known works in the orchid and horticultural literature. Seventeen volumes (each comprising twelve folios) with 813 plates were published between 1885 and 1906. Jean Linden remained director of publications until 1895, while his son Lucien worked as co-editor-in-chief with Émile Rodigas. The following year, Lucien was first mentioned as his father's co-director and, in 1897, listed as sole director. Two years later, he would claim the titles of founder, director and publisher. The *Lindenia* was always a family concern. Reading between the lines, we can see that Jean Linden retained control over all aspects of publication until 1896.

The *Lindenia* is exclusively dedicated to orchids. Its subtitle "Iconographie des Orchidées" – which is the same as that of the *Pescatorea* – reveals its fundamental connection with the magnificent work that came to an abrupt end following the premature death of Jean-Pierre Pescatore.

The *Lindenia* ends with plate 814. Plate 795 – *Cattleya trianae* Lind. var. *Memoria rodigasi* L. Lind. – is missing in all known copies, however; it would appear that it was never published. The reason for this, although nowhere documented, may be found in the fact that the description of the plant indicates that it was an orchid of hybrid origin, and by no means a variety of *Cattleya trianae*. This must have been realised at a time where it was no longer possible to replace that part of the publication. Eventually, 166 plates would illustrate hybrids.

Eight artists contributed to the creation of the colour plates. Two of these, P. De Pannemaeker and A. Goossens, are ranked amongst the finest botanical illustrators of their time. Eight hundred of the plates are full page, twelve are double (twin plates) each covering two full pages. Most plates are accompanied by an overview of the history of the species or origin of the hybrid. This is followed by a discussion, a relatively comprehensive description and information on cultivation techniques. A wealth of secondary information dealing with the wider aspects of horticulture is also provided: minutes of horticultural meetings, the arrival of new

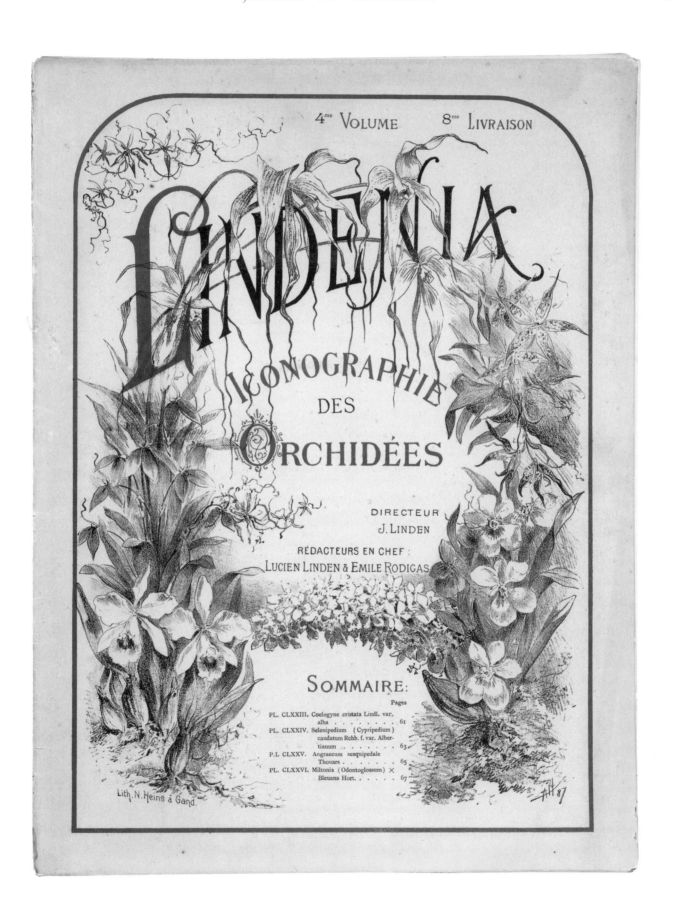

4me VOLUME   8me LIVRAISON

LINDENIA

ICONOGRAPHIE

DES

ORCHIDÉES

DIRECTEUR
J. LINDEN

RÉDACTEURS EN CHEF :
LUCIEN LINDEN & EMILE RODIGAS

Lith. N. Heins à Gand.

SOMMAIRE:

Lindenia. Iconographie des orchidées,
cover of vol. 5, 1888.

Lindenia. Iconographie des orchidées,
cover of vol. 6, 1889.

species and lists of plant genera. Altogether, the work extends to over 2500 pages.

The details of the end of the *Lindenia* remain an enigma. There may have been many factors involved. The end of the nineteenth century marked the beginning of the decline of "big money" in orchids. Orchids became popular. New introductions became rare and more and more hybrids were being produced. The prices were falling, in line with the "general mood" in Europe.

Its readership was not informed that the *Lindenia* was to be discontinued. Lucien Linden did, however, drop a hint in *La Semaine horticole,* where the suspension of trading can be read between the lines. The director seemed exhausted, and was having to cope with several problems. From 1903 to 1906, Lucien Linden was involved in several court cases relating to the sale of orchids, and lost each one. Although there is no direct evidence to substantiate our theory, this was probably a significant, if not the only, reason behind the discontinuation of the *Lindenia*. In the issue of 5 January 1907, the editor of *The Gardeners' Chronicle* writes: "After a considerable interval between the publication of Part 8 of this illustrated work of orchids, Parts 9, 10, 11 and 12, necessary to complete Volume XVII, have come to hand together, and complete the work on the original lines, if the intention to discontinue it in its present form recently expressed is adhered to." The editor remains silent as to the source of this information.

From February 1892 to July 1898, Jean Linden headed the so-called American edition. The latter begins with the second half of Volume VI (plate 265) and was edited by Émile Rodigas and Robert Allen Rolfe. This edition is often, though erroneously, cited as an English translation. In fact, with the exception of some passages clearly written by Rolfe, the English descriptions are very short, with the rest of the text remaining in French. Such a hybrid edition could not hope for success. The discontinuation of the publication due to lack of demand, at Volume XII (plate 624), is therefore hardly surprising.

L'ILLUSTRATION HORTICOLE (1854-1896)

This monthly[10] publication, launched by Verschaffelt in 1854, presented the most remarkable plants, focusing on new introductions and the most interesting horticultural facts. When Jean Linden purchased Verschaffelt's Ghent nursery, he also "inherited" the journal. The transfer of the latter was announced in the issue of July 1869 and was completed by October that same year. Édouard André immediately replaced Charles Lemaire. After sharing responsibilities from 1870 to 1880, André would finally hand over his position as editor to Émile Rodigas, as of 1881. For the sixth series, Rodigas would be assisted by Max Garnier and Charles De Bosschere[11].

Paphiopedilum charlesworthii (formerly *Cypripedium charlesworthii*). Plate from the *Lindenia*.

The periodical was dedicated to plants in general. It also contained information on aspects of culture and notes relating to social events such as conventions and orchid society meetings. In most volumes, publicity was generally limited to the Linden companies' advertisements, but the volumes in series 6 contain 12 pages of general advertisements per issue, possibly indicating that subscriptions were no longer sufficient to cover expenses.

The December issue of volume 20 (1873) announced that the series would be published in English as of 15 February 1874. Three months later, the issue of March 1874 carried a note to the effect that the English botanist, W.B. Hemsley, was working on a translation. We have yet to find any indication, however, of an English version of *L'Illustration horticole* ever appearing in print.

Altogether, six series covered the period 1854 to 1896:
- Series 1 (vols 1-10): 1854-1863, approximately 3 colour plates per issue;
- Series 2 (vols 11-16): 1864-1869, approximately 3 colour plates per issue;

10. The magazine became twice-monthly after series 6, in 1894. Before that, only vol. 19 of 1872 had comprised 24 issues.

11. Rodigas took charge of the issue that appeared on the 15th of each month. As for the issue published on the 30th of each month, this was entrusted to Garnier (vols 1 and 2) and then to De Bosschere (vol. 3).

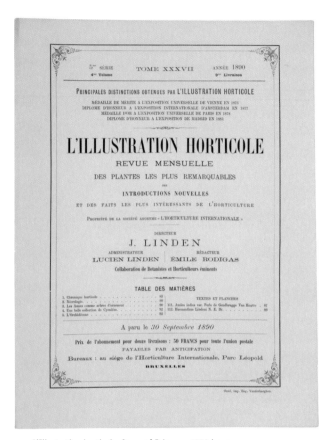

L'Illustration horticole. Cover of February 1870 issue,
vol. 17, series 3.

› *Odontoglossum triumphans.*
L'Illustration horticole, 1869.

- Series 3 (vols 17-27): 1870-1880, approximately 4 colour plates per issue;
- Series 4 (vols 28-33): 1881-1886, approximately 3 colour plates per issue;
- Series 5 (vols 34-40): 1887-1893, 2-4 colour plates per issue;
- Series 6 (vols 1-3): 1894-1896, approximately 1 colour plate per issue.

Over these four decades, the journal would be issued in several formats.[12] It regularly included colour lithographs, some of which were embellished by hand.

LE JOURNAL DES ORCHIDÉES.
GUIDE PRATIQUE DE CULTURE (1890-1897)

This bi-monthly journal, which was founded by the Lindens, was first issued on 15 March 1890. It consisted of 16 pages, with no colour illustrations. Towards the end, the journal was no more than a compilation of general, amateur information, similar to that found in the auxiliary texts of the *Lindenia*. It could easily be defined as a "*Lindenia* for the poor". Its production costs were much lower. In 1890, the latter carried an announcement concerning the launch of this new publication, as follows:

"*Le Journal des orchidées* is the title of a new bi-monthly magazine, to be published by Mr Lucien Linden in collaboration with both amateur and professional gardeners, beginning on 15 March next. It will have 16 pages of text and will appear on the 1st and 15th of each month. Its only aim is to be an aid to orchid growers, large and small; it will be a practical guide to cultivation and an indispensable companion to the modern gardener. It is not a scientific publication. The subscription is fixed at 10 francs per annum. Easy terms will be made available to gardeners. A sample copy will be sent free on request. The offices of *Le Journal des orchidées* are situated at 100 rue Belliard, Brussels."

Le Journal des orchidées was the Lindens' smallest publication. It was aimed at gardeners and amateurs who could not afford a subscription to the *Lindenia* (which cost 60 francs a year – the equivalent of two months' salary at working-class level). It is likely that it was initiated at the request of

12. The first four series were published in a format of 27 x 18 cm. The fifth series saw its dimensions enlarged (35.5 x 27 cm) but the sixth series reverted to more or less the original format (26.7 x 18 cm).

Etab. Lith. de L. Stroobant, à Gand.

A. Verschaffelt, publ.

ODONTOGLOSSUM TRIUMPHANS. *REICH. FIL.*

Colombie (Serre-froide)

P. De Pannemaeker, ad.nat.pinx in Horto Lind   Etab. Lith. de L. Stroobant, à Gand

Linden clientele, who were not too keen on leaving their precious copies of *Lindenia* in the hands of their gardeners, who yet needed practical documentation on the cultivation methods of the plants.

Lucien Linden argued for combining *L'Illustration horticole* with *Le Journal des orchidées,* citing the need to reduce the articles on orchids and come a little closer to the readership.[13] This reason can be regarded as factitious, however. The publication of *L'Illustration horticole* was proving costly, due in no small part to its colour illustrations. Furthermore, business in 1896 was not flourishing as well as it was in the years before. An obvious solution consisted in using the journal format of *Le Journal des orchidées* and applying it to a weekly publication that was devoid of colour, thus slashing costs. After all, the publication of the *Lindenia* was being maintained, even if problems were looming.

Le Journal des orchidées, which was administered in Brussels but published in Ghent, ran for seven years. Production ceased on 1 March 1897.

LA SEMAINE HORTICOLE (1897-1900) [14]

From the first volume, Lucien Linden fulfilled the dual role of editor-in-chief and proprietor. The editorial board consisted of Émile Rodigas[15], Georges Tourret-Grignan, Charles De Bosschere, A. Dallemagne and Max Garnier. At the end of 1899, in the issue of 30 December, a managerial change was announced: subscribers were informed that Lucien Linden would once again assume the position of editor-in-chief. This implies that the position had been someone else's responsibility for a time.

The weekly gazette was published on Saturdays. Its format consisted of 16 black-and-white pages, printed on very thin, white newspaper. The black text was printed in three columns.

La Semaine horticole was designed as the continental counterpart of *The Gardeners' Chronicle.* It was not as independent as it claimed, however. Linden's omnipresent influence was clear. Nevertheless, the four volumes contained a vast quantity of information, covering every aspect of botany and horticulture. Again, orchids took centre stage. Reports on species were complemented by information on hybrids, which were becoming increasingly widespread.

In December 1900, Lucien Linden announced the discontinuation of *La Semaine horticole* for a one-year period, in order to spend more time on his duties within the three societies of *L'Horticulture coloniale.* This "see you soon" quickly proved to be a final "goodbye".

‹ *Microstylis bella.*
L'Illustration horticole, 1885.

13. *La Semaine horticole,* vol. 4, p. 603.

14. The third volume (1899) displayed the complete title *La Semaine horticole et Revue des Cultures coloniales.* This extension was dropped again in vol. 4.

15. Émile Rodigas (1831-1902), a Belgian botanist and zoologist, was the director of the Zoological Gardens in Ghent, later professor and director of the Collège d'Horticulture de l'État in the same city.

La Semaine horticole,
29 December 1900, p 603.

LES ORCHIDÉES EXOTIQUES ET LEUR CULTURE EN EUROPE (1894)

This is the only book by Lucien Linden. It was published around 1 July 1894. The work comprises 1034 pages – numbered I-XIV, then 1-1019. It also includes a page of advertisements for the *Lindenia* and *Le Journal des orchidées.* As a self-publication, this book testifies to the healthy finances of the Linden enterprises, which were then at their peak with Lucien at the helm.

The book is co-authored by Alfred Cogniaux and Georges Tourret-Grignan. It contains a number of illustrations from *The Gardeners' Chronicle* and the *Journal of Horticulture,* thereby demonstrating the good relationship enjoyed with M.T. Masters, publisher of the former, and D. Hogg, director of the latter.

17. *La Semaine horticole,* 1897, vol. 4.

To date, *Les Orchidées exotiques* is one of the best general books on orchids. It contains comprehensive coverage of almost every aspect of orchid science and horticulture. The section on taxonomy no longer corresponds exactly with present-day classification, of course, and the information on certain other aspects (such as geographic distribution) is naturally a little outdated. For the most part, however, this book is as useful today as it was at the end of the nineteenth century, and the publication of an annotated version would be much more worthwhile than a plethora of so-called "modern" treatments. I can do no better than quote the review by *The Gardeners' Chronicle*:[16]

"Simultaneously with the receipt of our seven-times-tried friend, [the reference here is to B.S. William's *The Orchid-Growers Manual*] comes a new candidate for public favour, and we can at once say that its success is assured. In Mr Lucien Linden's *Les Orchidées exotiques et leur culture en Europe*, we have a portly volume of over a thousand pages of large octavo, well printed, well arranged, well indexed, and with numerous illustrations but no maps. [...] It is the work of a tried expert, who has known how to avail himself judiciously, and with due acknowledgement, of the writings of others, and to incorporate them with his own. Thus the name of Mr Cogniaux, which finds a place on the title-page, is ample guarantee that the botanical portions are correct, while the portrait and dedication to John Linden [*sic*] will remind the reader of the unrivalled opportunities that the son has had. This dedication is as well turned as it is appropriate. [...] The primary object of the work is to afford the Orchid-loving public information and practical advice in a form more compact and convenient than the pages of a periodical journal like the *Journal des orchidées*. The special competence of Mr Lucien Linden as a cultivator is acknowledged on all hands, and many will be glad to have in so convenient a form a summary of the general principles of cultivation followed in the remarkable establishment at Brussels, of which the author has been the responsible director for many years. The introductory chapters are devoted to the botanical history of Orchids and to the conditions under which they grow naturally. In this portion of the work Mr Lucien Linden must have derived great assistance from his father as well as from Mr Cogniaux and Mr Grignan. [...] The classification adopted is that of Bentham, as given in the *Genera Plantarum*, itself a slight modification of that proposed by Lindley. [...] We have said sufficient to show how comprehensive the book is. Little or nothing related to Orchids seems to have been forgotten, though naturally

Alfred Cogniaux, portrait in *Le Journal des orchidées*, 1896.

16. 1894, 3rd series, 16, p. 42.

some sections are better and more thoroughly treated than others; the chapters on insects and fungi attacking Orchids are, for instance, somewhat meagre. The work is sure to fulfil the main object of its projector, to diffuse the knowledge of Orchids and their cultivation in Europe; whilst as a book of reference for the expert it will be invaluable."

THE CATALOGUES

The Linden establishments produced a huge number of sales catalogues. Some were illustrated with De Tollenaere's colour paintings (1856, 1857). Eighty-nine catalogues have hitherto been identified, but there were probably many more. Going back to 1847, the first catalogue was published in Luxembourg; the last catalogue is dated 1900. Most of these catalogues were in French, although some were published in English. Some treated exotic plants in general, whilst others dealt with azaleas, camellias, rhododendrons and even palms.

CONCLUSION

Over a period of 50 years, Jean Linden and the establishments he directed produced a multitude of significant publications. Although the most voluminous, elaborate, best-known and most important publication is *Lindenia,* all the others are likewise significant in the history of horticulture. The *Pescatorea* is undoubtedly one of the most magnificent horticultural works ever published. Even "lesser" publications, such as *La Semaine horticole* and *Le Journal des orchidées,* deserve their place in the pantheon of orchid literature.

Overall, Jean Linden's publications (many of which were produced with the help of his son Lucien) reflect the huge importance of both Linden and his companies in the horticultural world. This is true from his return to Europe at the end of his third voyage through to his death and beyond. His reputation travelled well beyond Belgium, France and England, reaching distant places like Saint Petersburg. In the horticultural circle, none of his competitors – neither Sander, Low nor even Veitch – could rival Linden in his production of journals, periodicals and scientific publications.

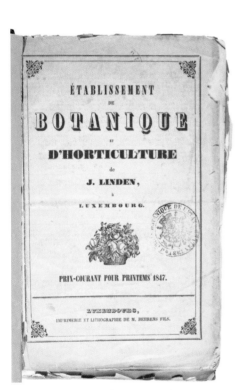

Catalogue des Établissements de Botanique et d'Horticulture de Jean Linden. Prix courant pour printemps 1847.

LINDEN AND THE ORCHIDS

At the turn of the century

The *Picon*. Jean Linden (seated, left) with members of the Otlet family, on Levant Island, 1886.

‹ Bust of Jean Linden in the Parc Léopold, Brussels, by Alphonse de Tombay, 1899.

ean Linden "retired" in 1875, entrusting the management of his horticultural companies to his son Lucien. Subsequently, he often stayed with the Otlet family on Levant Island. In a photograph of 1886, a relaxed Linden is sipping his *Picon* in a local bistro. This retirement was, however, an illusion. We have seen how the former explorer continued to place orders with collectors, drawing up their itineraries and scrutinising their shipments. In the south of France, he still visited the horticultural sites on Levant Island and at Cap Nègre. In 1891, *L'Éclaireur de Nice* describes Linden's role in "the almost tropical transformation of [the city's] vegetation, through the introduction of all these wonderful plants offering such a delightful contrast to the monotony of date palms, eucalyptuses and mimosas".[1] There follows a list of the species that Linden imported and which featured in *L'IIllustration horticole* over the years.

It is at the end of his life that we discover the more intimate side of Jean Linden. Schlim, his half-brother, José Triana – who learned his trade from him before the two quarrelled – and Lucien in *La Semaine horticole* all reveal, each in his own way, the daily life of Linden the man. "During his expeditions, he always remained even-tempered. He never seemed tired, enjoyed a good meal, which he would eat slowly, savouring each mouthful, and smoked endlessly. He needed his little comforts to sleep; besides his suitcases, he inevitably kept a pillow with him."[2] Triana recalls his perplexity on another occasion when, while on expedition, he wrote to Linden proposing to send him seeds and plants in exchange for a set of specialised botany books he particularly wanted. Linden replied that he would rather have a quantity of Ambalema cigars, and a sombrero... With

1. *L'Éclaireur de Nice*, 15 May 1891.
2. Santiago Diaz Píedrahita, *Triana, El Caballero de las Flores*, Colciencias, 1999, p. 20.

his air of bonhomie, Linden probably owed many of his friendships and good working relationships to his affability and good manners. The same picture of a big, placid and jovial man was evident in family anecdotes and people's memories of him.

Our last views of him offer a sharp contrast to the earlier, convivial Linden. He was now a tired, old man, marked by illness and the premature death of his son Auguste in 1894. He died in Brussels on 12 January 1898. *La Semaine horticole* brought out a special issue, whilst his elaborate funeral provided a final testimony of his companies' floral resources. At Ixelles cemetery, his mortal remains were laid among *Cattleya trianae* and *Odontoglossum crispum*, while a spray of *Malpighia ilicifolia* was placed on his heart. The hearse was literally submerged under flowers; more filled another two carriages. The rest of the cortège was equally impressive. The carriage carrying the king's representative, Lieutenant-General Bocquet, followed immediately behind the family members in their mourning black – his sons, Lucien and Gaston, and sons-in-law Victor Alesch and Édouard Otlet. The Count d'Ansembourg, chamberlain to the late King of the Netherlands and the Grand Duke of Luxembourg, was also in attendance, along with every leading Belgian scientist and botanist. A military guard of honour paid Linden the respects due to his rank of Commander of the Order of Leopold. In a gesture of affection that profoundly moved those present, the king sent his personal musicians to lead the procession. During the funeral orations, homage was paid to Linden, notably by Paul Hymans on behalf of the alumni association of Brussels University. Ferdinand Kegeljan, Charles De Bosschere and Émile Rodigas were also among the speakers. Count Oswald de Kerchove de Denterghem, President of the Société royale d'Agriculture et de Botanique de Gand, emphasised Linden's major contribution to horticulture: the adaptation of greenhouses to the requirements of imported specimens. Numerous eminent persons sent notes of condolence to the family, among them Sir Trevor Lawrence, President of the English Royal Horticultural Society; Alexis Varjenevsky, Grand Marshal of the Russian nobility in Moscow;

Jean Linden. Oil on canvas by Gaston Linden, 1890s.

‹ *Dressed for an excursion*. Jean Linden (second from left) with members of the Otlet family on Levant Island, 1886.

Lucien Linden. Portrait in *Le Journal des orchidées*.

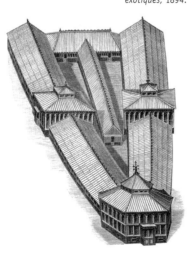

A greenhouse complex for the amateur. Design by Lucien Linden for the collector Mr Maloux. Engraving from Lucien Linden, *Les Orchidées exotiques*, 1894.

Maxime Cornu, Curator of the Muséum national d'Histoire naturelle in Paris; Baron de Meylhand; and Charles Palice, Director of the public gardens of Rome.

On the death of their honorary director in 1898, the Linden companies were in full production and enjoying a well-established international reputation. What followed was to prove distinctly less glorious. The successful progress of the business between 1875 and 1898 can doubtless be attributed to the continuing presence of Jean Linden in the wings. Over the next decade, however, things fell progressively into decline. Could the ageing Jean Linden possibly have foreseen this? Eight years after his father's death, Lucien fled the sinking ship and put an end to the activities of the company, which had no third generation of Lindens to come to its rescue. Lucien had only two daughters, Lucienne and Yvonne, and in those days women were not destined to enter the world of business.

Admittedly, the general obsession with exotic plants had noticeably faded. The huge scale of their production had had the effect of diminishing their exclusivity and hence their price. At the turn of the century, a reversal of fortune prevented many collectors from settling their accounts: even the Warocqué family's enormous capital was dangerously drained by the purchase of orchids! Lucien Linden himself was not entirely innocent of financial extravagances. Less prudent than his father, and lacking perhaps the latter's grasp of changing times, he incurred excessive expenses, publishing luxurious, large-format sales catalogues (32 x 25 cm) and launching a massive sale of orchids "at reduced prices".[3] He remained confident, relying on the loyalty of a handful of important clients and even designing greenhouses for connoisseurs. A skilled landscape architect, he also went into partnership with Maurice Otlet, selling heating systems for greenhouses. Finally, jumping at the chance to exploit the new colony in the Congo, Lucien founded L'Horticole coloniale, a company dispatching seeds and plants to the Congo for cultivation *in situ*. A series of legal wrangles and court cases swallowed up most of the Linden capital, however, with war dealing the bankrupt company the final *coup de grâce*.

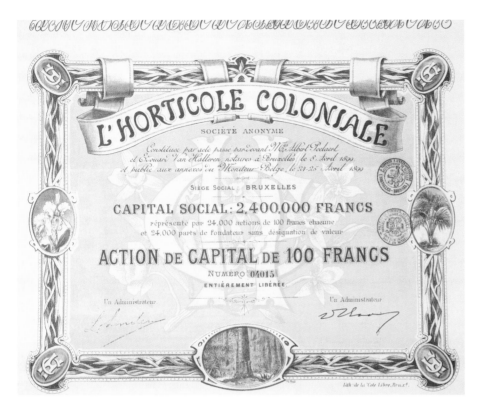

4. Letter from the Collège de la Ville de Bruxelles to the Comité Jean Linden, dated 17 March 1899. Brussels, Archives de la Ville de Bruxelles.

Share certificate,
L'Horticole coloniale, 1899.

THE LAST RELICS

Today, nothing remains of the Linden companies. The advance of the European institutions on the site of the Parc Léopold has erased virtually all trace of the work of Jean Linden. Only the "director's house", where he lived for over half a century until 1896, still stands in sad isolation behind the European parliament building (called *"Caprice des Dieux"* in Brussels). There are also a few foundations of lost greenhouses behind the Institut royal des Sciences naturelles de Belgique. The *Victoria* House was moved to the Botanical Gardens. Acquired by the state in 1877, it was moved again to Saint-Josse-ten-Noode until building work on a new north-south railway junction required it to be dismantled and re-erected for the last time in Meise, where it was restored to its former splendour in 1983.

There is no trace of Linden's tomb at Ixelles. The family did not maintain the monument, which was then removed from the cemetery. Another memorial, however, does survive in Brussels. A bust of Jean Linden, which can be viewed today in the Parc Léopold, was erected on the initiative of Count Oswald de Kerchove de Denterghem. He circulated a subscription among plant lovers, inviting them to "preserve, with a modest monument, the memory of the man to whom our gardens and homes owe so many precious and delightful plants".[4] The bronze bust created by the sculptor

Foundations of greenhouses belonging to L'Horticulture internationale at the back of the Parc Léopold.

Current view of the director's house in the
Parc Léopold.

Bust of Jean Linden (detail of base) in the
Parc Léopold, Brussels, by Alphonse de
Tombay, 1899.

Alphonse de Tombay (1843-1916) was placed with the agreement of the
Collège de la Ville de Bruxelles on the spot where the *Victoria* House once
stood. It was later re-sited to face the "director's house".

Elsewhere, in Woluwe-Saint-Lambert, a street bore the name of Jean
Linden until the end of the Second World War.

MEMORIALS OF ANOTHER KIND

What remains of Jean Linden today? Books. Some of these occasionally
come the way of antique dealers and specialist libraries. It is very rare, however, to find a complete edition of the seventeen volumes of the *Lindenia* —
or a copy of the *Pescatorea,* of which only a few copies survive worldwide.
The hand-coloured plates generally sell for a small fortune, whether they
are presented in their original context or not.

History bears little record of Jean Linden's name. The lack of primary
sources — even I, his great-great-granddaughter, suffered from this in my
research — has helped perpetuate numerous errors in the specialist literature.
Sometimes regarded as a botanist — although he had no formal scientific
training — Jean Linden has been described in a multitude of ways, some
more accurate than others: gardener, plant hunter, "the father of orchids",
horticulturist, professor of botany, etc. Some of these designations also tes-
tify to the professional jealousy that was already rearing its head in the
nineteenth century. Critics have, for instance, unfavourably compared
Linden and Van Houtte with the collector Charles Vuylsteke (b 1844),

denouncing their practice of sending out plant hunters, whereas the latter would acquire his specimens from suppliers already on site, such as diplomats and missionaries. These exaggerations betray an uncritical reading of the historical facts.

If there is another, less tangible vestige of Jean Linden's contribution, it is surely to be found in the literature of his times, when there was undoubtedly a mania for exotic plants among the higher echelons of society. *Le Monde illustré* commented on an auction of exotic plants where "the frenzy to buy reached the point of wanton extravagance".[5] France especially, under the Second Empire, developed an immoderate taste for tropical imports. In Guy Sagnes' study of boredom in French literature,[6] we find the following: "The desire to possess and grow exotic plants, which apparently knew neither spring nor autumn, developed from around the 1850s. In this respect, novels mirrored the times, with many works incorporating the new fashion."

In 1867, the Goncourt brothers turned to the winter garden of Princess Mathilde at Saint-Gratien for inspiration. In *La Curée* (1871), Zola enumerates the exotic plants recently introduced to Europe. What seemed to fascinate people was the hot, humid atmosphere of the greenhouses and the scents that pervaded them, or perhaps the strangeness of the new species. Cattleyas, palms and carnivorous plants were especially popular. The snobbery and passion for things exotic that typified collectors does not entirely explain the phenomenon, however. To curiosity about the unusual we must add boredom with the traditional use of plants and an ardent desire to redesign Nature through human ingenuity. Favourite plants were those with an artificial appearance heightened by continual selective breeding. "Everything that comes from the East", declared the Goncourts, "is as the work of an artist's hands, whereas in Europe, all Nature appears manufactured."[7] In his turn, Joris-Karl Huysmans sought out natural flowers that resembled artificial ones: his *monstres séduisants* [enticing monsters]. In his 1884 novel *À Rebours*, the character des Esseintes has quantities of exotic plants brought into his house to fulfil his need for powerful sensations. The heady descriptions and incantatory names sound as if they have been lifted straight from Linden's catalogues – the author had probably

In the novel *À Rebours*, the central character, des Esseintes, overcomes his boredom by purchasing tropical plants, prominent among which are species imported by the Lindens. Joris-Karl Huysmans, *À Rebours*, 223 coloured wood engravings by Auguste Lepère, Paris, Les Cent Bibliophiles, 1903, p 93.

5. *Le Monde illustré*, 4 May 1861.

6. Guy Sagnes, *L'Ennui dans la littérature française de Flaubert à Laforgue*, Paris, 1969.

7. Edmond and Jules Huot de Goncourt, *Renée Mauperin*, 1864.

"*Anthurium*, recently imported from Colombia" (p. 189)
[*Anthurium lindenianum, IH,* 1882, p. 107]

"*Cypripedium* with complicated, incoherent shapes,
the work of some demented inventor."
[*Cypripedium spicerianum, IH,* 1883, p. 8]

It is possible to link each of
J.-K. Huysman's plant descriptions in the
1884 novel *À Rebours* (*Against the Grain*)
to a plate from *L'Illustration horticole*
or other Linden publication.

"Specimens of *Tillandsia lindeni [sic]*, resembling a broken-toothed curry-comb, the colour of wine must ..."
[*IH*, 1880, p. 93]

"... the ghouls of the plant world, the carnivorous fly-catchers from the West Indies – *Drosera, Sarracena [sic]*, and *Cephalothus* opening its voracious cups that can digest and absorb real meat; and last but not least, *Nepenthes* whose fantastic shape exceeds every known limit of the bizarre."
[*Nepenthes bicalcarata, IH*, 1881, p 9]

TILLANDSIA LINDENI, MORR.
Pérou Sept¹ (Serre tempé)
A. Verschaffelt publ.

L'ILLUSTRATION HORTICOLE

NEPENTHES BICALCARATA, J. D. HOOK.

Cibotium spectabile

The tree fern Joris-Karl Huysmans refers to deserves special notice, being a good example of the link between the list of plants and the Linden catalogues. "A *Cibotium spectabile*, outdoing its fellows in the insanity of its structure, defying the wildest nightmares, its enormous tail like an orang-utan's emerging from among its palmate foliage, a brown, hairy tail with its tip curled over in the shape of a bishop's crosier." [À *Rebours*]

On 16 October 1861, Linden wrote to Hooker that he had 73 species of tree ferns and suggested sending some to Kew Gardens, "Some would give a marvellous effect in the large greenhouse at Kew, in particular *Cibotium princeps*. I have some gigantic samples of tree ferns, their stems the thickness of a man's body, and covered with long, fawn-coloured tan hairs."

The name "tree fern" is loosely bestowed on tropical ferns if the stem reaches a significant size. Hence, not all tree ferns necessarily belong to the same family or genus. The ferns mentioned above are from the "classic" group that includes representatives of the genera *Dicksonia, Cibotium, Culcita, Cyathea, Alsophila,* etc. The names *Cibotium princeps* (mentioned by Linden) and *Cibotium spectabile* (in the Huysmans novel) do not seem to have appeared in official publications of that time. In a purely botanical sense, therefore, they did not exist. Perhaps Linden used a provisional or temporary name in his letter.

John Smith, Curator of Kew from 1864 to 1886, confirmed the consignment of botanical specimens described by Linden as *Cibotium*, admitting he renamed this plant, allocating it to the genus *Cyathea*; the reference is to the *Cibotium princeps* in Linden's letter. We can thus deduce that Huysmans in turn referred to the catalogues for botanical names and descriptions. To date there is a *Cyathea princeps* (or *Cyathea insignis*), a tree fern originating from Central America, mentioned by Linden. Another small species of tree fern called *Cyathea spectabilis* was not described until 1929. [RONNIE VIANE]

acquired a catalogue from the company's outlet in Paris, which had opened in 1879 at 5, rue de la Paix. Huysmans had also gained some horticultural experience in the specialised greenhouses at Fontenay-aux-Roses in 1881. He gives his own summary of contemporary attitudes: "In just a few years, Man can operate a form of selection that would take Nature in her slothfulness a matter of centuries. Decidedly, horticulturists are the only true artists."[8]

At the turn of the century, with the Art Nouveau movement in full swing, orchids became a favourite motif in the decorative arts.

Here we have a rare surviving relic of the family: these Limoges plates were a gift to Lucien Linden. Painted by the artist Mary Gasparoli (1856), they feature

flowers of identifiable orchid genera: *Paphiopedilum* and *Odontoglossum*.

In 1884, Lucien Linden married Marguerite Van den Hove. Her cousin, Maurice Maeterlinck, portrayed flowers as sentient beings aiming to conquer the surface of the globe through various ruses and subterfuges. His book, *L'Intelligence des fleurs* (1907), echoes the discoveries of Charles Darwin. He also mentions William Jackson Hooker, but never once Linden. Maeterlinck, a Belgian, won further renown with works now regarded as landmarks in Symbolist literature, one of the foremost of which was the collection of poems entitled *Serres chaudes*.[9] In *Le Côté de Guermantes*, Marcel Proust would later quote a passage from *L'Intelligence des Fleurs*. Better known, to French speakers at least, is the expression *"faire cattleya"*, which Proust coined in *Un Amour de Swann* (1893): Swann uses it to signify "making love" when he is with his mistress Odette, thus recalling their first embrace and the flower she wore on her dress that night.

Thus, Jean Linden entered the collective memory without necessarily stamping it with his name. Similarly, if he seldom features today in history books or memorabilia, he enjoyed the highest honours both during his life and on his death. Always a modest man, he nevertheless revolutionised contemporary society. Beyond the good relationships he enjoyed with the luminaries of 19th-century Belgium, he contributed through his activities to the birth of a lifestyle reflecting the times in which he lived.

The fabulous adventure of exotic plants would last for half a century. It was enough to emblazon the names of Linden, Verschaffelt, Van Houtte and so many others on the world of horticulture. These were pioneers whose names we barely remember, whose influence on our current way of life we do not even suspect. Without the developments in horticulture they introduced over 150 years ago, we would be unlikely to find such a vast array of exotic specimens in our florists' shops and plant nurseries. Yet it has ever been the fate of pioneers to be forgotten.

Lucien Linden and
Marguerite Van den Hove-Linden,
first cousin of Maurice Maeterlinck.

8. Joris-Karl Huysmans, *À Rebours*, Paris, Auguste Lepère for Les Cent Bibliophiles, 1903, p. 194.

9. "The title *Serres chaudes* was a natural choice" according to the author, "because Ghent is a city of horticulture and especially of flowers. Greenhouses, heated, cold and temperate, are abundant there."

D. De Keghel
1894

JEAN LINDEN REDISCOVERED

Conclusion

Jean Linden and Anna Reuter, pictured on the occasion of their 50th wedding anniversary in October 1896. *La Semaine horticole*, 12 February 1898.

‹ *Bouquet of orchids.* Painting by D. de Keghel, 1895.

When I began this project, the prophets of conventional wisdom warned me against the danger of canonising Jean Linden. Faced with a "young" author researching her great-great-grandfather, they were concerned the result would be an interminable panegyric. This was the opinion of many professional botanists as well as authors who had touched on Linden in the past. On countless occasions, too, any mention of my ancestor elicited the laconic reply: "Linden? Never heard of him!" Such remarks often betrayed a measure of indifference but, far from inducing me to abandon the project, they only strengthened my resolve. There were, however, other moments when I came across individuals who really paid attention to my goal and helped to point me in the right direction.

It was never my intention to glorify this explorer turned horticulturist. My initial aim was to bridge the considerable gaps in the history of Jean Linden. His exploits as an adventurer and explorer were well documented, but not the circumstances that gave rise to these. The world knew of his success in business – especially the golden years of L'Horticulture internationale under his son Lucien in Ghent from 1875 – but nothing of how he began. Today the material evidence of his prominence in Brussels, abundant enough at the beginning of the last century, has all but vanished. Everyone knows what an orchid is, but few are aware of its provenance ... As for myself, I was scarcely better informed about an ancestor so far removed from my everyday life, so little was there to connect my world with his.

Given the impossibility of producing an exhaustive study of a man who left so few traces, I decided to assemble the fragments into a kind of mosaic: a portrait with many facets – and countless gaps where the pieces should fit together. This meant unravelling the myths handed down by past

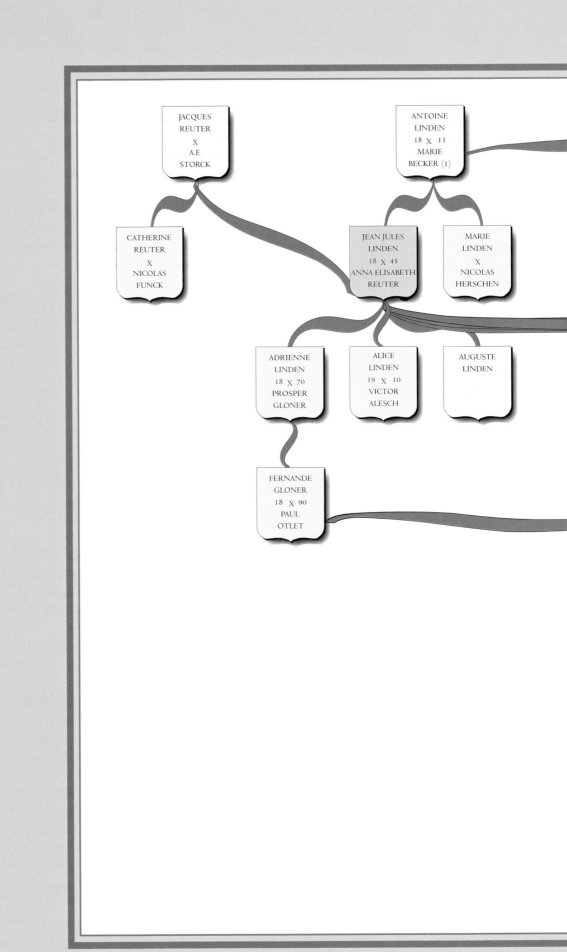

JACQUES
REUTER
X
A.F.
STORCK

ANTOINE
LINDEN
18 X 13
MARIE
BECKER (1)

CATHERINE
REUTER
X
NICOLAS
FUNCK

JEAN JULES
LINDEN
18 X 45
ANNA ELISABETH
REUTER

MARIE
LINDEN
X
NICOLAS
HERSCHEN

ADRIENNE
LINDEN
18 X 70
PROSPER
GLONER

ALICE
LINDEN
19 X 10
VICTOR
ALESCH

AUGUSTE
LINDEN

FERNANDE
GLONER
18 X 90
PAUL
OTLET

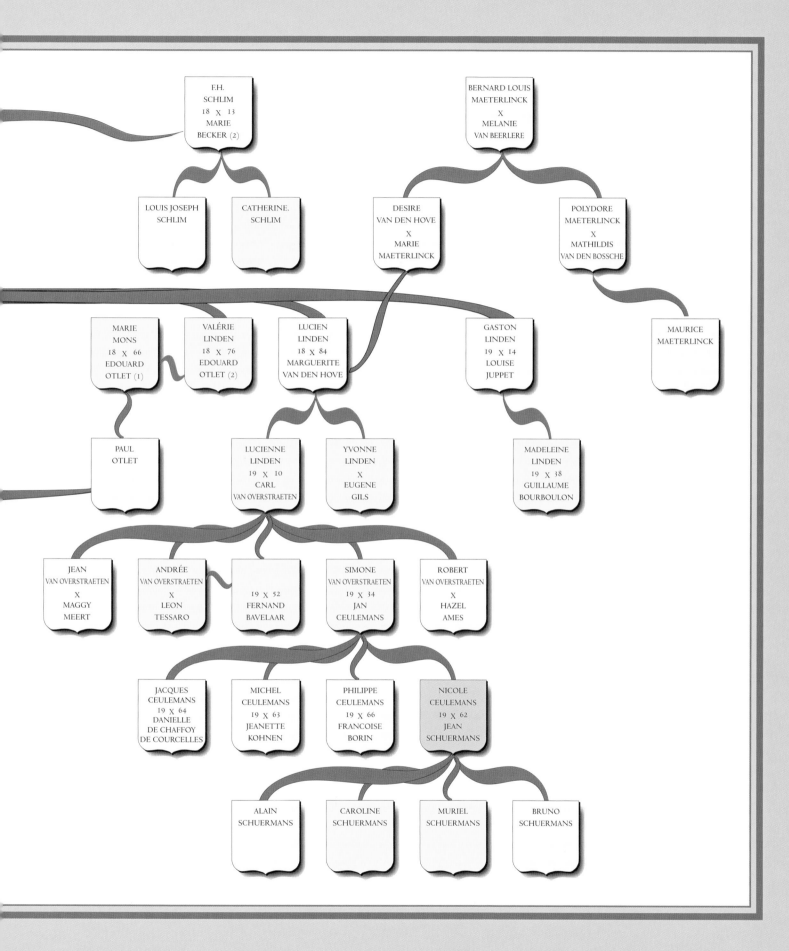

generations and replacing fiction with fact, a task further hindered by the lack of documentation. The Linden businesses disappeared in the swiftly changing landscape of Brussels, together with family memories of the man and his enterprises. It was as if all the achievements of that indefatigable pair, Jean and Lucien, had been deliberately wiped from the record.

Throughout my research, the person of Jean Linden has only appeared as if through obscured glass. Furthermore, as if to mitigate somewhat those early concerns about putting my ancestor on a pedestal, the rare evidence I came across had nothing but good to say of him. Although this evidence has been included, it was with the conscious decision not to dwell on effusions of praise, the most flattering of which were doubtless uttered at his funeral.

To paint the most realistic portrait of Linden, I have distanced myself from the perspective of a direct descendant. It seemed preferable to present him in terms of his various activities: explorer – first in person, then by proxy – horticulturist, author and publicist, but also as an immensely astute man of business with a gift for making profitable contacts. Rather than being a dusty figure excavated from the past, Jean Linden appears as very much the modern man. Even today he is regarded as one of the greatest explorers Belgium has ever known, while his published works remain of fundamental value to professional botanists.

Cattleya labiata.

Starting from nothing, he sought to infiltrate the influential elite who could make his dreams come true. A glance at our family tree underlines this. Apart from the links that connect me, Nicole Ceulemans, to an ancestor whose name I no longer bear, the genealogy reveals a number of names of historical significance in Belgium. Adrienne, the eldest of the Linden children, married Prosper Gloner who, after four years in charge of the Linden businesses in Ghent, assumed a key position with the bank owned by Gerson von Bleichröder, one of whose clients was Otto von Bismarck. Adrienne gave birth to five children. Elsewhere we have witnessed the short life of Auguste, who died without issue, as did Alice, who married Victor Alesch, a lawyer from Luxembourg. Lucien, the fifth child, is my direct ancestor. His elder daughter, Lucienne – the other sister also died childless – was my grandmother. I was also fascinated to discover that his wife, Marguerite Van de Hove, was a cousin of Maurice Maeterlinck, the dramatist and a native of Ghent who was to be awarded the Nobel Prize for Literature in 1911. Valérie became the second wife of Édouard Otlet, none other than the father of Maurice and Paul Otlet. The couple had six children. Gaston took a wife at an advanced age; his daughter Madeleine

("Madé") married Guillaume Bourboulon in Paris. The family tree also connects Jean Linden with Nicolas Funck and Louis-Joseph Schlim, who feature throughout these pages. Thus Linden moved in a world of explorers and political hierarchy, emphasising once again the extensive network of connections enjoyed by a man of considerable stature yet by nature the soul of discretion. I knew nothing of this when taking the first tentative steps in my research.

Many questions remain unanswered; a biography, in fact, never ends. My aim was, as earlier stated, a mere sketch; there are other lines of enquiry still to pursue. I was unable, for example, to access the archives that might reveal the contribution made by Linden to a major exhibition at the Cercle artistique et littéraire de Bruxelles or shed light on his role in the Société royale linéenne et de Flore de Bruxelles, of which he is listed as director from 1861 and president in 1879. There is also room for a further, in-depth study of the circumstances surrounding his first expedition; or perhaps an analysis of his first contacts with the British collectors who were so reluctant to collaborate with the young Belgian. These are all questions that may hopefully be addressed at a future date.

For my own part, I choose to end on the few remaining images of my great-great-grandfather. From the start, photographs and engravings powerfully affected me: I was impressed by this fine, much decorated gentleman; moved by his kindly, smiling figure in old age; struck with admiration by his clear ambition and determination. The family legends that enticed me to delve into the past finally come face to face with the facts in which they are rooted. As well as shedding fresh light on the figure of Jean Linden, the great explorer who became the Grand Old Man of Belgian horticulture, I hope that I have made it easier for his present-day descendants to accord him the honour that he deserves.

Cattleya labiata.

Nicole Ceulemans, November 2005

BIBLIOGRAPHY

SOURCES AND DOCUMENTS

Archives used by the authors and a partial bibliography of books, periodicals, etc consulted during the preparation of this work.

ARCHIVAL SOURCES

In Belgium

Académie des Sciences des lettres et des beaux-arts de Belgique, Brussels

Archives de la Ville de Bruxelles

Archives générales du Royaume, Antwerp

Archives générales du Royaume, Brussels

Archives of the Ministry of Foreign Affairs, Brussels

Bibliothèque royale de Belgique, Brussels

Institut royal des Sciences naturelles de Belgique, Brussels

Musée Mundaneum, Mons

Musée royal de Mariemont, Morlanwelz

National Botanic Garden of Belgium, Meise

Société royale d'Agriculture et d'Horticulture, Ghent

In France

Institut de France, Paris

Muséum national d'Histoire naturelle (MNHN), Paris

In the Grand Duchy of Luxembourg

Archives municipales de la Ville de Luxembourg

Archives nationales, Luxembourg

Bibliothèque nationale, Luxembourg

Muséum d'Histoire naturelle, Luxembourg

In the United Kingdom

Lindley Library, London

Natural History Museum, London

Royal Botanic Gardens, Kew

In Colombia

Academia colombiana de Ciencias, Bogotá

Archivio general de la Nación, Bogotá

In Mexico

Archivio San Cristóbal de las Casas, Tabasco

Archivio Villahermosa, Tabasco

In Venezuela

Archivio Mérida

Biblioteca Nacional, Caracas

Family archives

PARTIAL BIBLIOGRAPHY

ANDRÉ, Édouard. *Le Voyage dans les Andes 1875-1876. L'Amérique équinoxiale*, published in *Tour du Monde,* Paris, Hachette, 1877-1883.

Artistas y cronistas extranjeros en Venezuela, Caracas, 1993.

Les Bacheliers de l'Athénée de par le monde, Luxembourg, Bibliothèque nationale, nd.

BALIS, Jan and LAWALRÉE, André. *L'Orchidée en Belgique,* Brussels, Bibliothèque royale Albert I, 1961.

Les Belges et le Mexique, Leuven, Presses universitaires de Louvain, 1993.

BRAUMAN, Annick and DEMANET, Marie. *Le Zoo, la Cité scientifique et la ville,* Brussels, AAM, 1995.

CHABAUD, B. *Les Palmiers de la Côte d'Azur,* np, 1915.

COATS, Alice M. *The Plant Hunters,* London, 1969.

DE HERDT, René. *Gentse Floraliën,* Ghent, Stichting Mens en Kultuur, 1990.

DÍAZ-PIEDRAHITA, Santiago. *La Botanica en Colombia,* Bogotá, Academia Colombiana de Ciencias, 1991.

DÍAZ-PIEDRAHITA, Santiago. *José Triana, su vida, su obra y su epoca,* Bogotá, Academia Colombiana de Ciencias, 1991.

DÍAZ-PIEDRAHITA, Santiago. *Triana, El caballero de la Flores,* Bogotá, Colciencias, 1999.

DÍAZ-PIEDRAHITA, Santiago and LOURTEIG, Alicia. 'Genesis de una Flora', *Revista de la Academia Colombiana,* vol. XVII, 1990.

DUMONT, Georges-Henri. *Histoire de la Belgique,* Brussels, Le Cri, 2000.

EISCHEN, Linda. *La Collection de tableaux de Jean-Pierre Pescatore 1793-1855,* Esch-sur-Alzette, Schortgen Éditions, 2004.

Ferdinand Bellermann, Ein Berliner Maler, Berlin, Staatliche Museen zu Berlin, 1987.

Ferdinand Bellermann en Venezuela, Memoria del Paisaje. 1992, Caracas, Consejo Nacional de la Cultura, 1991-1992.

KURY, Lorelai. *Histoire naturelle et voyages scientifiques (1780-1830),* Paris, L'Harmattan, 2001.

LASÈGUE, A. *Le Musée botanique de Benjamin Delessert,* Paris, Librairie de Fortin, Masson & Cie, 1845.

LINDLEY, John. *William T Stearn,* np, 1999.

MORREN, Ch. *La Belgique horticole,* Brussels, various years.

PIRONET, Ewald. *Venezuela, Promotie en corrosie van een 'paradijs',* Leuven, 1983.

PLATIAU, René. *L'Orchidée à Mariemont,* Morlanwelz, Musée royal de Mariemont, 2003.

PODEVIJN, Dirk. *Charles Vuylsteke, Sr en Jr., Fine fleur van de Belgische sierteelt,* Ghent, Raphaël Vuylsteke, 1995.

REINIKKA, Merle A. *A History of the Orchid,* nd, np.

RÖHL, Eduardo. *Exploradores famosos de la naturaleza Venezolana,* Caracas, 1948.

ROVIROSA, José N. *Pteridografía del sur de México,* Mexico, 1909.

Mexico about 1850, London, nd

SARTORIUS, Carl and RUGENDAS, Moritz. *México y los Mexicanos,* London, 1859.

STERN, Fritz. *L'Or et le fer,* Paris, Fayard, 1990.

SWINSTON , Arthur. *Frederick Sander: The Orchid King: The Record of a Passion,* London, Hodder & Stoughton, 1970.

PUBLICATIONS BY JEAN AND LUCIEN LINDEN

Orchidaceae Lindenianae, Brussels, 1846.

Preludia Florae Columbianae, Brussels, Académie royale des Sciences, des Lettres et des Beaux-Arts de Belgique, 1853.

Pescatorea, Brussels, 1854-1860.

Hortus Lindenianus, Brussels, Hayez, 1859-1860.

Plantae Columbianae, Brussels, 1874-1875.

Lindenia, Brussels, 1885-1906.

L'Illustration horticole, Ghent-Brussels, 1854-1896.

Le Journal des orchidées. Guide pratique de culture, Brussels, 1890-1897.

La Semaine horticole, Brussels, 1897-1900.

Lucien Linden, *Les Orchidées exotiques et leur culture en Europe,* Brussels, 1894.

INDEX

Colophon

Editorial Coordination

Aline Lambilliotte, Geneviève Defrance and Ann Mestdag, Fonds Mercator, Brussels

Fabrice Biasino, Mot à mot, Brussels

Editorial concept

Fabrice Biasino, Mot à mot, Brussels

Copy-editing

First Edition, Cambridge

Translation from original French

First Edition, Cambridge

Paula Cook, Brussels

Picture Research

Nicole Ceulemans, Guido Braem, Fabrice Biasino

CAD, maps

Lodewijk Imkamp, Roermond

Layout and typesetting

La Page, Brussels

Photogravure and printing

Die Keure, Bruges

Binding

Splichal, Turnhout

This edition was published with the support of the Banque Degroof Luxembourg

Photo Credits

The numbers below refer to the pages where the photos appear.
We have done our best to trace all copyright holders, but in some cases this has proved impossible.
Anyone wishing to assert their rights in this matter should contact the publisher.

Jean Linden. Explorer – Master of the Orchid
was published by Fonds Mercator
in May 2006
in simultaneous English and French editions.